1750

WITHDRAWN
NDSU

BURT FRANKLIN: RESEARCH & SOURCE WORKS SERIES 479
Selected Essays in History, Economics, & Social Science 131

THE STRUGGLE FOR THE FREEDOM
OF THE PRESS

THE
STRUGGLE FOR THE FREEDOM
OF THE PRESS
FROM
CAXTON TO CROMWELL

By

WILLIAM M. CLYDE, M.A., Ph.D.

BURT FRANKLIN
NEW YORK

237718

PN
4748
G7
C5
1970

Published by BURT FRANKLIN
235 East 44th St., New York, N.Y. 10017
Originally Published: 1934
Reprinted: 1970
Printed in the U.S.A.

Library of Congress Card Catalog No.: 70-122223
Burt Franklin: Research and Source Works Series 479
Selected Essays in History, Economics, and Social Science 131

To
A. BLYTH WEBSTER

PREFACE

IN substance, this volume is a Thesis submitted in 1929
to the University of St Andrews in fulfilment of the
conditions for the degree of Ph.D. The Thesis was written
during my tenure of a Carnegie Research Scholarship from
1925 to 1927 and of a Carnegie Research Fellowship from
1927 to 1929. I am further indebted to the Carnegie
Trustees for a generous grant of money in aid of the
publication of this volume. I wish also to thank Sir James
C. Irvine, Principal of the University of St Andrews,
whose interest in my behalf is typical of the encouragement
he gives to research in all departments of the University.
I am indebted also to the University Court for its decision
to include this volume in the series of University publications and for granting the rest of the money required to
meet the cost of publication.

To Professor A. Blyth Webster as Head of our School of
English at St Andrews, as colleague and as friend, I owe
more than I can say. In gratitude the least I can do is to
dedicate to him this volume which, but for his instruction
and encouragement over a period of a dozen years, would
never have been written.

I acknowledge, too, the valuable help given me by
Professor J. W. Williams of St Andrews, whose compre-
hensive and detailed knowledge of the seventeenth century
of English history has saved me from many blunders, and
led me to some discoveries that I should not otherwise

have made. Also I have to thank Professor G. C. Moore Smith for guidance in the routine of research and for his helpful interest in my work : Dr. William A. Laidlaw of St Andrews, for reading the proofs of this volume and correcting many errors that I had overlooked : Mr. George H. Bushnell, librarian, St Andrews University, and, not least, the officials of the Reading Room at the British Museum, for unfailing courtesy and expert services.

My indebtedness to other scholars in the same field of study is difficult, I find, to assess. I have made acknowledgment wherever I have been conscious of a debt. If I have borrowed anything without acknowledgment, it has been done unwittingly and I offer my apologies. Perhaps I may be allowed here to mention my indebtedness to Mr. J. B. Williams, for though I find myself in disagreement with much that he states in his *History of English Journalism*, I have had that book beside me in all my work and had valuable help from it.

WILLIAM M. CLYDE,
St Andrews.

25 March, 1934.

THE ARGUMENT

The object of this inquiry is to discover the truth about the struggle for the freedom of the press in England during the period 1640 to 1658 when that struggle was at its height. Control of the press was then in the hands successively of the Long Parliament, the Army, the Council of State and finally the Protectorate. We shall see how each of these ruling powers dealt with its own particular problem of controlling the press, and how the principle that a man might publish his thoughts at will gradually evolved.

It will be necessary first to give a summary of the struggle for the freedom of the press from 1476, when printing was introduced into England by Caxton, to 1640 when the Long Parliament began.

Certain questions at once present themselves—for example, what is meant by the freedom of the press ? How did the principle that a man should be free to publish his opinions at will come to be regarded as a natural right ? When the system of licensing books was introduced, with what measure of tolerance was it applied ? Was it easy to smuggle into the country unlawful books printed abroad, and what were the risks attached to surreptitious printing and publishing ? Were the laws restraining the press regarded at any time as dead letters like so many of the laws on the Statute Book to-day ?

Again, something must be said of the Stationers' Company and the organisation of the book-trade ; for whatever government might nominally control the press, some measure of control rested with the Stationers' Company. What part then, we shall inquire, did the Company play in the struggle for the freedom of the press ?

These are the chief objects of this inquiry.

CONTENTS

CHAPTER III. 1645-1646

CHAPTER IV. 1647

APPENDIX

ABBREVIATIONS

H.C.J. = House of Commons' Journals.

H.L.J. = House of Lords' Journals.

Hist. MSS. Comm. = Royal Commission on Historical MSS.

C.S.P.D. = Calendar of State Papers, Domestic Series.

INTRODUCTION (1476-1637)

PRINTING AND THE ROYAL PREROGATIVE
1476-1637

A^T first, printing was held to be an art and a mystery rightly to be exercised only by men set apart for that purpose. It was not for the vulgar or profane. Like coining it was accounted among the regalia of government and looked upon with a jealous and strict eye. As late as 1651 William Ball, a pamphleteer, wrote :—

' . . . the most Christian *Potencies* (or Republicks) and Illustrious *Potentates* have thought fit *to comprehend the liberty of Printing, (even as of Coyning) within the sphere of their severall Powers*: . . . well per-ceiving *that the Eye of understanding might be subject to be deceived by erroneous principles in Print, as may the bodily Eye by counterfeit Coyne;* In Regard whereof they propagated wholsome Orders, and Decrees for the Regulating of Printing, and Printers ; which rightly considered, can-not be defaced, no not blemished by the notion of *Tyranny.*'[1]

It was not then considered an inalienable right of man to publish his thoughts and opinions. From the first, the allowing of printing and the granting of privileges was regarded as a just and unquestionable right of prerogative.

Printing was introduced into England by Caxton in 1476, and one of the first acts of Henry VII was to take over control of the Press. A certain Peter Actors was appointed stationer to his majesty, and thereafter official appointments of printers were made by special patent, ' king's printer ' became a privileged office and the crown granted to printers special patents at will.

[1] See Appendix, B.

1

The Patentees and the Stationers' Company

The printers and stationers so increased in number that some organisation of the printing trade became necessary. They formed themselves into a Company which was granted its charter in 1557. Even so, there remained one considerable difficulty in the way of controlling printing, namely, the continuance of certain printers to print by special royal patent. These men formed a privileged class, and a powerful one. The unprivileged naturally objected.

Then began a lengthy and acrimonious controversy over rights between the queen's printer, Christopher Barker, and the rest of the printers in London, which is retailed in the Council Register, 5 June, 1578. Five years later a compromise was agreed upon and the master, wardens and assistants of the Company of London Stationers wrote to inform the bishop of London that the differences between the patentees and the Company had at length been happily settled, ' the patentees being very charitably inclined and ' willing to yield to any reasonable motion '.[1] Henceforth the greater would include the less.

But though the holders of patents and the Stationers' Company had settled their differences, the king had not resigned his prerogative. At any time he might exercise it ; and from a suit presented in 1635 it appears that the granting of exclusive privileges of printing remained ' as ' absolute a right of his majesty's prerogative as that of ' coining ',[2] and one which his Ecclesiastical Court was still

[1] *C.S.P.D.*, April, 1583, Vol. 1581-90, p. 107.
[2] *Ibid.*, Feb., Vol. 1635-6, p. 223.

prepared to defend. Thus Sir John Lambe, high commissioner, pursued a policy of supporting the rights of individual patentees against the Stationers' Company which was becoming dangerously powerful.

The Stationers' Company and the Universities

There was another obstacle which the Stationers' Company had to overcome before it could hope for supremacy—the claim of the Universities to be outside its control. From the time of Henry VII the Universities had enjoyed the royal patent. They owed no service to the London stationers, nor were they 'very charitably inclined to them or willing to yield to any reasonable motion' of theirs. It was an additional strengthening of the king's prerogative that they should maintain their independence, and in this they had the royal support. In 1623 the king interposed on their behalf and demanded from the Council a statement of the grounds on which they had forbidden Cambridge men to print certain books, 'as it was his desire to grant them favours'.[1] Probably with a desire also to maintain his own traditional rights the king issued in 1627 a confirmation of former charters and privileges granted to the University of Cambridge touching printing. Encouraged by Cambridge's example, Oxford petitioned to share in the same privileges, and the petition was granted. A decision of the judges in 1629 went in favour of three Cambridge men who had claimed the right to print books approved by the University notwithstanding patents already granted to the Stationers' Company.[2]

[1] *Ibid.*, Oct., 1623, Vol. 1623-5.
[2] *Ibid.*, Vol. 1628-9, p. 496.

In all this it is difficult not to see an attempt on the part of the king to maintain his prerogative. On one occasion he went so far as to interfere with a decision of the Commission that had discharged the author of a certain unauthorised publication though he was admittedly guilty. The king forbade his commissioners to liberate him and imposed instead a fine of a thousand pounds, which sum the king declared to be no more than the profit received from the book in question.

The Stationers' Company and the Royal Prerogative

The power of the Stationers' Company nevertheless increased and its relations with the king were not unfriendly. The position had been defined by the charter of 1557, and while so much power resided in the Company the stationers raised no objection to the royal censorship. But there was always a danger of the Company becoming too powerful and forgetting the traditional principle that no subject might publish his thoughts and opinions without the king's consent. This is indeed what happened. The king had been free with his patents : any little obscure printer applying for a patent was likely to have his application granted if the king chanced at the moment not to be favourably disposed to the Stationers' Company. The Universities further asserted their independence of the Company.

Thus the free exercise of the royal prerogative led to confusion. The Stationers' Company found its authority weakened, and as a result of the divided control there was less control. Abuses in the printing trade were frequent, and in 1627 there was open conflict. The Stationers' Company set the king's commands aside and asserted its right to print in defiance of them. The wardens were summoned before the Council for disobeying the king's command concerning the printing of the late bishop of Winchester's works. The bishop of London, official licenser for the king, presented his complaint and besought the Council ' to ' bring the stationers to better obedience ; they are exceed- ' ing bold in their printing .'[1]

Royal patents were granted not to individual printers alone but also to the Stationers' Company, which was gradually adding to the number of books in which it had the sole rights ; but although the power and wealth of the Company increased there could not be complete centralisation of control or co-ordination of printing so long as the king's printers were answerable to the crown and not first to the Company. A royal patent such as the king's printers enjoyed was more profitable to possess than freedom of the Stationers' Company, and there were frequent petitions for exclusive privileges. As late as 1576 someone petitioned for a monopoly of printing ballads and all books of twenty-four sheets and under. A protest, *The Humble Suite of the Stationers*,[2] was sent to the lord high treasurer, beseeching her majesty ' to have pity upon them and their families ' and not to allow any such grant. It is at least arguable that the stationers would not have presented

[1] *Ibid.*, Vol. 1627-8, p. 28.

[2] Arber's *Transcript of the Stationers' Register*, 1. 468.

this counter petition had there been no likelihood of the other being granted. Had it been granted, the dissolution of the Company must have followed, and in the crown would have resided all control of the press.

The Protecting of Patents

If the right of granting patents was to have any real value, the rights of patentees had of course to be protected. This was done. Heavy fines were imposed for infringement. For example, the ecclesiastical commissioners in March, 1616, fined T. Dawson forty pounds for his contempt in printing certain books contrary to a patent granted to another stationer. Obviously there were great difficulties in the way of protecting patentees; so that whenever an infringer of copyright came before the commissioners he was likely to be severely dealt with. In this way, by the systematic attempt of the commissioners to defend the rights of patentees, the royal patent gained in value.

There was a danger, though of a different kind, on the other side. If the rights of patentees were inviolable and the privileged printer certain of being free from competition, the incentive to produce good work would be lacking. There would be no competitors. Books would be carelessly printed, the printer being assured that the buyer would have to take what was offered—there would be no other editions to choose from.

It is to the credit of the high commissioners that they did not permit careless printing by the privileged to pass unrebuked. So eminent a man as Barker, the king's

6

printer, was called to account for misprints in his 1631 edition of the Bible. That the prosecuting bishops were chiefly moved with concern for the Reformed Church of England is true, but their prosecution of Barker was at the same time an attempt to arrest the deterioration of printing :—

'THE BISHOP OF LONDON would have the Church sett upright in her reputacion, that we are as carefull in printeing the Bible as they are of their Jesus' psalter : and whereas the Printers say this is stirred up by the malice of one man against them ; the Bishop saith he stirred not till the Bible was sould into his house, bought by his footman : and he saith the printinge is so bad and the paper too that, if it be not mended shortlie, they wilbe put downe by those of Amsterdam and their trade spoyled, and showed the two grossest errors, vizt. "Shalt commit adultery" and "great asse" ; for "shalt not committ adultery" and "greatnesse": THE ARCH-BISHOP OF CANTERBURY saith, that the Printers that print for his Matie have a very profitable place, and therefore should be more carefull. I knew the tyme when greater care was had about printeing, the Bibles especiallie, good compositors and the best correctors were gotten being grave and learned men, and the paper and letter rare and faire every way of the best ; but now the paper is naught, the composers boyes, and the correctors unlearned : There is a farmer and he makes the benefitt, and careth for nothing about it. They heertofore spent their whole time in printeing, but these looke to gaine, gaine, gaine, nothing els : if it be good to bribe, to give hundreds, thousands, what to doe ? not to benefitt the people, but to make a gaine, then they are to be commended : Well, let them looke to it : and let the cause proceed, saith the Arch Bishop. LONDON "There was a great deale of doo betweene you of this Citty and those of Cambridge heertofore about the priviledge of printeing the Bible and psalmes which they of Cambridge claymed ; then the Bible was exactlie printed, now you have forced the Cambridg printer to an agreement, now noe bible is right printed ".'[1]

The printers, Barker and Lucas, were heavily fined ; which was a salutary rebuke to the privileged.

The Sale of Patents

The value of the royal patent was enhanced by the action of the Attorney-General in taking Star Chamber proceedings against Bonham Norton and thirteen of his

[1] *Cases in the Courts of Star Chamber and High Commission* (S.R. Gardiner, *Camden Society*, 1886), p. 364-5.

associates ' for spreading false and scandalous rumours
' that the Lord Keeper had received a bribe of 600 *l.* for
' making a decree betwixt Barker and Norton for the office
' of king's printer '[1] which had then fallen vacant.

The practice of patentees selling their rights, of which
there is evidence, had it been general would have weakened
the royal patent which it was the policy of the King's
Commissioners to strengthen, and would have led to further
abuses. Here are two examples of the practice. From a
petition presented by one Clement Cotton in March, 1630,
it seems that the petitioner, the holder of a patent to print
a small Concordance with the Bible, had been ' constrained
' to assign that privilege to one Nicholas Bourne for a sum
' of money, being the only means to support petitioner and
' his wife in very aged and sickly estate '.[2] The king granted
a similar petition in 1631 wherein George Weckherlin
' trusted the king would vouchsafe him some gracious
' acknowledgment of his service, lest he should undo himself
' and his family thereby '. The late king had granted licence
to one of his footmen for twenty-one years to cause to
print certain books, and, that term being almost expired, the
petitioner prayed for a patent in reversion for thirty-one
years for printing the same books and several others specified, ' whereby he might get some small recompence, as the
' footman did, by letting the same grant to the Stationers'
' Company '.[3] His request was granted. But the selling of
patents was not to be encouraged.

[1] *C.S.P.D.*, Vol. 1629-31, p. 285.
[2] *Ibid.*, p. 208.
[3] *Ibid.*, p. 514.

' The Freedom of the Press '

So long as printers and stationers held their patent from the king, so long were they under his control. Privileged printers and stationers could not be regarded as safe custodians of the subject's liberty to publish his thoughts and opinions uncensored. But that liberty was not part of the Englishman's birthright, and measures of repression which now seem tyrannical were not then understood as such. The principle of the freedom of the subject to publish his thoughts had not been formulated. To the sixteenth century Englishman it would have seemed a dangerous and undesirable claim for anyone to make. Yet when events proved that it was equally dangerous and undesirable for anyone to have full control of the press, the principle was not long in being enunciated.

Protests against the Royal Prerogative

The trouble began with the unprivileged printers prosecuting their trade in defiance of the privileged, which they did, not from any unselfish regard for the liberty of the subject, but in order to make money. The most profitable books were in the right of a few favoured stationers to print, and to print books for which there was little demand was not lucrative enough if the small printers were to make a living. The demand for books was small, work was scarce, not enough to go round, and the trade was overstocked with journeymen and apprentices. There was, of course, no patent required to print the lighter, ephemeral pamphlets, and it was from the printers of such that the privileged were chiefly threatened.

The first protest against the crown's assumption that no subject could publish his thoughts without royal permission followed the printing of the first English New Testament in 1525, when seditious books were privately printed at home or smuggled over from abroad. Special edicts were issued against them that the king's subjects might be kept pure and clean of all contagion from books ' swarm full of heresies and detestable opinions '. The bishops, with authority from the king, prepared *A Public Instrument*[1] ' for the abolishing of the Scriptures and other books to be read in English ' ; one, John Gough of London, ' pryn-' ter, was sent to the Flytt for prynting and selling of ' sedycyous books ',[2] all Lutheran books (including some like *A Pleasant New Nosegay* and *Christmas Carols very new and very godly* whose connexion with Luther was less obvious) were banned and copies burned in public. During Henry VIII's reign the measures taken against printers were for offences in common law and not for unlicensed publication, for there was as yet no act which required men to obtain permission before proceeding to print.

THE EARLY HISTORY OF LICENSING
The Religious Motive

The motive prompting the earliest attempts at licensing was largely religious. The invention of the printing press had first put the Bible into wide circulation. But if the Scriptures had been made more easily accessible, so had the

---

[1] *Foxe's Acts and Monuments*, Vol. 5, p. 569, 1530.

[2] *Ibid.*, p. 831, 1541.

writings of heretics : and the cause of true religion had to be protected from the attacks which an extension of the liberty of printing to the vulgar would certainly produce. It was felt that religious controversies should not be allowed to be conducted in print, but a sanctified use of the press would be in the interest of the faith once committed to the saints :—

'the art of printing has been and is a great help to the furthering of God's true religion, the renoun of both Universities, and the salvation of souls both in this kingdom and all the world. By this mystery the happy enjoyment of the Holy Bible and all other good books has been and is, through God's mercy, a great blessing to this kingdom. . . .'[1]

As we have already observed, Henry VIII, acknowledged by the clergy in 1531 as Defender of the Faith, had maintained his right over the press. In 1534 the first act for the regulating of printing was passed. It may be that his experience of foreign interference in other matters helped to secure an easy passage for this act which aimed at protecting native printers against foreign printers, and at providing against the importation of foreign books. The earliest printers had been foreigners and there were enough foreigners amongst the stationers to justify complaints that the native craftsmen were suffering through their competition.

The Reformation released a flood of books of controversy in England, most of them imported. The means of censorship proved ineffectual against them, surreptitious books in defence of the Lutheran doctrines being widely circulated.

The first licensing restrictions came into force in 1549, in the time of Edward VI. They were directed against

[1] *C.S.P.D.*, Vol. 1640-1, p. 509.

papistical books : ' Mr. Secretary Peter, Mr. Secretary
' Smith and Mr. Cicill or the one of them being authorised
' to examine all English books '[1] for the press.

Again, the religious motive is to be found in the granting
of a Charter to the Stationers' Company in 1557. The
Charter was intended as a precaution against the spread
of heresy, as well as a safeguard to the authority of the
crown to control the press. The opening words of the
Charter make that clear :—

> ' Know ye that we considering and manifestly perceiving, that several
> seditious and heretical books, both in verse and prose, are daily published,
> stamped and printed by divers scandalous, schismatical, and heretical
> persons, not only exciting our subjects and liegemen to sedition and dis-
> obedience against us, our crown and dignity, but also to the renewal and
> propagating very great and detestable heresies against the faith and sound
> catholick doctrine of holy mother the church. . . .'[2]

In the following year, 1558, Queen Mary reversed the
licensing machinery, directing it against Protestants
instead of Papists. Protestants were given no freedom
whatever to publish their opinions. According to Arber,[3]
her proclamation of June, 1558, against Protestant books
of ' heresye, sedityon and treason ' fairly out-Herods
Herod. The mere possession of a ' wycked ' book made one
a rebel in the eye of the law and liable to be executed without delay. Mary had embarked on a religious persecution
and to that end exercised her prerogative over the press.

When Elizabeth came to the throne she set herself to
undo what Mary had done. Her *Injunctions given by her
Majestie*, issued in 1559, provided (*inter alia*) for a strict

[1] E. Gordon Duff's *Century of English Book-Trade*, Introd. p.xxv.
[2] *Ibid.*, Introd. p. xxvii.
[3] Arber's *Transcript of Stationers' Register*, Vol. 1, p. 92.

censorship of the press. Thus she sought to consolidate her own royal right of control over the press. In the fifty-first Item of the *Injunctions* the religious motive plainly appears. The document, though it is reprinted in Arber's *Transcript of the Stationers' Register*,[1] is worth quoting here, if only for the reader's convenience :—

51. *Item* because there is a great abuse in the printers of bokes, which for covetousnes cheifly regard not what they print, so thei may have gaine, whereby arriseth great dysorder by publicatyon of vnfrutefull, vayne and infamous bokes and papers : The Quenes maiestie straytly chargethe and commandeth, that no manner of person shall print any manner of boke or paper, of what sort, nature, or in what language soever it be, excepte the same be first licenced by her maiestie by expresse wordes in writynge, or by vi. of her priuy counsel, or be perused and licensed by the archbysshops of CANTORBURY and YORKE, the bishop of LONDON, the chauncelours of both vnyuersities, the bishop being ordinary (i.e. *Ecclesiastical Judge as well*), and the Archdeacon also of the place where any suche shalbe printed, or by two of them, whereof the ordinary of the place to be alwaies one. And that the names of such as shal allowe the same, to be added in the ende of every such worke, for a testymone of the allowaunce thereof. And bycause many pampheletes, playes and balletes, be often times printed, wherein regard wold be had, that nothinge therin should be either heretical, sedicious or vnsemely for Christian eares : Her maiestie likewise commandeth, that no manner of person shall enterprise to print any such, except the same be to him lycenced by suche her maiesties commyssioners, or iii of them, as be appoynted in the citye of London to here, and determine divers causes ecclesiasticall, tending to the execution of certayne statutes, made the last parliament for vnyformitye of order in religion. And yf any shall sell or vtter, any manner of bokes or papers, beynge not licensed as is abouesaid : That the same party shalbe punyshed by order of the sayde commyssyoners, as to the qualitie of the faulte shalbe thought mete. And touchinge all other bokes of matters of religyon, or polycye, or governaunce, that hathe ben printed, either on this side the Seas, or on the other side, bicause the diuersitie of them is great, and that there nedeth good consideration to be had of the perticularyties thereof : her maiestye referreth the prohibition, or permission thereof : to the order whiche her saide commissioners within the Citie of London shall take, and notifye. Accordynge to the whyche, her maiestye straightly commandeth al manner her subiectes, and specially the wardens and company of Stationers, to be obedyent.

Prouyded that these orders to not extend to anye prophane [i.e. classical] aucthours, and workes in any language, that hat ben heretofore commonly receyued or allowed in any the vnyuersities or Scoles : But the same may be prynted and vsed, as by good order they are accustomed.

[1] Vol. 1, p. xxxviii.

Further evidence of the religious motive behind the early attempts to regulate the press is to be found in Elizabeth's appointment of ecclesiastics as the first licensers, men who approached their censoring duties remembering that they were trustees of the national religion. Elizabeth had thus captured the press for the Protestant Episcopal Church, whose bishops now become arbiters of the public taste in books. Prelates decide whether Puritan books shall be licensed or not, the Lords Spiritual may now ban any book which they consider disadvantageous to the ' religion, or polycye or governance ' of the country.

The *Injunctions* served the purpose for which they had been designed, but there are not wanting signs that the man with the private press and the courage of his convictions continued to print. In 1560, as appears from a letter[1] from the High Commission to the Stationers' Company, ' certayne evill desposyd persons ' having ' secretly taken upon them to prynte ', kept ' pryvye presses ' for that purpose.

To prevent such evasions of the law, further legislation was necessary. Hence Elizabeth's Star Chamber Decree of 1566.

It is significant that Robert Caley,[2] chief Roman Catholic printer in Mary's reign, gave up printing at the same time. One of the most successful printers of his day, yet he did not consider it profitable or expedient to conduct his business surreptitiously. There would have been a market for

[1] *Arber, ibid.* II. 62.
[2] Duff's *Century of English Book-Trade.*

14

his work—Roman Catholics who had openly bought his publications in the days of Catholic Mary would have found means to buy them secretly with Protestant Elizabeth on the throne.

Apparently the 1566 ordinance was enforced. Searchers were employed to bring the law-breakers to account. The study of John Stow, the Annalist, was searched by order of her majesty's licensers in 1569[1], and the Bishop of London reported the papistical nature of the books discovered. They were described as ' unlawful books '. It was sufficient that they were papistical, and the searchers contented themselves with drawing up a catalogue which exposed him to a more serious charge than that of being in possession of unlicensed books.

Again, it was for offences against other laws of the realm than those which provided for the regulation of the press that a printer, W. Carter, was hanged at Tyburn in 1584. He had several times been imprisoned ' for printinge of lewde pamphelettes ', and was described by the Bishop of London in a report to the Lord High Treasurer as ' a very lewd fellow '. A search of his house authorised by the Bishop brought to light, amongst ' other naughtye papystycall bookes ', dangerous pamphlets establishing a charge of sedition against him : for which, rather than for his contempt of the licensing laws, he was condemned to be ' drawne from Newgate to Tiborne and there hanged, bowelled and quartered '.[2]

[1] Arber's *Transcript of the Stationers' Register*, 1, 393.
[2] Stow's *Annals*.

The First Puritan Protest

So long as the unlicensed printer was a Roman Catholic and could be summoned on a charge of publishing heresy, the laws for controlling the press were not to blame for his punishment. It was then a question of religious toleration, and the country's recent experience of a Roman Catholic queen prevented a popular agitation against the tyrannies of censorship when Carter was hanged, bowelled and quartered. He was seen as a traitor to a now Protestant throne and not as a fellow countryman whose ideas on the freedom of the press were two centuries in advance of his time. But when the unlicensed printer was a Protestant there was a disposition to rebel against what was at once felt to be a tyrannical censorship. There were signs of public agitation. In her zeal for the newly established Protestant Church the queen failed to distinguish between the loyal Puritans and the disloyal Catholics. Protestant reformer and Catholic heretic were classed as one, for both threatened the stability of the Episcopal church. Hence her proclamation of June, 1573, which was intended to put an end to puritan books, which could only ' breede talkes and disputes agaynst common order '.

' . . . Her highnesse strayghtly chargeth and commandeth al and every Printer, Stationer, Booke bynder, Marchaunt, and al other men of what qualite or condition he or they be, who hath in theyr custodie any of the sayd bookes, to bring in the same to the Byshop of the diocesse, or to one of her hyghnesse priuie Counsel, within twentie dayes after that he shal haue notice of this Proclamation, and not to kepe any of them without licence or allowance of the sayde Byshop, vpon payne of imprysonment, and her highnesse further displeasure.'[1]

When this period of twenty days had elapsed the bishop

[1] Arber's *Transcript of the Stationers' Register*, 1, 464.

16

reported that not a single copy of any proscribed book had been brought to him.

'. . . and I can hardly think yat your Lordships of hir Maiesties privey Counsell haue receyued many, whearby it may easily appeare, what boldnesse and disobedience the new writers have already wrought in the myndes of the people : and that agaynst the Ciuill Magistrates, whome in wordes they seme to extoll, but whois authoritie in very dede they labor to cast downe, for he seeith litill yat doth not perceyue how that their whole procedinges tend to a mere popularitie . . .'[1]

The objection to Episcopalian bishops as licensers was one that appealed strongly to the loyal Puritans. It was a recognition of the dangers of committing the power of licensing into the hands of any one dignitary of the Anglican church that inspired a certain William Lambarde in 1577 to draw up a proposed *Act of Parliament for the Establishment of The Governors of the English Print,*[2] which would have placed that power, so far as the metropolitan press was concerned, no longer in the hands of one man, the Bishop of London, but in the hands of a Committee of twelve, eight of whom should be lawyers. The author of this curious document did not propose the abolition of all licensing, but that provision should be made against the injustice of licensers all belonging to the same religious party.

John Wolfe and the Royal Prerogative

The first noteworthy statement of the subject's liberty to publish at will came from an unprivileged printer, John Wolfe, who had a highly developed sense of personal liberty. He is described as a fishmonger. The most

[1] *Ibid.,* 1, 466.
[2] *Ibid.,* II, 751.

flagrant of the early offenders against the royal prerogative in printing, he set up several secret presses and defiantly printed whatever he pleased, disregarding other men's patents and privileges. The queen's patentees, although hard hit by the pirating of Wolfe and his associates, were ready to do everything in reason or in courtesy to amend their differences with the pirates. But John Wolfe in the name of liberty was not ready for any agreement : ' he ' generally affirmed that he may and will print any lawfull ' booke notwithstanding any commandment of the Quene, ' and to that end he hath incensed the popularitie of ' London, as in a common cause somewhat Daungerously '.[1]

Unlike Carter who suffered for his religious convictions, Wolfe could not be indicted on a charge of heresy. Carter had printed and disseminated opinions held to be damaging to the religion and government of the country, and was the victim of a public policy which barely tolerated the Roman Catholic in the midst and certainly would not tolerate Catholic propaganda. The question of the freedom of the press was merely a forgotten part of the larger and more pressing problem of religious toleration. And when he went to Tyburn in the cart, the ' popularitie ' were not incensed, for there went a Roman Catholic, and they remembered Mary. But with Wolfe it was a different matter. He was a Protestant and a printer trying to make a living despite the royal prerogative which had given exclusive privileges to other printers. He was a printer, not a religious propagandist : so that when he came under

[1] Norton's Letter to Goring (*Arber* II, 773).

the displeasure of the Privy Council it would have been an act of folly to have hanged and bowelled him. Of course, the law allowed no such penalty to be inflicted, but it would have been impolitic to have inflicted any punishment which might have made a martyr of him. A public discussion of the whole question of the subject's liberty in the matter of printing, the government would have found most inconvenient. If Wolfe had been punished there might have been an incensed populace to deal with. Therefore he was not bowelled. Instead, he was promoted and became a privileged printer himself, and put up the sword which he had unsheathed so mettlesomely in the cause of freedom.

Great interest had been shown in Wolfe and in his protest against what he held to be an entrenchment on the subject's traditional liberty. It would be unkind to say that he objected to monopolies so long as other men held them, and lost his zeal for the cause of unprivileged printing only when some of the privileges came his own way. Yet his indignation against the authorities abated so suddenly that it is difficult not to look for the explanation in the fact that he was himself singled out by the stationers for special employment. At the time, however, there was every prospect of an uproar. Even when he was in the Clink ' divers poore men of sundry companies ' resorted unto him. His behaviour was described as insolent and contemptuous. His agents ran up and down to all the fairs and markets throughout the country selling cheap, pirated books. There were demonstrations of public opinion : conventicles of people gathered in his house, in the Exchange, and in the Church called St Thomas of Acres, ' so disorderly that some of themselves fearing some ' hurley burley to follow, departed away, as they confessed '.[1] He professed himself the ' Luther of the book-trade '.

Nothing more is heard of the ' incensed popularitie ' of London, although none of the grievances which had caused their fury had been removed.

The 1586 Star Chamber Decree

Archbishop Whitgift, far from relaxing the restrictions, made them more severe. He had good reason for so doing. According to Strype :

' many disaffected books and scurrilous libels were daily published and dispersed against the government, especially against that of the Church, in respect of its religious worship, and episcopal jurisdiction, whereby many men became prejudiced against conformity, and a peaceable compliance with the Church's orders ; and their minds blown up with discontents and doubts, about the usages and present practices of the Church. The Archbishop therefore thought it highly necessary to have a strict watch there, and to stop any copies going to the press before they had been seen by the Bishop of the diocese, or some reverend and able persons, diligently read over and allowed. And not to permit any to be printed or published, that impugned the doctrine or discipline, or that made any unworthy reflections upon the Queen or the State.'[2]

In 1586 Star Chamber made another effort to control the press, and sent forth *The newe Decrees of the Starre Chamber for orders in printinge*, which is the most important act of its kind till the Star Chamber decree of 1637. In the preamble it is definitely stated that there were ' dyvers ' contentyous and disorderlye persons professinge the arte ' or mysterye of Pryntinge ', and that ' abuses and enormities ' were increasing. The decree announced that the most Reverend in God the Archbishop of Canterbury and

[1] *Arber*, II, 779.

[2] *Life and Acts of Archbishop Whitgift*, by John Strype (Vol. 1, p. 422).

the Bishop of London were appointed licensers, that nothing was to be printed that had not first been perused by both or one of them, and that all printing was to be confined to London and the two Universities. The Stationers' Company were to search for printing presses hidden in obscure corners and to seize unlawful books and bring them to Stationers' Hall. The Company were forbidden to elect new printers without special recommendation from the licensers. And severe penalties were fixed for infringements of the law.

The question now seemed to have been resolved. The authority of the crown had been strengthened, its right to grant privileges reserved and respected ; the Stationers' Company was little more than the privileged executor of royal decrees and likely to remain satisfied so long as its privileges were safeguarded and secure ; and the penalties for unlicensed printing were heavy enough to warrant the hope that there would be no more ' Luthers of the book-trade '. Yet it must not be supposed that any of these decrees for regulating printing was completely successful. They suppressed more or less effectually the professional pirates, but whenever there was any cause, religious or political, to be advocated in opposition to the established religion or government, and the printing press presented itself as the most successful method of advocacy, there were not wanting private persons who would take the risk incurred by illegal printing. Books so produced were either printed surreptitiously at home or else printed abroad and smuggled into the country.

THE INCREASE IN FOREIGN PRINTING AND THE IMPORTATION OF UNLICENSED BOOKS, 1476-1637

From the beginning there was a close connection between foreign and native printing. The first printers had been foreigners. From them Caxton had learned the art : and the best printing came from foreign presses. The less skilled English printers suffered from their competition, and disputes began as early as 1500 : they ended, naturally, in favour of the native craftsmen.[1] When it became expedient to limit the number of presses and of printers, a measure of protection was given to the native printers, and the importation of books was regulated. England ceased to be an open market for foreign books, though the denizened stranger retained some of his privileges. Even by the seventeenth century many foreign names were to be found among the printers[2]

As late as 1638 the ancient right of certain foreign printers to sell their books in England was respected : in 1640 Adrian Vlack, printer at Amsterdam, petitioned Sir John Lambe about the liberty given him by Star Chamber for two years to import ' lawful books printed beyond sea, which time is almost expired '. Having a great many Greek books still unsold he prayed for the continuation of his liberty.[3]

[1] Strype says that at Basel ' Englishmen were chosen for the overseers and correctors of the press, being noted for the most careful and diligent of all others '. *Memorials of Archbishop Cranmer*, Vol. 1, p. 511.

[2] See R. B. M'Kerrow's *Dict. of Printers*.

[3] *C.S.P.D.*, Vol. 1640, p. 27.

However, there was much smuggling of unlawful books into this country. It went on in spite of all attempts by the government to stop it. The Puritans suspected that it was more difficult to import Puritan than Roman Catholic books, and they accused Whitgift of giving a private licence to a bookseller to import Popish books secretly for a member of the Privy Council.[1] In 1630 Robert Barker, the king's printer, informed the Council of the importation of secretly printed English Bibles, liturgies and other church books of right belonging to him,[2] the which tended to corrupt the text and foster heresy. Search was made for ' persons probably suspected to imprint or import such books '. By the severities of its penalties the High Commission Court sought to prevent such illegalities—for example, the Lady Eleanor Davies was fined 3000 *l.* and committed to the Gatehouse for importing books printed at Amsterdam.[3] And there were government searchers in plenty. The Master and Wardens of the Stationers' Company, all justices of the peace, mayors and sheriffs were employed in the search for smuggled books.

It was more difficult for the searchers when the unlawful books came from Scotland, for books could be smuggled more easily over the border than across the Channel, and were harder to detect. Printing had been introduced into Scotland by Henry VII in 1507 : the office of king's printer was duplicated in Edinburgh. Robert Young,[4]

[1] *History of the Puritans*, Vol. 1, p. 385.
[2] *C.S.P.D.*, Vol. 1629-31, p. 306.
[3] *Ibid.*, Vol. 1633-4, p.261.
[4] Plomer's *Dictionary of Printers.*

appointed to that position in 1632, exported into England so many copies of the Bible that holders of the patent to print Bibles in England complained that they had been thereby ' damnified to the extent[1] of 1000 *l.* '. Growing numbers of secular books also were imported from Scotland. The Journeymen printers of London whose trade had consequently suffered, appealed to Sir John Lambe to suppress the Scottish books and to see them well supplied with work before permitting Scotsmen to export ' all sorts of books ' into England.[2]

Thus from the beginning of the history of printing unlawful books were smuggled into this country. It was a common method of circumventing the law ; and so long as it remained possible to evade the law in this way the tyranny of the Government over the press could not be absolute.

IRREGULARITIES AND ABUSES IN THE PRINTING-TRADE, 1583-1638

The disputes among the Stationers' Company, unattached privileged printers and the Crown had weakened the control of printing and given the secret printer his opportunity. With the settlement of these disputes, and the consequently increased vigilance of the authorities, the risk attached to surreptitious printing was great enough to deter all except the enthusiast who for the sake of his ' cause ' was ready to brave the penalties.[3]

[1] *C.S.P.D.*, Vol. 1636-37, p. 267.
[2] *Ibid.*, p. 478.
[3] *Circa* 1588.

Martin Marprelate, 1586

Martin Marprelate, an enthusiastic Puritan pamphleteer, in his zeal for championing the cause of Puritanism against the established form of Protestantism, defied the licensing system, and set up a private printing press. Whitgift ordered a thorough search to be made for the bold printer of Martin's tracts, who was not easily unearthed from his hiding-place. The printing press was kept on the move, travelling from Kingston-on-Thames to Northampton and as far as Manchester, where the printers were finally discovered and arrested. Martin escaped, but the chase had become so hot that he deemed it unsafe to provoke the bishops to further pursuit. In a final pamphlet he promoted himself as champion of the Puritan cause which he offered publicly to debate with the bishops. His offer was ignored.

The Marprelate controversy was a theological one. It was not about the freedom of the press, but it plainly showed that the press was entirely in the hands of the bishops, and certainly not free.

Michael Sparke's Protest against Monopolies

Within the book trade itself—to which, of course, Martin Marprelate did not belong—a successor to John Wolfe was found in Michael Sparke,[1] ' a vigorous opponent of monopolies '. From 1621 to 1631 he was frequently admonished and imprisoned, and ' although he promised ' to submit to his governors as other moderate men did, yet ' [he] grew more refractory and offensive than ever '.[2] He

[1] Plomer's *Dict. of Printers*.

[2] *C.S.P.D.*, Vol. 1631-3, p. 3.

was not disposed to submit to any restriction of his liberty to print whatever he pleased. If by so doing he infringed any man's copyright, he protested the illegality of the Crown to confer any such rights. He was also ready to print in defiance of the licensers' taste in books. He was made to stand in the pillory and heavily fined for printing Prynne's books. There was much that was disorderly about Sparke— he was indisputably greedy—but after Wolfe had allowed prosperity to silence his protest against privileges, Sparke was the only printer or stationer to offer any considerable opposition to monopolies. Summoned before the Ecclesiastical Commissioners in May, 1629, he had the courage to deny the binding authority of the Star Chamber decree for regulating printing, as directly entrenching on the hereditary liberty of the subject's person and goods, and being contrary to Magna Charta, the Petition of Right and other statutes.[1] He denied having done anything which was not for ' the glory of God, the honour of the king, the ' good of the Church and the welfare of the doctrine of the ' Church of England '.

Licensing Frauds

Sparke was not above uttering books falsely purporting to have been printed[2] at Cambridge by the authorised printers. This was but one of the many less creditable but common methods of defying the law. One of the least commendable of these evasions was the practice of altering the text of a book after it had received the licenser's

[1] *Ibid.*, Vol. 1628-9, p. 538.
[2] S. R. Gardiner's *Cases in Star Chamber.*

imprimatur. There is a curious record of a book being printed and sold whilst the stationer was still awaiting the licenser's decision concerning a dedicatory epistle which had been written after the book had been delivered to the stationer. The epistle remained in the hands of the licenser for three weeks. Meanwhile the stationer, with a keen eye to the marketable value of the book, saw it hurriedly through the press and had five or six hundred copies sold before an injunction to restrain its publication came from the Archbishop. What advantage this was to the stationer is not easily determined. He was committed to prison for fourteen days with the loss of his books. The book was intended as propaganda by the Earl of Essex' party : so perhaps the stationer was paid out of the party funds. The point of present interest is that the stationer, publishing a book of that kind, should have tried to get it by a quirk past the licenser.[1]

It continued to be a common practice to tamper with the text of a book after it had passed the licenser. In 1635 a corrector of the king's printing house in Blackfriars complained to the king that it was too frequent a thing to vitiate copies of books after they had come from the licenser, and for schismatical additions to be inserted to the disquiet of both State and Church. The remedy he proposed was a simple one, namely, that books should not be divulged before examination and that there should be an office to view printed books.[2]

[1] *C.S.P.D.*, Vol. 1598-1601, p. 450.
[2] *Ibid.*, Vol. 1635-6, p. 75.

The licenser's name and *imprimatur* were frequently affixed to publications which had no legal title to them. Admittance was thus gained to markets which were closed to unlicensed books. There were other abuses, too, which, however much the subject might wish for complete freedom to publish, made a certain amount of control necessary. For instance, fictitious speeches professing to be the actual words of the king were printed and they no doubt imposed on the credulity of the undiscerning, and at the same time injured the cause of liberty. In 1637 John Donne, the poet's son, complained to the Archbishop that since the death of his father many scandalous pamphlets were published under his name which were none of his. The offending printers were men well known and reputed in the trade, yet they paid little heed to Donne's remonstrances.[1]

The Government Searchers

The cause of the unprivileged printer further suffered from the vigilance of the stationers who, appointed by the Crown to see the printing laws enforced, had a personal interest in seeing the law obeyed ; for it was to the advantage of the Stationers' Company that the secret printers who threatened their prosperity should be ferreted out of their obscure hiding places and clapt in gaol. Probably Queen Elizabeth had realised what incentive the registered stationers would have to obey her when she commanded them to help in suppressing the disorderly. It was the

[1] *Ibid.*, Vol. 1637-8, p. 25.

policy of the government, declared by all subsequent legislation, to work *through*, and not apart from, the Company. It was to their own advantage that the stationers should do the work thoroughly, hermetically nail up the irregular printing houses and irreparably break the secret presses. No more conscientious executors of the laws against disorderly printers could have been found than those who had a material interest in their suppression. John Wolfe's value to the Company and to Archbishop Whitgift may thus be appreciated. Stationers' Hall was made the headquarters of the fight against the pirates. The stationers had no cause to complain of neglect nor the government of the negligence of the stationers. They were commanded to ' take notice what every printer had in working ', and their right of search was based on the royal Charter.

When objections to this right of search were raised they were based on the more ancient rights of personal liberty. As far back as October, 1582, the Wardens of the Stationers' Company had complained to Lord Burghley that a certain printer and his family had refused to let them search their house :

'. . . upon occation of Distruste of the contemptuous dealinge of certain lude Prynters, against her Maiesties Letters Pattentes as otherwyse againste all goode Orders of our poore Companye, we caused a searche and viewe to be made, by tow discreate persones in everye Pryntinge house, thereby to understand and take notice what everye Printer had in workinge accordinge to a laudable use warranted by Charter to our saide Companye under her Highnesse greate seale of England. But so it is right Honorable and our singular good Lorde, that comminge to the howse of one *Roger Warde* A man who of late hathe shewed himselfe very contemptuous againste her Maiesties high prerogative and offering to comme into his pryntinge house to take notice what he did, the saide *Roger Warde* fainynge himselfe to be absente, hys wyfe and servantes keepeth the Dore shutte againste them, and saide that none shoulde comme there to searche neither woulde in any wyse suffer any man to enter into the howse, by lykelyhoode whereof, and of tow good proofe he printeth what he lysteth, and persisteth in the same behaviour tyll your Honoure of your singular goodnesse vouch-safe to take order to the contrarye, as we hope of your vertuous inclination to Justice you will as well againste the saide *Roger Warde* as other most presumptuous and insolent persons, of whome the most Honourable master Secretarye WALSINGHAME can further informe your Lord-shippe. . . .'[1]

The government searchers rapidly acquired a reputation for dishonesty. Those employed at the Custom House, for example, were accused of opening cases and reserving some of the books contained in them for their own use. For a similar offence one, John Egerton, was sent to the Gate-house in 1635. Having private intelligence that certain uncustomed books lay at an inn at Aldgate, he had gone thither and seized them. Opening the packs he found them to contain Bibles printed and brought from beyond seas. Instead of reporting the affair, he bargained with the owner for a large sum of money to be given him in return for which he agreed to say no more about it. After the discovery of Egerton's corrupt dealings the Court of High Commission decreed that the Customs' searchers should not suffer any packs of books to be opened till the Archbishop of Canterbury or the Bishop of London had appointed his chaplain with the Warders of the Stationers' Company to be present.

George Wither and the Stationers' Company

A certain dispute which took place about 1624 between George Wither, the poet, and the Stationers' Company,

[1] *Arber, T.S.R.*, II, 777.

while not important in itself, shows that the power of the Company was such that even a royal patent might be worthless unless it had the approval of the Company. The story of the dispute is, therefore, worth retelling.

Wither had applied to the king for sole rights in his *Hymns and Songs of the Church* which he had prepared for publication and which he desired to protect from the pirates. The king granted him a fifty-one years' monopoly and commanded that no copy of the *Psalms in Metre*—a book in the privilege of the Stationers' Company and one for which there was a steady demand—should be printed without containing Withers' new songs and hymns as a supplement. The stationers protested that their own ancient privilege was cancelled out by the new one granted to Wither. Therefore they boycotted the book, the book-binders refused to include it within the covers of the *Psalms in Metre*, and Wither complained of the book-sellers' dissuading people from buying it. In his *Schollers Purgatory*[1] he replied to his critics, making it clear that his quarrel was not with the stationers in general but only with the dishonest stationers. This document is chiefly interesting for its lively sketches of typical stationers, honest and dishonest. The dishonest are accused of

' . . . taking upon them to publish bookes contrived, altered, and mangled at their owne pleasures, without consent of the writers : nay and to change the name some-tymes, both of booke and Author (after they have been ymprinted) and all for their owne private lucre ; like traders in stuffes, who under new names, many tymes shift off their old wares. And yet further also, to disparage, or censure maliciously, both writers, and their labours and so usurp unto themselves the high authority of the Church and State. . . .'

[1] *circa* 1624.

From which it appears that Wither regarded the power of censorship as residing in the authority of the Church and the State.

Naturally he resented the stationers' rebellious attitude towards himself and the privilege conferred on him by letters-patent from the king, for the power of the Stationers' Company was sufficient to nullify the advantages he had expected from the patent. Sir Sidney Lee[1] says it was anxiety to secure the full profits of his growing literary work that induced Wither to take this exceptional mode of guaranteeing his rights in his next volume, the *Hymns and Songs*. But Wither denied that his aim was at all mercenary :

' . . . Some give out that my booke contains nothing but a few needles Songs : which I composed, and gott privileged by Patent, merely for my private benefit, to the oppression of the Common-wealth. . . .'

While the hope of private benefit was not absent from his thought, his motive was at the same time to provide something good and godly *pro bono publico* : so that he resented the claim of mercenary booksellers to have their interest in every man's labour of that kind and their objection to him that he had compassed a privilege to the public grievance :

' . . . Good God ! how many dung-botes full of fruitless Volumnes doe they yearely foyst upon his Majesties subjectes, by lying Titles, insinuations, and disparaging more profitable Books ! . . .'

Let them cease talking of the public good who were thinking only of personal profit, and he would discourse of the matter peaceably, but—' Good God ! '

The Commonwealth of Stationers he described as a ' tyranny unheard of in former ages '. More than ten

[1] *Dict. Nat. Biog.*

years after the publication of the *Schollers Purgatory* the stationers and Wither met before the Council to determine their differences, and the stationers to answer for their contempt of the patent held by Wither. He had himself been guilty of irregular conduct—the printing of his *Schollers Purgatory* partly without licence, for which he had been summoned before the Ecclesiastical Court in 1623-4[1] Neither party, therefore, was blameless when the matter was sifted by the Commissioners in 1634, and the judgment given was in itself a compromise. Wither's patent was disallowed in so far as it forbade the publishing of the Psalter without his metrical supplement, though he still retained his rights in the book.

THE PRELATICAL TYRANNY OVER THE PRESS

The bishops went to Elizabeth's statute for their authority to ban as seditious all puritan as well as papistical books. It was an interpretation which the statute did not altogether justify. In 1592 a petition was ' directed to her ' most excellent Maiestie, wherein is delivered a proofe that ' they who write for Reformation, doe not offend against ' the Statute of Elizabeth and therefore till matters bee ' compounded, deserve more favour '.[2] The writer, not to run the risk of being persecuted by the bishops, preferred to remain anonymous, and hoped that no one would think any the less of his petition because it was unsigned—after

[1] *C.S.P.D.*, Vol. 1623-5, p. 143. Wither's excuse was that he *had* intended getting a license for it. He was sent to prison.

[2] *Brit. Mus.*, 108.b2.

all (he pointed out) no one thinks the less of the *Epistle to the Hebrews* because the author of it preferred anonymity. The argument of the bishops is put in syllogistic form :

' *Whosoever write bookes to the diffamation of her Maiestie, and to raise rebellion, doe offende against this Statute, and are felons.*

They that write for Reformation, make bookes to diffame the Queene, and raise rebellion.

Therefore the writers for Reformation offende against this statute, and are felons.'[1]

The writer denies the imputation of disloyalty which the bishops have laid upon the reformers. He protests the loyalty of the reformers to the queen, and suggests that it is the bishops who are guilty of disloyalty in doing in her majesty's name what is contrary to the spirit of her decrees. The reformer may not publish his thoughts :

' . . . The followers of Reformation lacke libertie to aunswere in their owne cause[2] If they speake, they be silenced : if they write, they want Printers. They be shut up in close prisons, their handes (as it were) bounde, & then buffeted. They are blindfolded, and then must reed, *who did smite them.*'

The ecclesiastical tyranny over the liberties of the Puritan was almost complete. *Habeas Corpus* seems to have been arbitrarily suspended by the bishops whenever it was inconvenient to bring Puritan prisoners to trial. Offenders were often committed without warrant and kept in prison, sometimes for over a year, before they were tried for their offences. The prisons were unhealthy, damp, ill-ventilated, insanitary : and the bishops could make use of them for the incarceration and effective silencing of their more obstinate enemies without much question. Several papers in the Harleian MS. Collection (No. 6848)

[1] *Ibid.*, p. 15.

[2] *Ibid.*, p. 26.

which are in part printed by Arber in his *Martin Marprelate Controversy*[1] give proof of the inhuman methods which the bishops had of dispensing justice.

In the course of a ' lamentable petition delivered to ye Queenes Maiestye the 13 of March 1588 ' the bishops are attacked for

' . . . Daily spoilinge, vesing, molestinge, hurtinge, pursuynge, Imprisoninge yea barringe and locking them up close prisoners in the most un(w)holsome and vyle prysones, and their deteyninge them, without bringinge them to their answeres, untyll the LORD by death put an ende to their myseries. Some they have haled ffrom theire honeste labours in their trades, and Caste them lo(a)den handes and feete with boultes and fetters of yron in to Cold and noysome prysons Close prisoners. Some they have Cast into the " Little Ease " : some they have put into the " Myll " Causinge them to be beaten with Cudgels in their prysones : others in the nighte tyme they have apprehended and drawen out of their houses yea out of their beddes ffrom their wiefes shuttinge them upp Close prysoners, separatinge them most ungodlye ffrom their wiefes, Children, famylies, Callinges, trades, laboures to their utter undoinge, and the affamishemente of their poore wiefes and children.

All this barbarous havocke they make without regard of age, sexe, estate, or Degree as may appeare by the lamentable estate of those which remayne, and by the Deathes of others by them murthered in the prisons, whose blood cryeth out ffrom under the aulter : some of us have bin kepte prysoners these 19 monethes for hearinge the scripture read unto us in one of our houses uppon a Lordes day morninge in all godly and peaceable maner, neyther have we bin all this tyme once produced to our answere, or had either errour or Cryme obiected against vs. . . .'

The surprising thing is not that there was ever a revolution in merrie England, but that it was delayed so long.

The Prynne Case

Star Chamber allowed no freedom of printing to its opponents. The ancient rights of the individual dwindled to vanishing-point. One, Peachman, was condemned to die for no other offence than that of having written a sermon which, when discovered, gave displeasure to the authorities, although the unfortunate man had neither preached nor

[1] p. 35.

published it.[1]   The Courts of Star Chamber and High Commission were tyrannical and cruel.   Laud, notably in his proceedings against William Prynne, a Puritan pamphleteer, acted with studied malice.   Deeper issues than the freedom of the press were involved, but the religious policy of Laud made it imperative that the freedom of the press should not be extended to Puritan writers, even the most innocent of whose writings were misconstrued so as to expose their authors to the most serious charges.   That Laud acted of deliberate malice against Prynne appears from the report of a High Commission trial in 1631-2 when three men were found guilty of professing false opinions, Laud urging that Prynne should also be articled against for the same—' we must not sitt heere to punish poore snakes, and lett him goe scot free ! '[2]

Clarendon admitted that in the opinion of most men Prynne was ' scurvily treated '.   Prynne's *Histriomastix*, published in 1632, was made the excuse for an attack on him.   Laud assiduously studied the book, which was mainly an attack on the stage, in order to find anything that might be construed as a reflection on the king.   He employed Dr. Heylyn to pick out all the offensive passages and to send a note of them to the Attorney-General urging the prosecution of the author.   The proceedings were altogether unreasonable.   The book had not been irregularly produced—it had been passed by the licenser,

[1]Cobbett's *State Trials*, Vol. 3, p. 575.

[2] Gardiner's *Cases in the Star Chamber and High Commission Courts*, p. 314.

Mr. Buckner, who had found nothing seditious or treasonable in it, and it had been printed by a registered stationer, Michael Sparke. Prynne's lucubrations on pastorals the Court interpreted as a veiled insult to the Queen, who had but lately herself taken part in the performance of a pastoral play. It was in vain to point out that the disputed passages in the book had been written long before the pastoral was performed and the book published quite six weeks before the queen's performance. A trifle like that was not enough to stay the prosecution of Prynne. One of his judges expressed surprise at the leniency of the Court in not making the charge a capital one. He harangued the prisoner at great length, working himself into a passion and convincing himself that the king's life was endangered by the publication of so libellous a book : whereat he protested that it ' made his heart to swell and the blood in his veins to boil '. Another of the judges noted with concern ' the fearful symptoms of this sick and diseased time ', the increasing murmerers among whom he classed ' this minor prophet ' Prynne, and he counselled a ' lustration to purge the air '. The lustration took a painful form. Prynne was fined five thousand pounds, deprived of his University degrees and condemned to lose his ears in the pillory and to suffer perpetual imprisonment.

The printer, Sparke, described by the Attorney-General as ' a common publisher of unlawful and unlicensed books ', had a fortunate escape. He went almost unnoticed by the Court, whose vindictiveness against Prynne reduced his own offence to comparative unimportance. He was charged with having printed the book, part of which according to the Court had not been licensed, and with having persuaded people to buy it after it had been prohibited : previously he had advertised it to his customers as ' an excellent Book which would be called in ', advising them to buy a copy before it was too late. The charges against him being proved to the satisfaction of the Court, he was fined five hundred pounds and condemned to stand in the pillory in Paul's Church-yard—the Archbishop hoped it would not be in Paul's Church-yard, because it was consecrated ground and not a fitting place for the unregenerate to suffer in. Sparke escaped with his ears.

The licenser was mildly dealt with, although he admitted having seen the book when it left the printers even if he had reviewed no more than a part of it before it went to the press. The only excuse he could offer was that he had been surprised and cozened into giving his *imprimatur*. He could not, of course, say that he had seen nothing offensive in the book when so many high dignitaries of Church and State felt so strongly in the matter and when it was plain to the judges that Prynne was lucky not to be on trial for his life. The licenser was admonished and fined fifty pounds.

Popular sympathy was with Prynne. After this remarkable trial and judgment he was a bold man who dared to publish his thoughts and opinions unless he knew they would be acceptable to Star Chamber. Yet the Englishman's developing sense of freedom was difficult to restrain. One of Prynne's judges observed that though the writing

38

and printing of books had been exceedingly found fault
with and had received sharp censure from the Court, it
grew every day worse and worse, ' every man taking upon
' him to understand what he conceiveth and thinking he is
' nobody except he be in print'. There was no improvement
after Prynne's ears had been publicly cropped and himself
shut up in prison for life. Unlawful books, many of them
libellous, issued from secret presses at the same rate. Even
Prynne continued his pamphleteering although it was part
of his sentence that he should be deprived of writing
materials.[1]

Just over four years later (*i.e.* 1637) he was again a victim
of Star Chamber proceedings, this time with Dr. Bastwick
and Henry Burton who were charged with ' writing and
publishing books against the hierarchy '. In his *Answer*
Prynne accused the Archbishop of Canterbury of usurping
upon his majesty's prerogative with innovations, and
licensing Arminian books. Laud was ' nettled thereat ',
and even more incensed when Prynne protested against
the injustice of men known to be his adversaries being
constituted his judges. His protest was not allowed.

There was an early incident in this second trial which
revealed the temper of his prosecutors.[2] One of them complained that Prynne's ears were not as closely cropped as
the law had a right to expect. The usher of the Court,

[1] *State Trials*, 145 (Vol. 3).

[2] One man was detained in prison for nine months for having in his possession a copy of Prynne's *News from Ipswich*. (*Hist. MSS. Comm.*, 5th Report, p. 91.)

therefore, was commanded to turn up the prisoner's hair and show his ears for the better satisfaction of the lords.

Prynne was again found guilty, sentenced to have his ears more closely shaved, fined another five thousand pounds and sentenced to perpetual imprisonment. Thus twice within less than five years was Prynne for different offences condemned to be imprisoned for life. When the first part of the sentence was being executed ' the light common people strewed herbs and flowers ' before the prisoners on their way to the Palace-yard, and ' at the ' cutting off of each ear there was such a roaring as if every ' one of them had at the same instant lost an ear '.[1]

The 1637 Star Chamber Decree

Laud's efforts to put down unauthorised printing were unsuccessful : the great number and severity of the sentences passed on convicted printers did not dismay the Puritans. And in 1637 the most repressive of the Star Chamber decrees regulating printing was issued. It was modelled on Elizabeth's statute which ' had been found by experience to be defective in some particulars ', for ' divers ' abuses had sithence arisen and beene practised by the ' craft and malice of wicked and evill disposed persons to ' the prejudice of the publike '. What those abuses were will appear from a study of the measures proposed for their remedy.[2]

[1] *C.S.P.D.*, Vol. 1637, p. 287.

[2] As all of these abuses have already been noted above, there is no need to recapitulate them here. The text of the 1637 Decree is given in the Appendix.

The Act was a failure : the abuses which it was designed to abolish went on unchecked. The promoters and executors of the measure were not to blame. The times were not normal, the government was divided against itself and the forces of rebellion against Laud and his Star Chamber methods were growing bolder and more violent. The unpopularity of the bishops' rule overshadowed even the good points in their legislation, for the Act, judged by the standards of its day, was not a bad one. It did not depart from already established principles, but sought merely to provide more thoroughly against the abuses which had taken the sting out of former acts for the regulating of printing. Henceforth properly informed licensers would be entrusted with the censorship. Books of State affairs for example, would not be rejected (or approved) by licensers whose profession enjoined them to be dead to this present world : books of heraldry would receive their *imprimatur* from men whose business it was to know something about heraldry. To prevent the unscrupulous author or stationer from altering the text of a book after it had been passed by the censor, a copy of every book in its licensed form was ordered to be preserved. Imported books were to be catalogued and a dignitary of the Church to be present whenever the packs and fardels were opened. The rights and privileges of the Stationers' Company were to be safeguarded : unauthorised persons to be prohibited from bartering or selling books : the number of master printers fixed, and the number of presses allowed to them : the master printers were to be compelled to give work to journeymen printers whose lack of regular employment had been the cause of their turning to secret and disorderly printing : and the thoroughness of searchers was to be guaranteed by choosing them from the stationers whose business stood to profit by a suppression of the pirates.

All this might have been approved if the tide against the bishops had not been running high. Coming from a popular government it might have been accepted as an honest, if forcible, attempt to bring order out of chaos. But it was only too well known that the aim of Laud and the bishops was to allow Charles to rule arbitrarily and tyrannically.

The decree did little to stop the importation of books printed abroad. In 1640 Adrian Vlack, the Amsterdam printer, petitioned Laud for the continuance of his right to import books from Holland, and for the privilege of printing and publishing certain well-known books abroad. He was found in London observing what were the most useful and vendible books. He had not come empty-handed—' divers bales or packets of books printed beyond sea '[1] had come with him. He went on his way ignoring the Star Chamber Decree.

He was not the only printer to do so. The business of importing into England books printed abroad was, to judge by the increasing number of pirated editions, lucrative. Books against the bishops and their Popish ceremonies continued, in spite of the new Decree, to be a popular import : e.g., the News from Ipswich printed ' to make the

[1] C.S.P.D., Vol. 1640, p. 41.

bishops' cruelty known to all nations ', and presumably to benefit an astute publisher : the *Practice of Piety* printed by 10,000 at a time.

It was profitable to print not only the Puritan pamphlets which no English licenser of the time would pass and for which there would be ensured a ready sale, but also school text-books such as *Lilly's Rules* which were in the privilege of the patentees.

How to escape the Customs House Officials was a problem which, notably in one way at least, called forth the ingenuity of the shipmasters. Matthew Symmons, the bookseller, volunteered information in 1638—' all the ' shipmasters are engaged in this traffic, and they have a ' way, as they say, to cozen the devil. They strike upon the ' sands at Queenborough, and send away their passengers ' and deliver all their prohibited goods in some small boats, ' and then come off the sands without danger '.[1]

Laud was alive to the danger to the Government of allowing the publication of uncensored and seditious English books on the Continent ; and magistrates abroad seem to have been aware of the inadvisability of permitting them to go unchecked. Some internal measures of repression were accordingly adopted, and, in May, 1639, Laud in his majesty's name thanked the Amsterdam magistrates for their diligence in repressing such libellous and infamous books as tended to the disturbance of his majesty's government.[2] It was an encouragement to the Amsterdam

[1] *Ibid.*, 14 April, 1638.
[2] *Ibid.*, 4 May, 1639.

magistrates to proceed with the repression : an earnest of things to come as much as an expression of gratitude for services rendered.

No Star Chamber Decree, however, could have coped with a similar state of affairs in Scotland, where religious feeling was running high, and with it resentment against the policy of the bishops. Scotland had covenanted with God to defend Protestantism and to resist all its ' contrary errors and corruptions '. The Scots, true to their covenant, carried the attack across the Border and demanded the abolition of all that offended them. ' Impertinent and damnable ! ' was the king's comment on the situation. War was imminent. Such was the temper of the Scottish people that the attempt to interfere with the liberty of the nation to choose its own religion roused them to fury. Jenny Geddes was only one among many who had flung stools and Bibles at the head of the bishop who, at St Giles's in Edinburgh, had attempted to read the new form of divine service. There were willing hands to roll the prelate in the mire ; and the war of aggression against the new tyrannies of bishop and king was carried into the enemy's camp by many an anonymous pamphleteer. It was essential that the English puritans should feel a like resentment at the tyrannical rule of the bishops, and the Scots looked for allies in their midst. Seditious books were conveyed across the border in growing numbers. At Newcastle,[1] for instance, they were cast in at doors and shop windows. (The persons engaged in

[1] *Ibid.*, Vol. 1638-9, p. 472.

scattering them abroad evidently did not wait to receive payment !) A proclamation was publicly made that copies of seditious books should be forthwith delivered to the mayor, and ministers were asked to preach against the doctrines of freedom as stated in the Scottish books.

The king found it necessary in February, 1638-9, to warn his ' loving subjects ' against such ' infamous libels, stuffed full of calumnies '[1] against the royal authority, and to give them timely notice of the traitorous intentions of the covenanting Scots. But the Scottish petty-chapmen, peddling more than appeared on their trays, were industrious and ingenious and still contrived to do their business *sub rosa*. They grew bolder as the volume of protest increased against the popish tendencies of the English bishops and court ; and one of the dispersers of Scottish pamphlets appeared openly in Gray's Inn dressed ' in ' satin doublet with his man following him with a cloak ' bag full of books, and his cloak laced with a great broad ' gold lace '.[2] There was also Captain Audley, dwelling in Bloomsbury near the great cherry garden, another notorious spreader of libels and Scottish pamphlets.

The Star Chamber decree proved powerless against the invasion of Scottish libels. It was no more successful in dealing with the home products of the now thoroughly roused Puritans. The work of the searchers became more exacting and arduous. The Stationers' Company requested[3]

[1] *Ibid.*, p. 507.

[2] *Ibid.*, Vol. 1640-41, p. 40.

[3] *Hist. MSS. Comm.*, 3rd Report, p. 75.

to have power with a constable to enter into all houses and places suspected of harbouring secret presses or unlawful books : but even the support of a constable could not suffice to make the searchers' work any the less difficult, or gain them an easier passage to houses and places suspected of concealing unauthorised presses. One, Bustian,[1] a constable, presumably in his capacity as a private citizen, assisted in repulsing certain searchers, stationers who were engaged in searching for copies of an unlawful book. The delinquent printers boldly dispersed and sold their stock of books in defiance of all authority. Yet the searchers appointed by the Stationers' Company cannot be accused of a want of vigilance, their own interests being materially engaged.

The searchers of the Customs House, however, seem to have displayed less zeal in enforcing the Star Chamber Decree of 1637. Often they did not delay opening packs and fardels of books till the arrival of the chaplains appointed by the Archbishop of Canterbury or the Bishop of London, but opened them themselves. Some were not above helping themselves to part of the contents and letting the rest pass privately without question.

Thousands of seditious books were imported from Holland in defiance of the Government. John Lilburne, then a youth of twenty, was accused of having sent over ten or twelve thousand of them, and was tried in the Star Chamber. Whether or not he was responsible for their importation (and he protested his innocence of the charge), their importation

[1] *C.S.P.D.*, Vol. 1638-9, p. 55.

was an accomplished fact. On his persistent refusal to take the oath, he was sentenced by the Court to pay a fine of 500 *l.*, to be whipped through the streets to Westminster, to stand in the pillory, and to be further imprisoned until he should conform himself in obedience to the orders of the Court. Lilburne was not lacking in courage. While in the pillory and suffering unduly through the neck-hole being too low for one of his stature, he inveighed very freely against the tyranny of the bishops, and referred to Dr. Bastwick, Mr. Burton and Mr. Prynne, former victims of Star Chamber justice, as ' those three renowned living martyrs of the Lord '. It is not altogether surprising that at length a gag was placed over his mouth by the officers in charge : but it was cruelly done. Blood gushed from his mouth, so that later when the whole case was reopened before the House of Lords one of his lawyers was justified in his comment—*ferocitas luporum in humana figura*. Incidentally, Lilburne was busy providing his judges with further cause for complaint even while he was undergoing his sentence in the pillory, for not only did he made seditious speeches, but he made it an occasion also to disperse copies of seditious books among the crowd.

47

CHAPTER II

1640-1645

THE LONG PARLIAMENT

Its Belief in a Free Press

THE temper of Puritan England was rising. It was obvious that Charles's conception of royal prerogatives would have to undergo some modifying change, and some other means of governing the country than by Star Chamber be found, if a revolt was to be avoided.

In August, 1640, the Scots followed their pamphlets across the border and extracted certain promises from Charles before they would consent to return. Their demand for money which he could not come by compelled him to summon Parliament. The Long Parliament assembled in November. Without delay it began to revise the proceedings of Star Chamber. The ecclesiastical tyranny was over. A Committee of Religion was appointed to examine all booksellers and printers ' who had been interfered with by my lord of Canterbury '. Henceforth the press was to be free, there were to be no oppressive restrictions. The authority of the Star Chamber and High Commission Court was called in question, and the Commissioners' right to search for and seize books on a general warrant denied, and the right to decide matters connected with the printing and publishing of books was declared to be out of their jurisdiction. The Court's judgment in the case of Prynne, Bastwick and Burton was promptly reversed : the three exiles landed at Southampton[1] and entered London amid scenes of indescribable enthusiasm : flowers and herbs strewed their path, and the crowds of people who had come forth to welcome them were as loud in their exclamations against the bishops as they were in their acclamations of ' such cruelly persecuted godly men '. Lilburne, who had suffered no less than Prynne, though his ears had been preserved, was immediately released from the Fleet and the sentence declared to have been ' bloody, cruel, wicked, barbarous and tyrannical '. The reparation which it was resolved to give him for his sufferings was, however, delayed for some years.

The Trial of Laud

Lilburne, a man (as Bastwick later described him) of a restless, boiling and unwearied spirit, wrote a libel against Laud which was posted upon the Royal Exchange. It so incensed the populace against the prelate that an attack was made on his house. His life was in danger and likely to have been sacrificed if it had not been that he had provided himself with arms and ammunition. A few windows were broken and the rabble retired after speaking their mind freely in violent and abusive language. Several arrests were made, and one man more mutinous than the rest was

[1] Prynne had been removed to the island of Jersey.

hanged, drawn and quartered.[1] A regrettable affair—but it showed how violent was the revolt against the bishops.

Laud was brought to trial on a charge of high treason.[2] The first article of his Impeachment affirmed that he had ' endeavoured to subvert the fundamental laws and govern- ' ment of the kingdom ; and instead thereof, to introduce ' an arbitrary and tyrannical Government against law '. Setting aside the question of his attitude towards the Press, there was enough evidence to sustain the charge. Prynne, speaking for the prosecution, held him responsible for the ' spiritual famine of God's Word '—' a miserable ' abuse of the Spiritual Keys, to shut up the Doors of ' Heaven, and to open the Gates of Hell '. The popish bias was, his accusers urged, manifest in all he did. It was to be seen in his attitude towards the press—and that is all that concerns us here.

The ninth article of his Impeachment declared that he had chosen to be his chaplains men ' notoriously dis- ' affected to the Reformed Religion, grossly addicted to ' popish superstition, and erroneous and unsound both in ' judgment and practice. And to them, or some of them ' [he had] committed Licensing of Books to be printed ; ' by which means divers false and superstitious Books had ' been published, to the great scandal of Religion, and to ' the seducing of many of his majesty's subjects '.

While the charges against him were in preparation, he was commanded to furnish the names and number of all

[1] Nalson's *Impartial Collection of State Affairs*, Vol. 1, p. 343.
[2] *State Trials*, 171.

books seized since 1627 either by himself or by any of his servants as forfeited goods.[1] Attention was paid to complaints by printers that licenses had been refused to books merely on account of their being Protestant in tone, whilst those that were Popish could be certain to pass the censor. As one man, the Protestant author of a book which had failed to satisfy the licenser, dryly remarked—' Italy has its *Index Expurgatorius*, England its *Imprimatur* '.

The Trial of Laud, which dragged on for four years, reflects no credit on Parliament. The enemies which he had made by his Star Chamber proceedings were implacable and not to be moved to pity by the venerable appearance and calm dignity of the aged prisoner. If he had prosecuted Prynne with malicious thoroughness, Prynne was no less indefatigable and vindictive in the impeachment of Laud. And there were others like him, only too willing to give evidence for the prosecution.

Laud conducted his defence with dignity and dexterity. The physical strain alone must have been considerable to a man of over seventy, quite apart from the mental exhaustion entailed by the protraction of the trial.

He refused to admit responsibility for the conduct of the licensers of books for the press. Nor was it fair, he argued, to impugn him singly and make him solely answerable for the decisions and decrees of Star Chamber. He had left the licensing of books to his private chaplain, Sir John Lambe. In this he was but following the practice of his predecessor. An archbishop had not the time to attend personally to the

[1] *C.S.P.D.*, Vol. 1640-1, p. 509.

censoring of books for the press : nor did his chaplains and licensers expect him ' to meddle with that troublesome business '.[1]

It was objected against him that he had printed, in defiance of a Proclamation against it, a certain book by Dr. Cowel which asserted the king's prerogative to be above Law. Laud denied the charge. Being out of town, he had required Sir John Lambe to look to it carefully that the Proclamation was obeyed, but his chaplain had slighted his commands. He was living (said Laud) and could answer for himself. As for the charge of suppressing the English Bibles with the Genevan Notes added to the text, he admitted that he had done so, but not from an objection to the Notes. The Bibles had come from Amsterdam better printed, better bound and in every way superior to those that issued from English presses. Therefore, in the interests of the native craftsmen he had undertaken their suppression—' there was a great and a just fear conceived that ' by little and little printing would quite be carried out of ' the kingdom '.[2]

The suppression of certain books in Holland was also laid to his charge. His accusers attributed to his power and influence the Proclamation made by the States against seditious books. Laud seemed surprised that anyone should object to the Proclamation, which appeared to him to be something to be grateful for. Whoever was responsible for it had, he thought, thereby placed the kingdom

[1] *State Trials*, 171, col. 483.
[2] *Ibid.*, col. 497.

and the Church of England in his debt. For ' till this had ' been done, every discontented spirit could print what he ' pleased at Amsterdam against either '.[1]

Laud was found guilty of more serious charges, and for these, rather than for his popish bias in applying the licensing laws, he suffered death on the scaffold in the seventy-second year of his life.

Dr. Bray, his chaplain and licenser of books, was not allowed to go scot-free. He was examined before the House of Lords for having permitted the writings of Dr. Pocklington to be published. Bray's defence was that he had granted his *imprimatur* without taking the precaution of first examining the books with proper care. He expressed regret. The House ordered him to make a public recantation from the pulpit on the following Sunday. When this had been done to its satisfaction, the House, with a taste for poetic justice, ordered him to print the sermon in which the recantation appeared.[2]

Parliament's Approach to the Problem

While the impeachment of Laud was wearily progressing, Parliament was not neglecting the question of the freedom of the press. The Puritans outside the House were eager to offer advice. In 1640 they humbly petitioned that the government by Archbishops and their courts should, roots and branches, be abolished. A catalogue of ' evils, Pres- ' sures and Grievances caused practised and occasioned by

[1] *Ibid.*, col. 498. See also p. 43, *supra.*
[2] Nalson's *I.C.S.A.*, Vol. 1, pp. 787, 797.

'the prelates' was subjoined, of which items 8 and 9 were as follows :—

'The swarming of lascivious, idle and unprofitable books and Pamphlets, Play-Books, and Ballads, as namely *Ovids* fits of Love ; *the Parliament* of Women come out at the dissolving of the last *Parliament, Barnes* Poems, *Parkers* Ballads in disgrace of Religion, to the encrease of all vice, and withdrawing of people from reading, studying, and hearing the word of God, and other good Books.' (8)[1]

'The hindering of godly Books to be Printed, the blotting out, or perverting those which they suffer, all or most of that which strikes either at Poperie or *Arminianisme*, the adding of what or where pleaseth them, and the restraints of reprinting Books formerly licensed without relicensing.' (9)[2]

There was also a petition,[3] presented by certain ministers who had been exercised over the kind of books that passed the licenser, to the effect that the power of licensing should be committed to 'orthodox and godly men, in order that 'all dangerous and poisoned treatises might be suppressed, 'and only books containing sound and wholesome doctrine 'allowed to be published'.

On one point, however, Parliament had made up its mind and required no advice. Parliament had determined that the press should henceforth be free—as free as was possible—particularly to Puritans, who under Laud had had no freedom to publish their thoughts.

At first there was no attempt to legislate for this new freedom. Meanwhile there was no doubt that Parliament differed from Star Chamber in its idea of what books should be licensed and what not. This change of idea is

[1] *British Lightning*, by G. L. V., translated from Low Dutch, 1643, says that Bishops in England 'forbad the printing of all good books, and, contrarily, suffered to be printed all arminianish, papish, vain books of Amadis de Gaul, and of commedies, to 40 thousand in a yeare'.

[2] Laud said nothing was ever cut out without good reason, as *e.g.*, where unfounded charges were made against Rome, the licenser advised the author that it would injure his own argument to leave such a passage in.

[3] *Hist. MSS. Comm.*, Part 4, p. 57 (*MSS. of H. of Lords*, 1640-1.)

brought out nowhere more clearly than in a Report[1] presented to the House by a Committee appointed to consider what should be done with the books formerly seized by the High Commissioners. In this Report the books are divided into three classes :—

1. Such as are fit to be delivered to the Owners, and to be sold by the Stationers as good and vendible Books, viz. :—

   The Holy Table, Name and King.

   Mr. Walker's *Treaty of the Sabbath.*

   A French Commentary on the Revelations, etc.

2. Books which the Committee thinks fit to be sold to choice Persons, as :—

   Thomas de Kempis *of the following of Christ, of which there are* 100 *in Decimo Sexto.*

   The Life of Sir Thomas Moor.

3. Superstitious Tablets and Books, which are fit to be Burnt, as *Missals, Primers and Offices of Our Lady,* etc.

The House ordered the first sort of books to be returned to the owners and to be sold by stationers : the second sort to be delivered to safe hands, to be sold to ' noblemen, gentlemen and schollars, but not to women ' ; and the third sort to be burned in Smithfield without delay.

Thus it was obvious from the start that though the Long Parliament intended that the press should be free, it did not contemplate extending that freedom to the authors of papistical books.

A Committee of Printing was set up, but not with the object of legislating for Parliament's new policy of freedom to all except Papists. It was set up, chiefly, it seems, as a precaution against the disorderly brethren in the book trade : and it served its purpose. A few disorderly printers were proceeded against[2]—Parliament's own printer,

[1] Nalson's *I.C.S.A.*, Vol. 2, p. 690.

[2] *Ibid.*, Vol. 2, p. 246 : printer of Elegy on Strafford committed to Gate House, 1641.

Overton,[1] amongst them. He was brought to the Bar of
the House of Commons to answer for his misprints, and there
reproved by the Speaker. The Committee suppressed a
few books of which there had been complaint : for example, a scandalous book published in the name of the
Archbishop of Armagh, though it was certainly none of his.[2]
And amongst those whom the Committee called to account
was Henry Walker, author of interminable pamphlets, who
was summoned to answer for his neglect of the licensing
laws.

The Stationers' Company occupied a difficult position.
Nominally the registered stationers were on the side of
law and order, benefiting by being themselves the executors
of the laws against unlicensed printing. But the law during
the rule of the Bishops had become aggressively anti-
Puritan. And not a few of the stationers were uncompro-
mising Puritans, and therefore disinclined to inform against
any secret printer of books which, being Puritan in tone, had
not been submitted to the licenser. In the MSS. of the
House of Lords is a memorandum of the year 1641—' that
' Simons and Payne, who have continually printed libels,
' are known to all the stationers, and have their presses in
' Redcross Street '.[3]

When no question of loyalty to a fellow-believer was
involved, there was every reason for diligence on the part
of the Company's searchers. Their own copyrights had

[1] *Ibid.*, Vol. 1, p. 719.
[2] *Ibid.*, Vol. 1, p. 773.
[3] *Hist. MSS. Comm.*, Part 4, p. 111.

perhaps been infringed. John Aston, printer, in 1641 fell foul of the stationers. He had been undermining their business and making a good profit out of the secret presses which he had installed in a house in an obscure part of Holborn. The Company's representatives, ' with the assistance of a justice and constables ', attempted to search the house, but Aston and his two associates, Walkenden and Winter, resisted them ' with naked swords, guns and ' pistols for upwards of two hours, until they had burned ' many papers and books. . . . '[1] Which shows that the searchers' lot was sometimes an unenviable one.

The Growth of News-Books

The growth of news-books introduced a new and disturbing element into the struggle for the freedom of the press. The ' Corantos ', as they were called before 1640, provided a ' running ' relation of foreign affairs. The first entry in the Stationers' Register of an English ' coranto ' occurs with the date 18 May, 1622. Foreign news alone was related. The innovation was, like the name, Italian in origin. ' Gazet ' and ' coranto ' were different names for the same thing ; ' Gazet ', the earlier term, has survived in modern journalism. An early eighteenth century writer records that those who wrote the Italian Gazettes

' were call'd *Menanti,* because (says *Vossius*) those loose Papers and the Writers thereof, intended commonly some Defamatory Reflections upon some Persons or other, and were therefore proscrib'd and prohibited in *Italy,* by *Gregory* the 13th, by a particular Bull under the name of *Menantes,* so call'd from the Latin Word, *Minantes,* threatening, because threats or defyances used to be the consequences included in defaming Libels, or necessarily understood thereby, etc . . . But Mr. *Menage* will have it to be

[1] *House of Lords MSS.* (*Hist. MSS. Comm.,* Pt. 4, p. 102.)

deriv'd from the *Italian* Word, *Menare*, signifying to lead at large, or spread abroad a far of, as those News-mongers were oblig'd to write spaciously, or a great deal, by reason of the multitude of the Copies, which were to be scatter'd abroad far and near . . .'[1]

At first the gazettes were mere translations of foreign news letters. There was no account taken of home affairs; certainly no 'defamatory reflections' upon statesmen or state affairs: no English 'menanti' had appeared. But Star Chamber, nevertheless, interfered in October, 1632, and, 'upon consideration of the great abuse 'in the printing of gazettes and pamphlets of news from 'foreign parts, and upon signification of his Majesty's 'express pleasure and command to the Board', all printing, publishing and selling of the same was suppressed and inhibited.[2] The reason for this drastic action may be inferred from a petition[3] presented in the following year by Bourne and Butter, stationers who had been chiefly concerned in the publication of gazettes. It was a cautiously worded document. The petitioners promised 'to be careful in 'time to come that nothing dishonourable to princes in 'amity with his Majesty should pass the press'. Five years later they were granted a royal patent to print gazettes and corantos[4] for the term of twenty-one years.

It was a royal prerogative to allow or forbid the printing of news. News was by no means common property. It was doled out to the general public by the royal hand: it

---

[1] *Athenae Britanicae*, Myles Davies, 1716.

[2] *C.S.P.D.*, Vol. 1631-3, p. 426.

[3] *Ibid.*, Vol. 1633-4, p. 222.

[4] On payment of an annual subscription of 10 *l.* towards the repair of St. Paul's. (*C.S.P.D.*)

came from the royal dispensary alone. Nothing ' dishonourable to princes in amity with his Majesty ' was
allowed to be published even if true[1]: and in England
nothing whatever concerning home affairs till 1641.

With the abolition of the Star Chamber and High Commission Courts fell the mighty bulwark and buttress of the
royal prerogative. The Commons passed the abolition
bill ' with great alacrity',[2] the Lords with expedition.
New laws were, therefore, required for the regulation of the
press : the old lapsed automatically when Star Chamber
proceedings were declared to have been illegal. The
situation, owing to the sudden birth of the news-book
chronicling domestic affairs, was unparalleled. The bishops
had, it is true, been faced with a mild threat of the corantos
and gazettes publishing news that might inconvenience the
government in its relations with foreign powers. Such
risk was not to be tolerated, and the corantos had been
suppressed until the writers thereof had guaranteed to
speak ill of none but the king's enemies.

Parliament had in 1641 to attempt the solution of
a problem which had been complicated by the rise of ' diurnals ' and ' mercuries ' divulging the proceedings of Parliament itself. In former days secrecy had invariably been
observed as to the doings of the House : they were not
proclaimed from the house-top. Now, with the spread of

[1] Secretary Windebank was advised by a correspondent in 1639, ' The
Gazette is an admirable way, and the French make a wondrous good use of
it in giving what impressions they think good to their subjects '. *C.S.P.D.*,
Vol. 1639, p. 234.

[2] *C.S.P.D.*

news-books, they are most inconveniently and incorrectly reported. The author of *A Presse Full of Pamphlets* (1642),[1] for example, regretted the advent of the ' unseemly ' and obnoxious ' diurnals, holding them responsible for fomenting the sores on the body politic with the

' diversity of their rumours mixt with Falsity and Scandalisme. Members of the State are abused, even the Proceedings of the High Court of Parliament, and the worthy members thereof, are by the same exposed to the view of all men. And were the same truly and really published, it would gain great Admiration and Renown. But in the description, it is so interlaced and intermixed with petitious devisings of idle and rash wits, that the same are not credulous, and by that means loseth that due and awfull respect, which otherwise ought to bee ascribed unto the same. Never Parliament so famous for Loyalty towards a Soveraign, Piety towards God, and integrity towards their Country ; so wise and politique in their Proceedings, for the settlement of the peace and tranquility of his Majesty and his Kingdomes, and of such courage and magnanimous spirits, that former Ages have not parallel'd the same : and never a Parliament so much abused, by scurrilous and fictitious Pamphlets, never so much printing of Parliamentary Proceedings, as hath bin during the sitting of this most happy and renowned one '.

The Need for Legislation

It will be seen that the Committee appointed by Parliament in 1641[2] to deal with the new situation had not been very successful. Strong reasons for immediate action were represented to the Committee (Sept., 1641) : it was pointed out that there was danger of a sudden increase in the number both of imported Popish books and of libels and loose pamphlets printed at home : that for the time being, the royal and ancient rights of patentees were without safeguard : that the unauthorised printing of parliamentary proceedings was producing immediate and embarrassing results. For example, one such unauthorised and, as it

[1] Printed for R.W.—either Robt. Wood, who was convicted for publishing a lying diurnal in 1643 ; or else, Robt. White, convicted for printing unauthorized news of Irish affairs in 1643.

[2] See p. 55 *supra.*

happened, inaccurate, report evoked a reply in which the
House was charged with disloyalty to the king.[1] On being
called upon to make good his indictment, the author
produced a copy of the unallowed report of certain parliamentary affairs.

The Long Parliament had to deal with such problems at
a time when the country was on the verge of civil war and
when there were in the House two irreconcilable views as
to what was and what was not sedition.

Whilst the proceedings of Parliament were of such
moment and fraught with such interest, the news-writers
found a large demand for their wares. If there was not
enough news to fill the sheet, more could so easily be invented when the source of authentic information dried up.
The knavery of those who supplied the growing demand for
printed news was the occasion and theme of a witty and
ingenious pamphlet[2] written in 1641 by a certain J. B.
who shows ' how impudently the poets have not only
' presumed to make extreme and incredible lies, but dared
' also to feign orders and proceedings from the Parliament
' with many fictitious speeches '. The whole city, he complains, is ' embroidered with incredible lies from the
' mintage of their roving fancies. Lying and nonsense are
' the two coincident twins that always distilled from the
' nasty dregs of their satyrical quills : Goose-quill censurers,
' nursing their viperous muses in Acharon and fomenting
' them in Stygian gall .'

[1] *C.S.P.D.*, Vol. 1641-3, p. 129.

[2] *The Poets' Knavery Discovered* (*Harleian Miscellany*).

No Parliament, particularly at such a time, could be expected to take measures against irresponsible scribblers that would be immediately successful. More urgent business occupied the attention of the Government—the quarrel with the king, jealousies between the two houses, the revolt in Ireland, the attempted impeachment of the five members of the House of Commons : finally the raising of the king's standard at Nottingham in August, 1642.

In the confusion that preceded the outbreak of civil war, the Committee found time to imprison an occasional printer of libels, and to restrain as many of the vendors of news-books and unlicensed pamphlets as it could lay hands on. But the hawkers were irrepressible. Dignifying themselves with the name of wandering stationers, they pursued an undignified calling, never certain where they would lodge for the night, escaping from Newgate only to recommence their old trade at once, crying ' Come buy a new Booke, a new Booke, newly come forth ! '[1] (They were always *new* books, no matter how old they might be.)

Again, the books of Irish news contained so much that was false and palpably feigned overnight in English alehouses that ' divers of gentry of Ireland now resident in England ', perceiving another injustice to Ireland, petitioned the House ' that no news be printed except by order of the House after examination of the truth of the same ' : and the petitioners recommended that a monopoly of printing Irish news be given to William Blayden, a stationer

[1] *Dounefall of Temporizing Poets, unlicenst Printers, upstart Booksellers, trotting Mercuries, and bawling Hawkers.* 1614.

then resident in London,[1] whose father was an alderman in Dublin.

Despite its preoccupation with weightier affairs Parliament felt that something had to be done immediately to restrain the authors and printers of scandalous pamphlets and news-books ; and so the Justices of Peace of London and Middlesex were ordered to take notice of scandalous pamphleteering and to punish offenders. The Committee appointed by Parliament to deal with matters of the press already had its hands fully occupied. It was overworked, but not very successful. Therefore, when John Bond, one of the numerous knavish poets engaged in concocting fictitious news for the gullible reader, was discovered to be the author of ' a scandalous letter in the Queens Majesties Name ', and arrested, the Committee made an example of him, condemning him to stand in the pillory. Later, in April, 1642, he published *The Poet's Recantation*, complaining because he had been the only sufferer—' I was exposed *Publico dedecore*, as the sole contriver ' of all such spurious news, whereas it was well known that he was only one among many similarly engaged.

There was work enough to keep the Committee constantly employed, but the abuses continued unchecked. In January, 1642, Parliament decreed[2] that every publication should thereafter bear the name of the author ; but

[1] *Hist. MSS. Comm.*, Pt. 4, p. 113.

[2] *H.C.J.*, 29 Jan., 1642 : Committee for Printing revived, and ' Master and Wardens of the Company of Stationers required to take special Order, that the Printers do neither print or reprint anything without the Name and Consent of the Author. . . .'

the decree failed to prevent the abuse of copyright, or to lessen the labours of the Committee. The Clerk of Parliament was appointed licenser. Thereafter his *imprimatur* was printed on the front page of licensed publications. It was easy, perhaps, to forge an *imprimatur*, and a false *imprimatur* enabled many an unauthorised book to evade detection. A bookseller vending such books could always plead that it was not for him to know that they were unlicensed. How was he to distinguish between those licensed and those not when both sorts bore the same printed sign—' Licensed by the Clerk of Parliament '?

The licenser's *imprimatur* was evidently an advantage to a book ; else it would not have been fraudulently printed so often. Perhaps the magic formula on the front page obtained for the unlicensed pamphlet admission to the best markets, where it was not safe to display any book which did not appear to have passed through the licenser's hands. It was a common practice thus to make use of a false *imprimatur*, and *A Paradox Usefull for the Times*[1] refers to the practice as presumably profitable :—

' . . . your lying Diurnals, your absurd Passages, your diabolicall newes from Heaven, your horrible, terrible, and fearefull tydings, and such like : to some of these I have seen an Order, a Vote, or the Clarke of Parliaments name inserted : But I beleeve the Honourable House, or Clarkes never did intend such things, and therefore rather thinke that the covetous Stationers doth it to make their Bookes sell. But such things being suffered, and winked at, I doe greatly feare will be a cause of ruine to this Kingdome.'

The Plight of the Stationers' Company

A more immediate effect than the ruin of the Kingdom was likely to be the ruin of the Stationers' Company. In

[1] 5 Nov., 1642.

the torrent of pirated and unauthorised books that poured
from the secret presses, their privileges and rights were
being swept away. A patent without the necessary safeguard was meaningless : and the privileged members of
the Stationers' Company, faced with poverty, humbly
remonstrated with Parliament to prevent the abuse of
copyright.[1] To this end Parliament's Decree of January,
1642, had been unsuccessfully directed.

John Taylor, the water poet, an entertaining scribbler
in the cause of the king, attributed the decline of the
Company to the attractive force of the rapidly multiplying
news-books and to the failure of Parliament to control
them :—

' This hath past without controlement to the abuse of Church and State,
the scandall of the whole Kingdome, the injury to this Honourable City ;
the raysing of strifes, divisions, and bad opinions in many people of weake
capacities and judgements ; and to the mighty impeachment and detriment
of the Worshipfull Brotherhood of the Stationers, who are at great charges
in paying all duties and Taxes, and that now (almost two yeares) the
Bread hath bin eaten out of their mouthes by these Vagrants, commonly
called Mercuries and Hawkers. . . .'[2]

George Wither was, as might be expected,[3] glad of an
opportunity to draw attention to the overweening importance
of the ' Commonwealth of Stationers '—' a Tyrrany unheard
of in former ages '. But the truth of the matter is that the
Company was never before, nor ever again, in such an enfeebled state. Very few books were entered in the Stationers' Register for the years 1641 and 1642, though not

[1] Arber reprints the ' *Stationers' Remonstrance* ' (Vol. 1, p. 585, *Trans-
script of Stationers' Register*.) Thomason dates the Remonstrance April,
1643.

[2] *The Whole Life and Progresse of Henry Walker the Ironmonger*, by John
Taylor, 1642.

[3] See p. 30 *supra*.

all that were unentered were unlicensed. For instance, Samuel Pecke's *Perfect Diurnal*, which was certainly authorised by the Clerk of Parliament in 1642, was not entered in the Register till July, 1643.

The Ordinance of June, 1643

The Ordinance[1] for the Regulating of Printing was passed in June, 1643. It was the Long Parliament's first serious effort to control the press. In the preamble reference is made to the diligent but unsuccessful efforts of the Company of Stationers to put ' in full execution the divers good orders ' of Parliament for the suppressing of the great abuses and disorders in printing. The new measures having been so long ' retarded through the present distractions ', some of the stationers had evidently determined to wait no longer on the government to protect their copyrights, and had printed whatever would bring them money, regardless of all copyright. It was a case of *sauve qui peut*. Others of the stationers, who were impolitic enough to inform against their delinquent brethren, suffered by having their own copyrights infringed deliberately in revenge.

By the new ordinance, no order or declaration of Parliament was to be printed except by order of the House : all books were to be licensed and also entered in the Stationers' Register : no book in the privilege of the Company was to be printed without the license or consent of the

---

[1] *H.C.J.*, 9 March, 1643 : Committee of Examinations given power to search for secret presses in Houses, Shops or Warehouses. J.P.'s and constables required to help in the search. Apparently the work of the Committee was not very successful.

Company : if any book were entered under a particular name or imported from abroad, the license of the owner was to be required : the Wardens of the Company, the Gentleman Usher of the House of Lords and the Sergeant of the Commons were empowered to make searches, apprehend delinquent authors, printers, etc., to seize unlawful printing presses together with nut, spindle and materials, and, in the event of opposition, to break open doors and locks : and all justices of the peace, captains and constables were commanded to assist.[1]

The position of the Stationers' Company was thus assured. Parliament had returned to the ancient custom of regulating the press by working *through* the worshipful company. The great change is in the personnel of the licensing board. The place of bishops and their chaplains is now taken by lawyers, doctors, members of parliament and one schoolmaster, while books of divinity are to be licensed by Presbyterian ministers, and ' small pamphlets, portractures, pictures and the like ' by the Clerk of the Stationers' Company.

It is important to notice that the Company owed its stability and salvation to the Government and was bound in loyalty, therefore, to the king's adversary. Not all of the stationers were parliamentarians : but all of them as freemen of the company were in the service of Parliament

[1] Hitherto, searchers had received insufficient support, *e.g.*, Joseph Hunscot (beadle to Stationers' Company) had in May, 1643, according to an Order of the House of Lords, assisted in seizing the press of William Ashton for printing scandalous pamphlets. Ashton thought it worth his while to bring an action against Hunscot. (*H.L.J.*, 12 May, 1643. See also, p. 57 *supra*.)

and were executors of presbyterian decrees. It could not be otherwise. The Stationers' Company could not avoid being the servant of whatever Government was in power. The king could leave London, the Stationers' Company could not. It could not have removed its privileges with its presses. But there is no reason to suppose that the freemen of the Company were more than ordinarily dissatisfied in 1643, or that they had any desire to emulate the king's flight from London. Many of the stationers, indeed, were confirmed Presbyterians and content now that they were no longer dictated to by Laud's chaplains.

Royalist Printing in the Provinces[1]

When Charles fled from London, he took printing materials with him, and a skilled printer. York became a centre from which printed manifestoes and pamphlets in the king's cause were issued. In 1642 a Roman Catholic printer, Stephen Bulkley,[2] had fled to York to escape a summons to appear before the Commons as a delinquent ; he took his printing press and materials with him, and continued his trade in the city of York. His sympathies were with the king. It was safe to print at York in the king's cause. One royalist author, writing and printing in London, expressed a longing for the greater freedom enjoyed at York :—

‘ . . . Now I should proceede to give you the reasons of this great alteration (*i.e.*, in Whitehall since the departure of the Court), and perhaps

[1] See *Bibliographica*, Vol. 2, 1896, for W. H. Allnutt's paper on ‘ English Provincial Presses ’.

[2] H. Plomer's *Dict. of Printers*.

had this beene printed at *Yorke* I might have done it, But as the case is I forbeare, I would be loth to have the House pul'd down where it is printed. . . .'[1]

The printing press moved with the royalist forces. A letter signed by one Basill Waring, and purporting to have come from Shrewsbury, communicated to interested readers in London that the Presse for Printing had arrived in that town :—' this day they are setting of it up in some vacant roomes in my house '. A few months later,[2] if current news-books are to be trusted, the royal press was moved to Oxford.[3]

In former days Martin Marprelate had taken his press with him on his travels.[4] From Kingston-on-Thames he had fled to Northampton, thence to Manchester. Now it is the king who owns the travelling press. The royal prerogative over the press has no longer any practical significance except in places where his army has its headquarters. His authority over printing in general has shrunk to a very little measure—his authority over one or two printing presses in particular.

News-Books and the 1643 Ordinance

Till January, 1643, there were no royalist news-books. This serious defect in the king's armoury was remedied by his Oxford friends who now began to issue a diurnal, *Mercurius Aulicus*, ' communicating the intelligence and affairs

[1] *A Deep Sigh Breathd Through the Lodgings at Whitehall.* 1642. (*Thomason Tracts.*)

[2] *England's Memorable Accidents*, 19-26 Dec., 1642.

[3] In 1646 to Newcastle.

[4] See p. 25, *supra*.

of the Court, to the rest of the Kingdome '. It was conducted by men of known scholarship, among whom John Berkenhead stands out as the wittiest and liveliest contributor. It was printed in Oxford and later duplicated in London.[1]

The parliamentarian diurnals had had London to themselves since 1641. Entries of them in the Stationers' Register begin to appear immediately after the passing of the 1643 Ordinance. They were, of course, strongly parliamentarian in tone : otherwise they would not have passed the licenser and would have had to be printed in holes and corners, if printed at all.

Mercurius Britanicus,[2] chief of the licensed diurnals, gave itself wholeheartedly to the task of contradicting *Aulicus*. *Britanicus*[3] was at that time conducted by Captain Audley, a former disperser of Scottish libels. In the ' war of the diurnals ' that succeeded, the dice were heavily loaded against *Aulicus*, for Parliament would naturally support the parliamentarian news-writer against the royalist. Yet Aulicus (so to call the writer of *Aulicus*) [4] was not without a friend in Parliament. On 10 October, 1643, according to the *House of Lords' Journals*, the Lords set themselves to inquire how Aulicus had obtained information, which he had printed, ' concerning certain things that passed privately in the House '. The House, to stop

[1] According to a Note by Thomason on his copy of *Aulicus* (the fortieth week.)

[2] Royalist scribblers made sarcastic comments on the mis-spelling of ' *Britannicus*.' See *Queres*, Thomason Tracts, 669 f. 11 (33).

[3] Marchamont Nedham later edited *Merc. Brit.* See also p. 45, *supra*.

[4] This method of reference will be used throughout this volume.

this leakage of news to Aulicus, ordered that anyone going or coming between Oxford and London without a warrant from Parliament should be apprehended as a spy or intelligencer. Yet the leakage continued. Nor was *Aulicus* likely to cease, said *Britanicus* (30 Dec.–6 Jan., 1644-5), so long as ' Digby sat voting in the Privy Junto '. *Britanicus* lamented ' the opening of back doors ' through which information was conveyed to Oxford.

Aulicus usually had the better of the weekly argument with Britanicus—the scholars of Oxford revealed a surprising talent for abuse as well as a greater smartness in repartee and the ability to lie more logically, though that is less surprising. Sometimes *Britanicus* was able to exult in the triumph of the militia of the city over *Aulicus*, and laugh with unbecoming heartiness when his rival's stock was seized in London :

' The grand newes is, *Mercurius Aulicus* was surprized on *Wednesday* last by the Militia of the City of *London*, a few onely escaped, and no fewer than five hundred lies were taken prisoners, it is thought as great a losse as befell his Majestie since the late losse at *Glocester*, but we hear they are recruiting him fast at *Oxford*, and I can assure you there is a *Presse* there at this very present for that very purpose. . . .'[1]

In his next number Aulicus appears to admit that he was taken before the Committee, that dealt with delinquent printers, in London the previous week : but it may have been ironically said.

The Committee, however, cannot be charged with negligence. Samuel Butler, speaking for his fellow scribes, declared that the Committee had ' bunged up all our mouths at once '.[2]

[1] *Merc. Brit.*, No. 4, 12-19 Sept.
[2] Letter from *Merc. Civicus* to *Merc. Rusticus* by S. Butler, 1643.

Nor can the Committee be accused of favouritism, for it kept an eye, no less vigilant an eye, on the professed parliamentarian news-writers. They were subject to the same surveillance. The same penalties were inflicted. For example, Samuel Pecke, a careful servant of the Parliament, spent several months in the Fleet prison[1] for having printed some unadvised reports in his weekly news-book : ' An ' Anabaptist that sometimes kept a Scriveners stall at ' Westminster ' (says the *Kingdomes Weekly Post*, Nov., 1643) ' that hath layne this halfe year and above in the ' Fleet, for writing of Lyes, where he complyed so far with ' the Cavaliers there, that they made him often so drunke ' . . ., and now his place of greatest residency is at a Sta- ' tioners in the Old Baily. This turn-coat. . . .'

If Parliament kept him in the Fleet prison for six months for such an offence, it is not surprising that he turned his coat.

The Failure of the 1643 Ordinance

The Stationers' Company had been saved from internecine strife, but it could not do much to help its saviour. The stationers had a more intimate knowledge than parliament could have of the ways and habits and likely

[1] *H.L.J.*, 24 April, 1643. ' Upon reading the humble Petition of *Sam Pecke, Francis Coles*, and *Francis Leach*, committed formerly to the " Prison of *the Fleete* ", for printing and making of scandalous and false Pamphlets, declaring their hearty Sorrow for their Offences, promising never again to commit the like : This House Ordered, That, if they shall find good security not to print any Thing concerning the Parliament without special Order of Parliament, that then they shall be released from their present Restraint '.

hiding-places of their disorderly brethren; but beyond tracing the sellers[1] of a foreign edition of the Bible which because of its many ' gross errors and foul dangerous corruptions ' had been banned, and making it necessary for the secret printer to be yet more secret still to avoid detection, the Master and Wardens of the Company did singularly little that was of much use to the Government in the year following the new ordinance. The keeping of the Register was probably their most helpful contribution.

The new ordinance had little authority outside of London. The printing presses that there were beyond the city were in the hands of royalists and mostly in the war area.[2] The provincial activities of royalist printers and pamphleteers were not confined to York, Oxford and Shrewsbury. Wales was ' infested with most dangerous books '.[3] Even

[1] ' Petition of Master and Wardens of Stat. Coy. against *Tooley* and *Hix* for selling and vending Bibles printed beyond Seas, wherein are many erroneous Faults in the Printing '. (10 July, 1644, *H.L.J.*) The Bible referred to is almost certainly ' the last Geneva Bible ', printed at Amsterdam in 1644 (I am indebted to Mr. A. W. Pollard for this suggestion).

[2] See *The Complaint of Mary Blaithwaite Widdow*, 19 May, 1654 (*Thomason Tracts*, E. 735, 15), who complained that she and her husband had been falsely accused at Cockermouth in 1644 of ' dispersing scandalous pamphlets for the Parliament ', apprehended when they were at public worship in the chapel and by warrant of the Commissioners of Array shamefully treated, stripped under pretence of searching for parliamentary papers, and tortured. She petitioned the Protector for compensation, all her troubles having sprung from the indignities put upon her by royalists in 1644.

[3] *The True Informer*, Numb. 59, 1644. ' . . . the Printer of Bristoll sent thither [*i.e.*, to Exeter] for paper, it is very observable, that that Printer infests the West and South Wales with most dangerous Books ; he did the like before he came to Bristoll, at Shrewsbury, and North-Wales : and, as it is reported, did the like before at York : it were well if it were searched out who put this Printer up first, and to know what he is : it is reported he was sent from London. '

the Cambridge University press, over which Parliament had an ancient right of control, was producing almost equally dangerous books. Here Parliament could, and did, interfere. Dr. Holdsworth, the master of Emmanuel College, was called to account for licensing ' books in prejudice, and to the scandal of Parliament '.[1] But the perambulating printing-presses were planted on royalist territory and beyond Parliament's control. It was hard enough to control those that were at no distance from Westminster.

The London diurnals, on the other hand, could not ignore ordinances with impunity. The letterpress type of every diurnal was distinctive and became familiar to readers, thus affording (should it be needed) a clue to the identity of the printer. Whilst the printer of an occasional unlicensed pamphlet might escape detection, the printer of a regular news-book had not the same chance of escape. His letters would in time betray him : the vendors and booksellers whom he employed regularly would hold important and disturbing information as to the source of their stock. The regular printers and publishers of news, for the most part, kept on the right side of the law, though few, even of the most reputable of them, could avoid giving offence to the Government.

There were two prevailing kinds of offence ; the first, that of publishing defamatory matter against prominent persons of state ; and the second, that of publishing news inexpediently. For example, Robert White, the printer,

[1] *H.C.J.*, 1643.

was summoned to appear before the Lords in June, 1644, to answer for certain scandals against the Earl of Stamford which he had printed in his *Kingdomes Weekly Intelligencer*.[1] An instance of the second kind of offence is recorded in the *House of Lords' Journals* for August. The States Ambassador complained of news-book references to the Prince of Orange : and Francis Coles, the bookseller, was again in trouble. A libel against Sir Richard Onsloe which appeared in a pamphlet was the immediate occasion of more serious trouble. This time it was the licenser, Mr. Walley, who suffered. The House of Commons[2] dismissed him from his office as licenser of ' small pamphlets ' and ordered that no pamphlet be printed but by the approbation and allowance of Mr. Rushworth, who was to take ' especial care ' what pamphlets were published.

Another common offence was the unauthorised printing of Parliamentary Declarations, Orders and Ordinances. The amount of confusion which this must have caused is incalculable : for the unauthorised copies usually differed from the original. After 1642 no Declaration or Ordinance in Parliament ends without some such words as ' And— ' [*i.e.*, the Parliamentary printer] to have the printing here- ' of, and none other to presume to print it '. Sometimes the pirate was warned that he printed it ' at his peril '. There were several prosecutions for offences of this sort—Royston,

[1] T. White confessed to have printed the particular number of K.W.I. in question. Captain Audley, he declared, had written it. (*H.L.J.*, 19 June, 1644)

[2] *H.C.J.*, April, 1644.

afterwards Master of the Stationers' Company, was attached for printing *His Majesty's Declaration to all his loving subjects*,[1]—and could not complain if he suffered for his loyalty to the king : John Wright suffered in 1643 for a false entry in the Stationers' Register by which it appeared that both Houses of Parliament had given him a monopoly to print the Ordinance of Excise, whereas his privilege was from the House of Lords alone. The Commons had appointed Joseph Hunscot a share in the privilege. Wright, bad-spirited and greedy, ' spake some unbeseeming words,' and suffered the loss of his liberty for a few days, at the end of which he acknowledged his sorrow and was discharged.

If it was difficult to control the news-books, it was more difficult, well nigh impossible, to control the pamphlets. There appeared no end to them. All the industry and zeal of the Committee for Examinations and the Stationers' Company failed to stop the advancing tide of scandalous publications. The failure of Canute on another occasion is not more difficult to explain than the failure of the overseers of the press. On 18 June, 1644, a[2] Committee was appointed to report to the House of Lords what course was ' fit for preventing the printing of scandalous pamphlets '. It was a confession that the 1643 Ordinance had failed completely.[3]

[1] June, 1643. (*H.C.J.*)

[2] *H.L.J.*

[3] Derby House Committee's letter to Sir John Meldrum, 8 October, 1644, ' . . . we earnestly desire you not to think of what is in printed diurnals or such books. The authors of them take too much liberty to themselves, but which for the present is not likely to be fully remedied '.

AREOPAGITICA

The Stationers' Complaint against Milton

On 13 December, 1644, one, George Jeffrey, was apprehended and examined by the Lords for dispersing a
libel against the Peers in London.[1] His explanation did
not sound convincing. He had, he said, found 22 of the
printed papers between the stall boards of his master's
stall, and had carried them into his master's shop. He did
not keep his discovery to himself, but shared it with neighbours, who promptly came " and got some of them away."
The Wardens of the Stationers' Company were invited to
investigate the matter and find out who printed or wrote the
libel. The Wardens reported failure—' the letter, being so
common a letter ', was not distinctive enough to afford a
clue as to what press had been used.

Probably (as Professor Masson has suggested)[2] it was in
order to distract attention from their own failures, that the
Wardens hastened to complain ' of the frequent printing of
' scandalous books by divers, as Hezechia Woodward and
' Jo. Milton '. Mr. Justice Reeves and Mr. Justice Bacon
were appointed to examine Woodward and Milton and
' others of whom the Master and Wardens of the Stationers
might complain '. The Gentleman Usher was sent to attach
the parties and to bring them before the Justices. The
stationers were invited to give evidence.

George Jeffrey and his ingenuous story, and the failure
of the stationers, seem all to have been forgotten in the

[1] H.L.J., Dec., 1644.

[2] Masson's Milton, Vol. 3, p. 293, 1873.

greater interest of pursuing Milton.[1] Not only had he disregarded the new licensing laws, but he was the author of a most heretical book, also unlicensed, on divorce. The Stationers' Company had not let the Divorce Tract pass unquestioned ; there was some unpleasantness before they let the matter drop. Then, a few weeks before Jeffrey was carried with his small illicit stock to the House of Lords, Milton had by issuing the unlicensed *Areopagitica* plainly declared that for his part he was not disposed to let the matter drop. His liberty as a subject was being interfered with : no man was free so long as the Ordinance of 1643 remained on the Statute Book. The Long Parliament, for all its reputed magnanimity, did not ' brook written exceptions ' against its proceedings any more gently than the jealous, haughty prelates had done in the days of their late usurpation. The Long Parliament had begun well by breaking open the presses which the bishops had closely sealed against all who were not of their party and persuasion. ' It was the People's birthright and privilege in time of Parliament, it was the breaking forth of light ',[2] said Milton, and included some of the members of the House in his eulogy of those who ' by their unlicensed books to the ' contempt of an Imprimatur first broke that triple ice clung ' about our hearts, and taught the people to see day '.[3]

[1] *H.L.J.*, 17 Jan., 1644-5 : Wardens of Stationers' Company found one *Tew* dispersing libels. They seized him and his stock. His ' letters being very like the letters of the libel against the peers ', he was further questioned. He was committed for contempt for refusing information. The Wardens had not forgotten.

[2] *Areopagitica*, l. 1088.

[3] *Ibid.*, l. 1646.

To his championship of the cause of unlicensed printing
Milton brought a store of learning, which included the
classical stock-in-trade of every writer of his time and left
enough over to proclaim the independent student and
scholar : eloquence and personal conviction, that raised
his tract above the level of an academic prolusion and made
it an impassioned utterance rather than a calm disquisition
of *pro* and *con* : and humour, which is as fresh to-day as it
was nearly three hundred years ago. Though the immediate effect of the *Areopagitica* was merely to involve him in
trouble with the authorities, Milton had settled the question
for every impartial and thoughtful reader, though licensing
was thereafter to be an unconscionable time in dying.
What he said in favour of unlicensed printing was indisputably true.

Milton and the Censorship of News

But Milton had remained silent on one of the main points
of contention. He had said nothing about news-books.[1]
Should the news-writer be permitted to issue false news and
no measures of prevention but only of retribution be
taken ? The Long Parliament had learned by bitter experience how much mischief spurious news in print could breed,
how much confusion unauthorised reports caused, particularly in time of civil war. It may be that Milton made
a mental reservation in favour of news-books being subject

[1] Except the following :—' . . . Do we not see, not once or oftener, but
weekly, that continued court-libel against the Parliament and City, printed,
as the wet sheets can witness, and dispersed among us for all that licencing
can do ? Yet this is the prime service a man would think, wherein this
Order should give proof of itself '. The reference is to *Aulicus* (l. 767).

to official examination before publication. A treatise on the right and scriptural observance of the Sabbath, for example, or a book of poems is obviously in a different category from a diurnal of parliamentary proceedings. The damage which a false report of a decision of parliament may cause is very considerable, whereas no one but the author himself will be held responsible for the views expressed in (say) a treatise on Sabbath observance, or in books of poetry or philosophy. In 1651 Milton became licenser himself, but as he seems to have been concerned solely with news-books, he must be acquitted of a charge of inconsistency.

Milton's Complaint against the Stationers

Milton and the Stationers' Company had been in conflict with each other before the publication of the *Areopagitica*, and they were so again afterwards. His attitude to the Company may, therefore, have been prejudiced : it is none the less important. He approved the right of copy :—

' For that part which preserves justly every man's copy to himself, or provides for the poor, I touch not : only wish they be not made pretences to abuse and persecute honest, and painful men, who offend not in any of these particulars. . . .'[1]

But while he approved the wisdom of the Order of January, 1642, by which the name and consent of the author was required for every publication,[2] he had less respect for the motive which had prompted the Stationers' Company to petition the Government to pass that order :—

[1] *Ibid.*, l. 116.
[2] See note on page 63 *supra*.

. . . ' And how it got the upper hand of your precedent order[1] so well constituted before, if we may believe those men whose profession gives them cause to inquire most, it may be doubted there was in it the fraud of some old patentees and monopolisers in the trade of bookselling who, under pretence of the poor in their Company not to be defrauded, and the just retaining of each man his several copy (which God forbid should be gainsaid), brought divers glozing[2] colours to the House, which were indeed but colours, and serving to no end except it be to exercise a superiority over their neighbours : men who do not therefore labour in an honest profession to which learning is indebted, that they should be made other men's vassals. Another end is thought was aimed at by some of them in procuring by petition this order, that having power in their hands, malignant books might the easier escape abroad, as the event shows. . . .'[3]

These are hard words but not altogether untrue. The Company is not guiltless of a charge of selfishness. Its own interest had come manifestly first. And the privileged freemen of the Company had laid themselves open to such a charge as this.

Methods of Censorship

The *Areopagitica* throws some light on the methods of censorship employed by the board of licensers which had been set up in June, 1643. It appears that licensing was bad for licensers, as well as being a continual discouragement to learning and the learned. Milton ' cannot believe ' how he that values time and his own studies, or is but of ' a sensible nostril, should be able to endure it '.[4]

' In this one thing I crave leave of the present licensers to be pardoned for so thinking ; who doubtless took this office up, looking on it through their obedience to the Parliament, whose command perhaps made all things seem easy and unlaborious to them : but that this short trial hath wearied them out already, their own expressions and excuses to them who make so many journeys to solicit their license are testimony enough. Seeing therefore those who now possess the employment by all evident signs wish themselves well rid of it, and that no man of worth, none that is not a plain unthrift of his own hours, is ever likely to succeed them, except he

---

[1] *i.e.*, that of Jan., 1642.

[2] Specious.

[3] *Ibid.*, l. 1682.

[4] *Ibid.*, l. 821-838.

mean to put himself to the salary of a press-corrector, we may easily foresee what kind of licensers we are to expect hereafter—either ignorant imperious and remiss, or basely pecuniary. This is what I had to show, wherein this Order cannot conduce to that end, whereof it bears the intention.'

Further reflections on licensers seem likewise to have a foundation in empiric fact :—

' . . . the hasty view of an unleisured licenser much his younger [*i.e.*, younger than the author who seeks his *imprimatur*], perhaps far his inferior in judgment, perhaps one who never knew the labour of book-writing. . . . '[1]

And if the author wishes to make an alteration in the text of his book after it has been licensed and before it has gone to the press, he must make another submission to the licenser :—

' . . . The printer dares not go beyond his licensed copy ; so often then must the author trudge to his leave-giver, that those his new insertions may be viewed ; and many a jaunt will be made, ere that licenser, for it must be the same man, can either be found, or found at leisure. . . .'

All that a man writes

' . . . is but under the tuition, under the correction of his patriarchal licenser to blot or alter what precisely accords not with the hide-bound humour which he calls his judgment ; when every acute reader upon the first sight of a pedantic licenser will be ready with these like words to ding the book a quoit's distance from him :—" I hate a pupil teacher ". . . .'

This was more than theory. Such things had already happened, if not to Milton, then to others of his acquaintance. One specific example is mentioned of a learned book being refused an *imprimatur* by a pedantic and perfunctory licenser.

' . . . And to what an author this violence hath been lately done, and in what book of greatest consequence to be faithfully published, I could new instance,[2] but shall forbear till a more convenient season. Yet if these things be not resented seriously and timely by them who have the remedy in their power, but that such iron-moulds as these shall have authority to gnaw out the choicest periods of exquisitest books, and to commit such a treacherous fraud against the orphan remainders of worthiest men after death, the more sorrow will belong to that hapless race of men, whose misfortune it is to have understanding. . . .'

[1] l. 882.

[2] This may possibly refer to Coke's *Institutes* published in 1641, seven years after his death. (Crook's *Areopagitica*, 1904.)

A curious and in every way remarkable[1] instance, corroborating what Milton had said, of the arbitrary methods of the licensers must (if it be true) be assigned to the period between 1643 and 1646. The record of the incident is found in *Philanglus*,[2] written by James Howell, afterwards Historiographer Royal to Charles the Second :—

'. . . Ther was one Master *Heron* a Printer, who being sent for by a Lady of good quality, she told him that now that there was a National Covenant com forth, which every one must take, she had a Sermon in a fair manuscript of that great light of the Church, Master *Brightman*, which treats of *universal Covenants, viz.* how far they are agreeable to Scripture, and consonant to the Word of God, and it had bin preach'd before the House of Commons thirty yeers before, therefore it wold be now very seasonable to print and publish it, The Printer giving her Ladyship many thanks, receiv'd the Sermon, (which she avouch'd upon her honor to be a *tru* Copy) and undertook the business, so he went to him who was appointed by the *Syncd* to license for the Press peeces of that nature, to get an *Imprimatur*, but the *Synodical* man having kept the Sermon above three daies by him, the Printer went for his Sermon, and found it formally licenc'd for the Press, but most pittifully *falsify'd, interlin'd* and *adulterated* in many places ; For whereas the opinion of *Brightman* throughout the whole Sermon, was, that a National and General Covenant was agreeable to the Word of God, Provided, *the King did give his Royall assent thereunto, without which it was both detestable and damnable* : The *holy Synodical* man had expunged the word *King* every where, and foisted in the room of it, sometimes the word *Parlement*, sometimes the *Trustees of the Common wealth* ; sometimes the *men in Authority* ; The Printer having perus'd the interlineations and expunctions, told him, that were he to get 1000 *l.* by printing the Sermon, he wold not be so arrand a knave as to wrong the dead so much, by making him speak what he never meant, nay things quite contrary to his meaning ; I saw the said Sermon, and the maner how it was so basely sophisticated.'

There is no valid reason for rejecting Howell's testimony. I had seen the said sermon after it had passed through the li nser's hands. He was not dependent on hearsay e ence, though writing presumably ten years after the

Attention is drawn to it in my letter to *The Times Literary Supplement*, 12 July, 1928.

[2] *Philanglus ; Som sober Inspections/Made into the/Cariage and consults/ Of the Late-long Parlement,/Whereby occasion is taken to speak of Parlements in/former Times, &c./With some Reflexes upon Govern/ment in general./ By Jam. Howell,* Esq., 1660.
The same passage appears in the first edition, 1655.

incident had taken place. And Master Heron, a printer, was known to him, being his own printer. In 1655, when the above passage first appeared, Howell had nothing to gain by drawing attention to the malpractices of former licensers. Had he reserved his animadversions till after the Restoration, they could not have been regarded as affording such trustworthy evidence. The date of the actual incident may be fixed somewhere between 1643 (when the National Covenant was adopted) and 1646 (when Heron ceased printing). The licenser, whoever he was, merits the description Milton gives of others of the Board—'iron-'mould, with authority to gnaw out the choicest periods of 'exquisitest books, and to commit such a treacherous fraud 'against the orphan remainders of a worthy man after 'death'.

Milton's eloquent comment on the failure of the *Areopagitica* to excite more than the mild interest of the mighty, and the spleen of the Stationers' Company, is well known :—

'I did but prompt the age to quit their clogs
    By the known rules of ancient liberty,
    When straight a barbarous noise environs me
Of owls and cuckoos, asses, apes, and dogs :
    As when those hinds that were transformed to frogs
    Railed at Latona's twin-born progeny,
    Which after held the sun and moon in fee.
But this is got by casting pearls to hogs,
    That brawl for freedom in their senseless mood,
And still revolt when truth would set them free.
Licence they mean when they cry Liberty ;
    For who loves that, must first be wise and good ;
But from that mark how far they rove we see,
    For all this waste of wealth, and loss of blood.'

When the barbarous noise of the Master and Wardens[1] of the Stationers' Company had died down, the real effect of the *Areopagitica* was seen.

[1] R. Mead, J. Parker and R. Whitaker.

CHAPTER III

1645-1646

A More Strict Censorship Required

POLITICAL events made a more strict supervision of the press imperative. The country was in an over-heated excitable condition of mind, and rumours were uncritically received. One third of England was in the possession of the king's forces : the king himself had entered into so many intrigues with the Irish, the Scots and the Parliament, and made so many fair promises which he had left unfulfilled, that even his friends hesitated not to believe the worst of him. Also, no one could with any confidence say what was happening in Parliament. The news-books variously reported the proceedings of the two Houses. Even the parliamentary news-writers drew their material from not too reliable sources, and *Britanicus*, whose position as one of the better established periodicals of the day might have led the reader to expect a more carefully authenticated relation of current affairs, was plainly more concerned to score off *Aulicus* than to provide news for the reader.

The uncensored retailing of domestic news was sufficiently confusing, but when it was foreign news that was inopportunely or unadvisedly published, confusion threatened to become more confounded. For example, one such printed

relation caused the ' Lords Ambassadors extraordinary from
the High and Mighty States General of the United Provinces
of the Netherlands ' some inconvenience in April, 1645.
Their valedictory speeches in the House had been printed
and circulated against their will.   On 2 June the States
Ambassador made further complaint to the House of
Lords of a ' feigned.letter in *Mercurius Civicus* supposed to
' be written from the Parliament to the States by way of
' complaint against the late Ambassadors ',[1] who had taken
leave of this country in no amicable frame of mind.   The
Lords, anxious to redeem the transgressions of the authors
and printers whom they had failed to control, hastened to
order the arrest of author and printer, and to inform the
ambassador of the innocence of Parliament.   Friction with
the Netherlands was undesirable at a time when Parliament
devoutly wished for all the security that the possession of
good allies could give.

THE LICENSING OF NEWS-BOOKS

The usual classification of news-books (1640-60) as
licensed and unlicensed has obscured an important fact,
namely, that a licenser's *imprimatur* was no guarantee of
immunity from prosecution.   A news-book might be duly
entered in the Stationers' Register under the name of
Mr. Rushworth, as the *Parliament Scout* was, for example,
(1645-46), and the author would still be held responsible
for the truth or falsity of the reports it contained.   Thus
Dillingham, whose *Parliament Scout* had given offence to

[1] *H.L.J.*

Parliament, suffered imprisonment for his indiscretion, although his was one of the regularly licensed news-books. The nature of the indiscretion is worth noting because it shows the sort of thing to which Parliament at that time objected. According to the *Lords' Journals* Dillingham's offence was the publishing of a passage which the Lords construed as ' a great defamation of Essex's honour '. The passage in question is not quoted in the *Journals*. Mr. J. B. Williams in his *History of English Journalism* implies that it was the following :—

' . . . Indeed it were sad if discipline should once be stretcht to *jure divino*, its true we had dayes in which sometimes this then that was *jure divino* but now we are growne wiser and set upon a form of Church government that is *alterable*.'

But that, surely, could not have been construed as a ' great defamation of the Lord General's honour '. The following is more likely, I think, to have been the cause of the trouble :—

' 27 Jan. The Commons agreed upon the Ordinance, for the maintaining of the forces to be commanded by Sir Tho. Fairfax, and had it sent up to the Lords, but that they rose sooner than they usually do : we hear they are as *jocund* at *Oxford* for this alteration, as they were, when they knew they were beaten at *Marston* Moore, and that *Yorke* was lost.'

Royalist scribes made merry over ' the cashiered Earl of Essex ' (*vide* e.g. *Merc. Anti-Britannicus*, Aug., 1645), and the *Parliament Scout* seems to have indulged in the same tasteless humour at the expense of those who had lost their military command on account of the new Self-Denying Ordinance, which had been but a thinly veiled excuse for getting rid of the incompetent. The fact that it was the Lords who found fault with the *Scout*—the Lords who had been opposed to the Ordinance—seems to bear out the contention that this was the passage that gave offence.

The Case of Mercurius Britanicus

The case of *Mercurius Britanicus* in 1645 throws further light on the working of the licensing system as applied to news-books.

On the first of February, 1644-5, *Mercurius Britanicus* was entered in the Stationers' Register under the hand of the Lord General (*i.e.* Essex) and 'perused by Thomas Audley'. According to the Ordinance of 1643 *Britanicus* should have been licensed by Walley; after April, 1644, by Rushworth. Yet so far as news-books are concerned, this rule does not appear to have been rigorously observed. A warrant from Essex was sufficient licence for *Britanicus*. The Lord General, it must be supposed, assumed no responsibility for what appeared in the news-book : Audley was solely responsible. Even after the death of Essex Audley continued to publish ' by warrant from the late Lord General ',[1] though after 30 September, 1644, Audley was deputy to Rushworth, the official licenser.

The true facts (about the writing, printing and licensing of *Britanicus*) came to light when *Britanicus* got into trouble in August, 1645. The occasion of the offence was a scurrilous attack on the king by *Britanicus* on 4 August. The Lords objected,[2] and the printer, Robert White, was sent to the Fleet although he disclaimed responsibility

[1] *Stationers' Register*, II., May, 1645.

[2] Sir R. Burgoyne to Sir R. Verney :—' *Britanicus*, as I hear, is sent to Newgate prison for being too saucy and uncivil with the King in his pamphlets. The parliament did much resent the impudency of his stile. I wish he may smart to purpose, and others learn better manners '. (*Hist. MSS. Comm.*, Pt. 7, p. 454.)

for what he had printed by order from Audley. He believed, but was not certain, that Audley had Rushworth's permission. Audley, being examined, said that he had allowed the news-book to be printed, but had objected to the passage in question regarding the king. Marchamont Nedham, the writer of it, had neglected to obey his injunction to alter it. The Lords committed Audley to the Gate-house : Nedham was discharged with a caution. A few days before this sentence was passed, *Mercurius Britanicus, His Apologie To all Well-affected People*[1] was published according to order, printed by R. White and duly entered in the Stationers' Register : ' I confesse I have overshot my self, though I hope, not beyond *Recovery* ', said *Britanicus* with a humility that profited him little. Two days later one of the most curious of all the entries in the Stationers' Register during this period occurs—that of a pamphlet entitled *Aulicus His Hue and Cry Sent forth after Britanicus*, which if not written by John Berkenhead is witty enough to have been so. That a royalist[2] who had given the licensing authorities so much cause to wish him in the Clink should have submitted his tract to the authorities and that they should have licensed it, argues either a greater tolerance on the part of the licensers towards royalist scribes than has hitherto been supposed, or else a greater dislike of *Britanicus*. Audley and his secretary Nedham were perhaps not popular even with their own party.

[1] 11 August, 1645, is the date Thomason affixes to his copy of the tract, which was regularly licensed by Mabbot on 9 August. *Anti-Britannicus* (*vide* p. 90) attributed the *Apologie* to Audley.

[2] If we attribute the pamphlet to Sir John Berkenhead.

Aulicus describes *Britanicus's* apology as ' the vomitting out of poysoned Crocodile teares in slanders ' : Britanicus announced in the next issue of his news-book (which came forth the following week despite his imprisonment) that it had been ' well accepted by many known sincere lovers of God and their country '.[1] Aulicus condoled humorously with his rival on misfortunes common to both :—' Your ' printer, R. White, is in the Fleet, so is my friend Royston,[2] ' the printer. Let us not grieve too much for them ; why ' should we shew more love to them than to our selves ? ' Hang them, let them goe '.

The author of an unlicensed pamphlet, *Mercurius Anti-Britannicus*, which appeared the same day, adds some picturesque details to the story. A few days before, if his word is to be trusted, he had seen Britanicus, whom he identifies as Captain Audley, through the grate at the Gate-House ' with his evil Genius in conjunction with ' him, busily penning what they have since published ' as their apology. Audley, ' short, swarthy and Chess-nut ' colour'd ', was aided by Nedham, who may or may not have been a ' Gentleman of Grayes-Inne '. We are told how the news-book was normally produced. Audley attended meetings of the Close Committee and received instructions. He made notes which it was Nedham's business to weave into a narration of suitable length. The one collected the matter, the other gave it form.

[1] *Merc. Brit.*, 11-18 Aug., 1645.

[2] Committed to prison for ' vending books from Oxford ' and for his ' correspondency for Oxford ' : released by the Lords, 15 August, 1645 (*H.L.J.*).

On 15 August Audley expressed deep regret to the Lords[1] and after engaging not to give like cause of offence again he was released from his imprisonment and ordered ' not to presume to license any more books '.[2] ' The storm was over ',[3] *Britanicus* was licensed by Mabbot who, as Rushworth's deputy, had already been licensing such pamphlets since March, 1645.[4]

After this decision it is, to say the least of it, surprising to read in the Stationers' Register an entry for 15 November, 1645, of *Britanicus* ' under the hand of Tho. Audley by Consent of Master Rushworth '. By an Order of the House of Lords Audley had been forbidden to license any more books. Yet three months later here is Rushworth, the official licenser, giving him permission to license *Britanicus* once again. It is unlikely that the entries in the Stationers' Register from 15 November, 1645, to 16 May, 1646, of *Britanicus* under the hand of ' Audley ' or ' Audley and Mabbott ' are false.[5] The stationer, Robert White, who entered the book every week could hardly have kept up the fraud for six months (*i.e.*, from Nov., 1645, to May, 1646). It is easier to believe that the entries are correct and that Rushworth had given Audley permission to license, in spite of what the Lords had ordered on 15 August, 1645.

[1] *Hist. MSS. Comm.*, Pt. 6, p. 74.

[2] *H.L.J.*, 15 Aug., 1645.

[3] Quoted from *Britanicus*, 18-25 Aug., 1645.

[4] J. B. Williams' date (*Hist. of Eng. Journ.*, p. 66), 15 Aug., is incorrect.

[5] In his examination before the Lords on 23 May, 1646, Nedham said that Audley was ' deputed by Mr. Rushworth to license ' weekly pamphlets (*H.L.J.*).

Britanicus, however, could not keep out of trouble. In his issue for 11-18 May, 1646, he brought himself into disfavour with Parliament for the tone of his reflections on the king, whom he did not scruple to call tyrant and to threaten with a hostile reception on his return from Scotland. The Gentleman Usher of the Black Rod was sent to attach the bodies of Mr. Nedham and Captain Audley and bring them before the House.

Nedham confessed himself the author of *Britanicus*, 11-18 May, but, as on the previous occasion of his prosecution for a similar offence, he excused himself on the ground that Audley had perused the news-book before it went to press. In August, 1645, Nedham had been truthful in his assertion, and he could truthfully (if we believe the evidence of the Stationers' Register) have said the same of the issues from 15 November, 1645, to 16 May, 1646. But the issue of *Britanicus* that relates the events of the week ending 18 May, 1646, was for obvious reasons not entered in the Register. Audley disclaimed all knowledge of that particular number of *Britanicus*, and he was released. Nedham was sent to the Fleet.[1]

[1] Mr. J. B. Williams' account of the whole story seems to me to be misleading. He says (*History of English Journalism*, p. 68) :—' [Nedham] stated that *Britanicus* was perused and licensed by Audley as Rushworth's deputy—which was untrue '. But it is almost certain that what Nedham said was true—*i.e.*, of *Britanicus* from 15 Nov., 1645, to 11 May, 1646. It was untrue only of the issue of 11-18 May, 1646. Speaking of the previous prosecution of Britanicus, Mr. Williams says (p. 66) :—' On 15 August . . . Audley was liberated and forbidden to license " books " again. From this date Gilbert Mabbott acted as licenser '. The implication of Mr. Williams' narrative is that from August, 1645, Audley ceased to license, and that, therefore, Nedham was not speaking the truth on 23 May, 1646, before the Lords : whereas, in point of fact Nedham was right about *Britanicus* from 15 Nov., 1645, to 11 May, 1646.

Thus, it may be believed, the lot of the parliamentary news-writer was not free from unpleasantness. If he assumed the rôle of critic (Britanicus, of course, exceeded the bounds of decent criticism), and was not content merely to catalogue current events, he must needs be extremely careful not to offend the authorities. Oxford Aulicus by comparison had a comfortable life. He acknowledged no licenser, his lodging was secure from government searchers, and the nut and spindle on which his printing press depended were out of the reach of Hunscot's itching fingers.[1]

It was not difficult for a royalist mercury, printed at Oxford and composed within call of the king's troops, to survive, and for author and printer to live a life of normal security ; but when either printer or author, or both, lived in London, short shrift was to be expected from Parliament. Britanicus, though imprisoned for speaking his mind too freely regarding the king, did not suffer the further indignity of having his mouth quite and permanently ' bunged up '.[2] *Britanicus* was suppressed (18 May, 1646) but Nedham and Audley did not cease writing news-books.[3] *Mercurius Rusticus*, however, which made little attempt to conceal its

[1] *Diutinus Britanicus*, 2-8 Dec., 1646, warned the Government against the danger of allowing *Aulicus* to continue unchecked :—' And it is a dangerous designe to our estate and affaires, to permit any *Paine* or *Aulicus* or *Oxford* Cavalier of them all to write, (And our Presses to print) against our friends, (The Parliament on the right hand, The Clergy on the left hand, or the Army that fights for both).' It should be added that *Diutinus Britanicus* was produced by Nedham and Audley !

[2] Samuel Butler.

[3] There is an interesting, hitherto unnoticed, entry in the Stat. Reg. of ' 2 *Brittanicus* ' under the hand of Mabbott, 16 July, 1646. The 2 *Brittanicus* are not to be found in the Thomason or Burney collections of newsbooks.

opposition to Parliament, was treated with the severity usually meted out to an enemy's publications in time of war—it was immediately suppressed.[1]

The Character of a London Diurnal

It may be of interest to notice, in passing, a witty, vivacious and biting satire on the London news-books of the time[2]—*The Character of a London Diurnal*, published in February, 1645, and written almost certainly by the poet John Cleaveland, of St John's College, Cambridge. A ripple of baffled rage ran through the London diurnals of the week following its publication. *The London Post* recorded with spiteful satisfaction that Cleaveland was taken to London to answer a charge of libel. *Britanicus* spoke at greater length :—' . . . this pamphlet costs half ' a crown now, whereas it cost four shillings at first : now ' one could probably get a copy of it for one and sixpence— ' all very dear, which shows how dearly the Malignants are ' in love with any treasonous by-blowe of scurrile wit from ' *Oxford* '. He described Cleaveland as ' a whelp of the same ' litter with Aulicus. . . . He is a poet too, one that hath ' taken a *nap* upon *Parnassus*, quaffes pure *Styx* instead of ' *Helicon*, to the confusion of *Round-heads* and *Reformation*; ' and by this means having taken a surfeit, he vomits up ' *characters*, and *spells* to charme and amaze the *people*. . . . '

Many people who were not Royalists sympathised with Cleaveland's attack on the London diurnals. So

---

[1] *H.C.J.*, 4 Oct., 1646.

[2] For a description of the news-books of 1645 by a man who was not a royalist, see *infra* p. 136.

popular was it that it was re-issued in several editions during the following fifteen years. To-day it is chiefly interesting because it contains the first unfavourable character-sketch (of any length) of Cromwell—a catalogue of inspired abuse of the Lieutenant-General before he attained eminence, before he had done more than prove himself the most successful soldier of his day, and when the greatest sin that could be laid to his charge was that he had driven Manchester from his commanding position in the army and remodelled the army to his own will.

PARLIAMENT AND THE SCOTTISH COMMISSIONERS

A curious but not uncommon example of the insufficient protection afforded by a licenser's *imprimatur* occurred at the end of 1645. The Scottish Commissioners' visit to London was then the most lively topic of discussion and news of their negotiations with the English Parliament was eagerly awaited. Parliament, however, had decided that secrecy was essential to success. R. Bostock, the printer, obtained news of the conference and determined to publish it. Dr. H. R. Plomer in his *Dictionary of Booksellers and Printers*, 1641-67, notes that Bostock ' was in trouble in ' 1645 and again in 1646, for publishing pamphlets relating ' to the disputes between England and Scotland '. It does not seem to have been noted that Bostock had the authority of an *imprimatur* for so doing. The Committee of Examination appointed to examine Bostock reported that he

' admitted having caused the first impression of the ' Scots' papers to be made, *but not without authority* '. The official licenser, Mr. Cranford, had, he said, given him licence to print the papers which had been brought to him by Mr. Buchanan ' without any knowledge ' or consent of the Scotts commissioners that he ' knoweth '. Bostock was dismissed with a caution. On 12 November, 1645, further news of the Commission was published in a pamphlet, *Truth It's Manifest*. Parliament appointed a committee to examine the author and printer. John Parker, Master of the Stationers' Company, testified before Parliament in January, 1645-46, that it had been licensed by Mr. James Cranford, the licenser. J. Hunscot (who became Master of the Stationers' Company in 1649) added that ' Buchanan entered it in Bostock's name, and ' after printing it at his own charge and there being some ' difference between him and Bostock regarding the price, he ' sold the whole impression to George Thomason ' (*C.S.P.D.*, Vol., 1645-7, p. 330). Cranford was fined five hundred pounds, according to *An Answer to Truth It's Manifest*[1] and imprisoned for breach of the privileges of the House.

In April, 1646, Bostock was again in custody on a similar charge, that of publishing (on 11 April) a pamphlet entitled *Some Papers of the Commissioners of Scotland given in lately to the Houses of Parliament concerning the Propositions of Peace, 16 March to 6 April* : Printed for Robert Bostock. The Copy of the Examination of Bostock as reprinted in the *Hist. MSS. Comm.*, Pt. 6, is an amusing as well as informative document :—

[1] Brit. Mus., E.811, 2, 12 Nov., 1645.

PARLIAMENT AND THE SCOTTISH COMMISSIONERS

' Bostock says that he printed the book entitled *Some Papers of the Commissioners of Scotland*, etc. On Thursday or Friday last, whilst he was absent, a stranger came to his shop and gave a bundle of papers to his wife, telling her to have them printed forthwith, upon which she distributed them between three printers. On his return she told him that she thought they came from the Scots Commissioners. On Friday last Mr. Buchanan sent for him to meet him in Paul's, and bid him make haste with the printing ; but not let it be known that the papers had come from him. The proofs were sent to Mr. Buchanan and were returned with corrections in his hand-writing ; and as soon as the book was printed, twelve copies were sent to Mr. Cheisley's man for the Scots Commissioners. Bostock, when summoned to appear before the Committee, heard on his way that the Commissioners had sent for him so turned into Worcester House, where Mr. Barkley asked him how he would justify the matter before the Committee, to which Bostock answered that he should say the book was printed without his knowledge, and presently wrote to his wife to answer to the same effect. Bostock says that the book was printed without license, and was not entered at Stationers' Hall because he was so hastened by Mr. Buchanan. 13 April. Examination of Robert Harrison confirming the preceding statement, except that he says that his master distributed the sheet to the several printers.'

Bostock was sent to prison and Parliament ordered that a reply be issued to undeceive the people who had believed *Truth It's Manifest* and *Some Papers of the Commissioners of Scotland*.[1]

There is further evidence to show that the Scottish Commissioners took it upon themselves to authorise London printers to publish without regular licence their accounts of the negotiation with Parliament, though Parliament were equally determined to prevent them. A certain poor journeyman called Liptrat promptly informed against some of his brethren in the hope of currying favour with Parliament. He gave information to the House of Commons regarding the printing of some papers relating to business transacted in Parliament.[2] Blaiklock, he said, a sharer in the printing of them, told him they were being

[1] *H.C.J.*

[2] *Ibid.*, 14 Oct., 1646.

97

printed at the houses of Field, Griffith and Leech : they would come forth on the following day and were printed by warrant under the hand of some of the Commissioners of Scotland. Parliament resolved to show printers and booksellers that a Scottish Commissioner's *imprimatur* had no recognised authority. Liptrat was ordered[1] to go to the houses of Field, Griffith and Leech, to bring back copies of the papers in question together with the original document from which they were made, and to stop the printing of them, and to summon the three printers to accompany him to the House of Commons : which he did. The document in question was a copy of Commissioner Lord Louden's speech in the House. Lawrence Blaiklock and Samuel Peck, stationers, had the full text in their possession and had delivered it to Ann Griffith, the printer's wife, to be printed.

John Field, caught red-handed at his printing press, was ready with his excuse—there was no intention of circulating the pamphlet till 8,000 copies had been printed. The *Scottish Dove*, reporting the examination of the culprits, said ' the Printer and the Booke-seller were both commited, ' for that they without Lycence should print any such things. ' It seems it was ignorance in them, and it is likely both they ' and others will be warned for the future '. The *Perfect Diurnall*, 12-19 Oct., 1646, confirms this statement :— ' The Stationers and Printers plead ignorance in what they ' did, not understanding the nature of the speeches they were ' to print, and that formerly Papers have been printed by

[1] *Ibid.*, 15 Oct., 1646.

' Authority of the Scotch Commissioners without other
' lycence, which made them undertake this ; but they are
' heartily sorry for their error. . . .' The plea of ignorance
of the law is remarkable, coming as it did after all that
Parliament had done to stop such offences, but it must
have carried some conviction, for the sentence passed on
Field, Chapman and Griffith was a light one.

The House of Commons made three observations upon
the matter :—

1. To have Arguments held forth to the Kingdom, against the judgment
of Parliament, in Matters of this Importance, is not for the good of the
Kingdom.

2. To have Arguments printed, all of the one Side, and none of the other,
is not to deal fairly with the Kingdom.

3. To desire the Lords, that a Committee may be appointed to join with
a Committee of this House ; and to consider of some way of righting the
Houses, and to prevent inconveniences of the like Nature for the future.[1]

It was now the Commissioners' turn to object. They
quite reasonably took exception to certain news-pamphlets
that had been published while the above matter was still
under consideration. One of these pamphlets bore the
title, *A Declaration concerning the miserable sufferings of the
Countries under the Scots Forces that quarter in the North
of England,* 31 Oct., 1646, and was unquestionably
licensed by Rushworth.[2] The Commissioners sent a plain-
tive note to the Lords asking them ' how they would
' construct of it if Diurnalls and Pamphlets of this kinde
' (*vide* enclosed specimen) were dayly lycensed in the King-
' dome of *Scotland* to be printed against the *English*

[1] *Ibid.,* 16 Oct., 1646.

[2] *H.L.J.* See also entry in Stat. Reg., 2 Nov., 1646.

' Nation or Army, and noe Cause taken for their Vindica-
' tion : but rather al Papers which may cleere their
' Proceedings denyed to be lycensed, or stopped and sup-
' pressed. . . . Having perceived that the Patience of the
' Houses hath animated the Authors of such Pamphlets to
' retorne to their former Boldnes, wee are necessitated to
renue our former Desires '.

The matter was settled only by the return of the Commissioners to Scotland.

THE PRESBYTERIAN TYRANNY OVER
THE PRESS

The importance of the years 1645 and 1646 in the history
of licensing and in the struggle for the freedom of the press
seems to have received less than its due recognition. The
history of the news-books during this period has been
fully dealt with by Mr. J. B. Williams in his *History of
English Journalism* ; but it was not the news-books that
provided the battle-ground for this struggle for freedom.
Rather was it the miscellaneous pamphlets of general
interest.

The dangers arising from the uncensored publication of
news, both domestic and foreign, had of late been clearly
demonstrated to the Parliament, and a more careful
supervision of the diurnals was not unsuccessfully attempted. This was by no means an impossible undertaking, for
the news-books came forth regularly and were more easily
traceable to their source : also, they did not aim at providing more than a compendium of news-items : there was

100

little, if any, attempt at criticism. But unlicensed pamphlets of occasional and topical interest afforded but little clue to their origin. The searcher who would surprise the surreptitious printer must needs be highly gifted as a detective.

Parliament in 1645 set forth on a crusade against sectaries and heretics. An Assembly of Divines whose decisions Parliament felt would be trustworthy, because it knew what they would be, was called upon to debate *de jure divino* in Church government. Could it be that there was a divine right of Synods and Kirk sessions, which to the presbyter already seemed so divinely right ? Presbyterianism threatened to become as tyrannical as the old prelatical rule. London became alarmed when the Lord Mayor and Counsellors revealed the same aggressive orthodoxy, actively supporting Parliament. It was plain that the printing presses were to be more than half shut to those who were not orthodox in the new sense of the term. In former days the press had been subject to popish authority, then to prelatical, now to presbyterian.[1] Under each dispensation there had been witnesses to a gradual faith in the freedom of the press. The Long Parliament had shared that faith in 1640, since many of its members had

[1] Parliament ordered the suppression of *Tender Conscience Religiously Affected*, 9 May, 1646. On the front page is a picture of Pope, Presbyter and Prelate, and an address to the reader :—' It is a priviledge in Parliament time, due to the freeborn Subjects of England, that the Printing Presses should bee free, especially to the friends of Tender Conscience. But this being now Monopolized from them by the persecuting Presbyters, Tender Conscience cannot have his dictats published with Imprimatur, although seen and allowed, but is forced to seek Corners, and by lanes to presse out Truth ; without interruption Thine is the Benefit, the Glory will be God's, and poore Tender Conscience must undergo the hazard '.

suffered under the prelatical tyranny : but that faith in freedom had degenerated into an exclusive belief in presbyterianism. Here the Scots concurred with the English Parliament, and the presbyterians appeared to be strongly enough represented, as well in the city and the army as in the Parliament, to make the erection of presbyterianism on the ruins of episcopacy a certainty even without the support of the complying Scots. The Independents in Parliament remonstrated, citizens not presbyterian remonstrated with the Lord Mayor and his Council. Unlicensed pamphlets hostile to the arbitrary extension of presbyterianism appeared in great numbers, testing the strength of the machinery by which the government regulated the press. Parliament determined to enlist the more active support of the Stationers' Company, and began by calling them to account, January, 1644-5.[1] The Master and Wardens were invited to inform ' by whose default it happens ' that such scurrilous, libellous and seditious Pamphlets are ' every day printed and published, they undertaking at the ' passing of their Ordinance, to prevent all those Incon- ' veniences that formerly grew by the Licentiousness of the ' press ' ; and they were enjoined to be more diligent in suppressing such licentiousness, as the House expected a better account of them, of their Proceedings therein thenceforth. Lilburne's pamphlets were among those that had determined the action of the House.

Some interesting facts about the surreptitious printing of these and other pamphlets were made known by Mr.

[1] *H.C.J.*

Plomer in his paper, ' Secret Printing During the Civil War '.[1] He has shown what books were printed at the following secret presses (1644-6) :—the Coleman Street press, Overton's ' Martin Mar-Priest press ', the Goodman's Fields press, and William Larner's press in Bishopsgate Street.

The working of the licensing system during this period, however, is a matter beyond the scope of Mr. Plomer's paper ; and the following facts, added to what Mr. Plomer has written concerning the productions of those secret presses, should make up a fairly complete record of unlicensed printing during the years 1644-6.

Lilburne and the Licensing Authorities

The story of John Lilburne's clash with the licensing authorities brings to light some information about the licensing system which has not yet been fully noted. Along with Prynne and Bastwick, Lilburne had formerly championed the cause of unlicensed printing against an episcopal tyranny, though of late he had bitterly quarrelled with his former companions in the pillory. Now he embarks on an equally bitter quarrel with the Long Parliament whose advent he had so devoutly wished and worked for and welcomed. At the same time he is engaged in petitioning for the money Parliament had promised but not paid him in respect of his many services during the first Civil War and his sufferings therein. He is now chiefly prominent on the side of the unlicensed pamphleteers in

[1] *The Library*, 1904, Vol. v, p. 374.

opposition to the Government, who are still paying him compensation for his former sufferings in a similar cause when the opposition had been provided by the bishops. There is added a touch of irony. Parliament alternately paid him for his previous sufferings[1] and prosecuted him for his new activity in the same cause.

The Committee of Examinations inquired in January, 1645, regarding a letter against Prynne printed under the name of John Lilburne, and proceeded to examine Lilburne.[2] To him, Prynne represented all that was intolerable in presbyterianism, though for the intolerance to which he objected he himself would be hard to match. There can be no doubt of his courage and sincerity. He had distinguished himself in the wars and had suffered imprisonment at Oxford by the Cavaliers in 1643. He was no less bellicose and intrepid with a pen than with a sword in his hand. It was his tongue, however, not his pen, that got him into trouble in July, 1645. Certain scandalous words of his concerning Speaker Lenthall were overheard by some of his enemies, who procured his examination before the House. His recalcitrance brought him into further displeasure. He appealed to the rights of freedom as laid down in Magna Charta, but this did not hasten the day of his release from prison, where he remained till October. It is worthy of note that while in Newgate he continued to publish letters which were printed and distributed to the further

[1] Lilburne received compensation from the Long Parliament both for his sufferings under the bishops and for his sufferings in the Civil War when he was captured and imprisoned.

[2] H.C.J.

discomposure of Prynne.[1]

England's Birth-right, by ' a well-wisher to the just cause ' for which Lieutenant-Colonel John Lilburne is unjustly ' imprisoned in New-gate,' was being sold in the streets of London on 10 October, 1645. It may have been written by Lilburne himself—who so great a well-wisher to Lilburne's cause as he ?—or it may have been the work of his associate and printer, Overton, or some friend unknown. Whoever it was had obtained his material from Lilburne, to whom the tract may, therefore, not unjustly be attributed.

Lilburne speaks more harshly of the Stationers' Company, the monopolisers of what should be free, than even Milton had done :—

'. . . that insufferable, unjust and tyrannical Monopoly of Printing, whereby a great company of the very same Malignant fellows that *Canterbury* and his Malignant party engaged in their Arbitrary *Designs,* against both the Peoples and Parliaments just Privileges (who turning with every winde, doe endeavour by all possible means, as well now as then, to sell and betray the Kingdome for their own gaine) are invested with an Arbitrary unlimmitted *Power,* even by a general Ordinance of Parliament, to print, divulge and disperse whatsoever Books, Pamphlets and Libells they please, though they be full of *Lyes,* and tend to the poysoning of the Kingdom with unjust and Tyrannical Principles.'

' They doe not rest here neither, but are yet further authorized with a generall Ordinance of this very Parliament, contrary to all law and justice, equity and reason, under pretence of searching for scandalous Books, to call numbers of deboyst men with Smiths and Constables, yea and the trained Bands also (when they please) to assist them, and in most bold and tumultuous manner to break open and rifle, even the Parliaments owne (in all their greatest dangers, troubles & distresses) most faithful friends Houses, Chests, Truncks and Drawers ; and from thence to rob, steale, and felloniously to carry away such of the Possessors proper goods, choice Linnens, and best things, as they please, as well as Books new and old, after they have put the owners themselves out of doores, and commanded Constables to carry them before a Committee, and from thence to prison.'

[1] Prynne replied with *The Lyar Confounded* in Oct., 1645. Lilburne retorted that Prynne in the House of Commons was as much use as a plague or an infectious disease.

' Where they may without any consideration rott, if they will not either betray both a good Cause, and some other of the Parliaments best friends, when they had few others, or else submit to their unjust lawes ; besides, it is a common thing for such lawlesse men to break in, and search honest mens shops, when neither the owners nor any of theirs are present to see what businesse they have there.'

' And yet as unjustly as all the rest, they doe not onely allow the weekly printing, divulging and dispersing of *Oxford Aulicus*, and other Malignant Books and Pamphlets tending to the ruine of the *Kingdome* and *Parliaments Priviledges*, but likewise the sending of Printing matterialls to the King, whereby to Print down both Power of Parliament, and freedome of People.'

' All which unjust dealings doe come to passe also with the privity of the Masters and Wardens of the *Stationers'* Company, as was openly proved to their faces at their publick Hall ; who therefore like wise men perceiving the Plague afarre off, would not goe on still and be punished, but most cunningly, both to hide themselves, and their treachery against the well-affected party, and divide their spoile, so unjustly obtained by lying in waite for blood, they have now procured by this their good service to the Parliament (as they did to the Bishops) the forme or power of a *Stationer-Committee* in *London* among themselves, that they may henceforth without either Censure or Resistance of *Higher Powers*, both absolve the wicked, and condemne the just, and so doe whatsoever they list.'

' The next *Monopoly*, it is to be feared will be upon *Bread* and *Beere*, for as justly may there be a Monopoly upon them, as upon the former.'

' Oh Englishmen ! Where is your freedoms ? . . . '

The Stationer Committee to which Lilburne refers seems to have been the result of a private arrangement between Parliament and the Stationers' Company for the better adjustment of abuses in printing, but the exact definition of its powers and privileges is not known.

The Master and Wardens were at loggerheads with the freemen of the Company who denied the power, which the Master and Wardens claimed, to make choice of their successors and to appoint whom they pleased as Assistants. The freemen favoured what may be termed a presbyterian, as opposed to an episcopal, system of government. They wished to be ruled from the bottom rather than from the top. Accordingly a Committee was appointed at the request of

Parliament to attempt a reunification of the Company as the first step towards resoldering it into a serviceable instrument for performing the will of Parliament in suppressing seditious books. But the freemen, prominent among whom may be noted the contentious Sparke, persisted in their demand for a revised constitution, and the Master and Wardens in their refusal to yield any concession. The Common Council of the city came to the support of the Master and Wardens ; and Sparke and his fellow reformers were summoned to answer a charge of contempt of authority.

After this victory for the presiding officials it may be that an unofficial Stationer-Committee, such as Lilburne describes above, was formed to help the authorities in return for the kindness received. Whatever the composition of the Committee, the presence on it of the Beadle, Joseph Hunscot, may be confidently affirmed.[1]

The Searchers

On page 41 of *England's Birth-right* Lilburne returns to the attack on the Stationers' Company in general, and the beadle thereof in particular :—

'. . . But to returne to our former matter, especially the grievances of the Nation ; (through the mistake of the Printer, in omitting of some

[1] Thomason Tracts, E.288.

To all Printers, Booke-sellers,/Booke-binders, Free-men of the/Company of Stationers./

You are desired by the Committee that was chosen by you at a Common Hall the first of Aprill last, to be at Stationers Hall the 23 day of this instant June, being Munday, at eight of the clock in the morning, to take an Account from the said Committee, of what they have done in pursuance of that trust you reposed in them, concerning Reformation and Printing, and to compleat the Subscriptions for the printing of the Bible &c. that the Manufacture of the Kingdome may not be utterly lost : of which you are desired not to faile, it being for a general good. Dated this thirteenth day of June 1645.

107

Manuscripts) and the absence of the Author, when the Monopolies in the former part of this Book were expressed ; as chiefly that soul-starving, or murthering Monopoly, in hindering the free passage of the Gospel, by extorting the prices of Bibles, which the false self-loving Stationers, as deadly enemies to all goodnesse, have been enterprizing a long time to obtaine, and against all common freedom, to engrosse into their owne hands the sole and only selling of them, by which meanes, they intend to sell at what rates soever they please, though already they sell at double the rate that honest wel-affected Common-wealths men may print and sell them, and also be conscionable gainers by them.'

' So of all Monopolies or Patents, next the monopolizing or ingrossing the Preaching of God's Word into the Tything and gripeing clawes of the Clergy ; this is the most wicked and intollerable, because it deprives many, both poore servants, and others of meane condition to buy any Bibles at all, by reason of the extraordinary dearth or dearnesse of them, that thereby they might be instructed in the way to heaven and happinesse ; and taught their duty also towards their Masters, and the Magistrates ; whereby it is evident, that those Stationers, thus enterprizing are self-seekers, and as great enemies to the Common-wealth as they are to all goodness.'

' And besides, they employ the Bishops old Theeves and Roagues about their robbing affairs, as *Hunscott* their Beadle for one, and a tall pale-faced fellow for another, who lately with their base crue of robbing Partners, under pretence of Parliamentary Authority, to search for dangerous Bookes, have robbed divers honest mens houses in *London*, who have been the Parliaments best friends and servants, and particularly, Lieutenant Colonell *Lilburnes* house, who being Prisoner in New-gate, and his wife with him, and she great with Child, & neer her time, these robbers took advantage of their absence.'

' And none being in the House, but an old Gentle-woman at that time, whom they much frighted ; as they did a young Gentlewoman in another place, to the great danger of her life (insomuch that she cryeth out in her extreame Fever, *Hunscott, Hunscott,*) they ranne up into the Chambers & stole out of his wives Drawers, divers pieces of her Child-bed linnen, and such other things as they pleased, and refused to show the Old-woman what they had stollen, though shee earnestly intreated them.'

' And in other the Parliaments friends houses, under the colour of Parliamentary Authority, they at least do rob all choice old books, as well as new, upon all occassions of such grievous oppressions, and unexpected persecutions.'

' And not only has this base fellow *Hunscott* this so needfull and profitable Office of Robbing, but it is reported, that hee hath also another as needfull and profitable, for he gathereth the Excise for Cattell, and Hats, &c. which with the former, is esteemed to be worth 500 *l. per annum* to him.'

' Oh ! what a cleer demonstration of future and intended slavery may be well and cleery perceived by any (who have but halfe an eye) to begin againe among us (though after more hidden and obscured ways than formerly) . . . .'

108

One morning in March, 1646, a man brought a bundle
of pamphlets entitled *The last warning to London* into the
shop of one William Larner, a bookseller in Bishops-gate
Street. Larner, after the manner of his trade, which was to
buy books of all sorts brought to the shop without examining the persons who brought them as to their name and
place of abode, bought twenty-five of the stranger's books
and allowed him to depart without enquiring his name and
place of residence. A little later, Hunscot and Miller of the
Stationers' Company came into the shop, searched it without displaying any warrant, and found copies of the pamphlet exposed for sale. *The last warning to London* was an
unlicensed and seditious book against which Parliament
was already taking proceedings.[1] The Common Council of
the city of London had the matter already in hand. Larner
was with the assistance of a constable brought before the
Lord Mayor and charged by Hunscot. He refused to answer
the usual interrogatories and was committed to the Counter
Prison.[2] Next he persisted in his refusal before the Committee, who sent him close prisoner to Maiden Lane. At
length before the Lords he maintained the same attitude
and appealed, as Lilburne had done, to the Commons to
be tried by his equals. The Commons turned him back to
the Lords, who had him locked up in the Fleet prison.

Larner appealed to Sir Harry Vane, the younger, and

[1] Hunscot described it as a book that sought to make mischief between
City and Army, this nation and Scotland, and to stir up opposition to the
House of Lords and to kingly government (Hunscot's *Petition*, 1646).

[2] Where the jailor charged him two shillings for two nights' lodging.
Larner refused to pay.

complained that he had been robbed and plundered by Hunscot[1] and his fellows ' who ever made it their trade, ' as well under, and by the *Bishops*, before this Parliament, ' as now under and by colour of Authority, from the Com- ' mittee of Examinations, to rob and spoile honest mens ' houses, under the name of *Searchers*. . . Yet could I never ' hear of any, whom they thus searched for, Imprisoned, ' and broken their houses, were ever convicted, or pro- ' ceeded against in any legall way. . . .'

He describes the methods of the Committee of Examinations as ' *just High-Commission-like* ', and reviles the stationers as ' old informers and *quondam* servants to the late Bishop of Canterbury '.

No answer was received from Sir Harry Vane.

Larner, meanwhile, petitioned the Lords against the unjust treatment he had received, and called attention to his services in the parliamentary cause. He had fought as a volunteer in the service of Parliament, he had suffered the impoverishment of his estate through receiving little or no pay—Parliament owed him nearly 50 *l.* for arrears— and he had lost two of his servants likewise in the war. Hunscot had been seven times to his house and pillaged his goods.

The unfortunate case of Larner called forth the sympathy of those stationers who were not bound in obsequious loyalty to the Company. They realised that what had happened to Larner might well happen to any of themselves. A

---

[1] It appears that Larner's wife, whose condition was similar to that of Mrs. John Lilburne, was equally frightened by Hunscot.

pamphlet in defence of Larner was printed with the apt title, *Every Mans Case*. It repeated with emphasis all the charges against Hunscot and his fellows and the malicious patentees. The alliance of the Committee for Examinations and the Stationers' Company was evidently proving oppressive of the liberty of the small printer and stationer.

The same terms of abuse appear in *Every Mans Case*— the ' tyranny of the late High-Commission Promoters and Informers, the Stationers, . . .', ' a naughty vexatious people, the patentees . .', ' Cankers of the Commonwealth ', ' Setting-Dogges in the Bishops times to hunt good men into Star-Chamber netts. . . .' : ' it is to little purpose to put down those Courts, and not punnish those wicked men, . . .', ' Mothes in the State. . .', '. . . and ' certainly their Honours [*i.e.*, the Lords] had past it over, ' and had not insisted thus upon you [Larner], but upon the ' *Stationers* instigation and misinformation . . .' : '. . . ' they have dealt treacherously with parliament '.

Mr. Hunscot must be given leave to speak for himself and reply to his critics. He did so in a petition presented to Parliament in June, 1646, most humbly shewing that Parliament owed him 40 *l.*, and humbly complaining of scandals laid upon him by Larner and Lilburne. Whilst engaged in active service for Parliament, he was superseded as printer by John Wright who ' by some friends got ' to be nominated Printer for the Lords House, and one ' Husbands Printer for the House of Commons, although ' neither of them are Printers (Wright being a Bookseller,

111

' and Husbands but a Paper Stationer).' Hunscot estimated the damage done to himself by infringement of his copy-rights at 100 *l*. He further complains of the public reproaches cast upon him for his trouble in searching for and apprehending the authors, printers and dispersers of malicious and unlicensed books. He is not alone in being reviled—the Stationers' Company, also, are called ' Theeves, ' Robbers, setting-doggs, the Bishops' old Rogues, persecut-' ors of the saints ', and openly reviled in the streets by Anabaptists and Sectaries, ' notorious impudent persons '. He had searched no one without warrant and command of parliament. To show that he was insufficiently supported by Parliament, he cited what happened to Brown, the woman whom he caught vending Lilburne's pamphlets in the streets. The woman had admitted to him that she had had the books from Lilburne in Newgate. Hunscot searched her father's house, where she lived, and, finding further incriminating evidence against them both, summoned them to appear before the Committee of Examinations the same afternoon. Brown failed to appear.

Meanwhile *England's Birth-right* came forth with further charges against Hunscot and the Stationers, which roused the Beadle to fury. The prosecution of Brown and his daughter, who was well known as a distributor of Lilburne's books, could not be urged forward fast enough to please him. The daughter, less fortunate than her father who though captured by a constable managed to escape, was clapt into the Marshal prison. Eventually Brown was taken also. Hunscot waited, and the Master and Wardens waited several days for a hearing which never came to pass ; they were not asked to present the case for the prosecution. Brown obtained his liberty. Hunscot felt he had a real grievance against the Committee. How could they expect their searchers to do their work thoroughly and diligently when their charges were so lightly dismissed ?

To give Hunscot further cause to regret his diligence as a searcher, Brown on his release threatened to sue him and the rest of the searchers for false imprisonment, and to knock out the brains of any searcher who came near his house again.

Hunscot in his petition represents William Larner as a man more sinning than sinned against. There was good reason to suspect that *England's Birth-right* had been surreptitiously printed in Goodmans Fields, and Hunscot and the Wardens of the Stationers' Company were employed upon a warrant from the Speaker of the Commons to search for the hidden press. A raid was made on the suspected house in Goodman's Fields, but the doors were barricaded against the searchers who, when they had at length forced an entry, discovered that the printers had got out of the window by a rope into the garden and so had escaped.[1] The press was carried off in triumph by the invaders.

It is hard to believe that Larner, in prison, presented his keeper with a copy of *Every Mans Case*, but Hunscot says he did ; which, he adds, was the cause why the Warden of the Company and himself were directed to search Larner's

[1] This was not the first time that Hunscot had been resisted. He and the Wardens were defied by Cole, Field and Mesole who refused to stop printing letters taken from the king, 1645 (*Hist. MSS. Comm.*).

chamber in the prison. The result of the search probably gave satisfaction to the searchers, for there were found divers papers in Larner's own handwriting which about a week later came forth in print with the title, *A true relation of all the remarkable passages and illegal proceedings of some satanicall, Doeg-like accusers of their Brethren, against* William Larner *a freeman of England.* Hunscot, therefore, petitioned Parliament to do justice upon Larner, to stop unlicensed printing of books to the dishonour of Parliament and the Stationers' Company, and to award him some satisfaction from Husbands. He pointed out that so far from receiving 500 *l.* a year from his occupation as searcher, which his enemies affirmed against him, he had not benefited by a single penny.

There is in the case of Robert Eeles further evidence in support of Hunscot's claim that the searcher was inadequately supported by Parliament. Eeles had been employed by a committee of the Lords to suppress seditious books. He had done so not without danger and expense to himself. He was responsible for the detective work which led to the surprise and capture of Lilburne's printer, Overton, the Anabaptist[1]; on which account he was ' set ' upon by some of the Anabaptist faction in the open street,

[1] Overton's wife gave a different account of the capture :—'. . . . the house was surrounded with divers armed men with swords and muskets, under the Conduct of one *Robert Eales*, and by the said Robert Eales (Deputy-Catchpole to the House of Lords) with his Sword drawne in his hand, and by one M. *Eveling* (dweller at the Greene Dragon in the Strand) with his pistoll ready cock'd, was suddenly and violently entred ', . . . and her husband ' by force of arms was in an hostile manner led captive to the House of Lords.' (*Mary Overton's Petition*, March, 1646-7).

' dragged before a justice and unjustly committed to prison,
' while the Stationers' Company, envying what he had done
' and what they ought to have done had they been honest
' men, threatened that they would shortly order him well ;
' but he was resolved still to prosecute his duty in bringing
' the authors of sedition to justice '.[1] Meanwhile perhaps the
Lords would dispatch the gratuity which it should please
them to confer upon him for services rendered ! Both
Eeles and the Stationers petitioned the Lords. The Stationers complained that Eeles with his wife was employing
the confiscated printing-press for the publishing of unlicensed books, instead of bringing it to Stationers' Hall
there to be defaced. The Lords ordered the press to be
destroyed at Stationers' Hall.

But that was not the end of the affair. A few months
later the Master of the Stationers' Company had just been
attending the House to give account of his proceedings
under an order to search for and seize copies of a libel,
Royal Tyranny, and was on his way out of Westminster
Hall when he saw a mercury-woman, whom he recognised
as the wife of Eeles, selling pamphlets. The Master of the
Worshipfull Stationers, seeing her lap full of books, searched
her in the hope of discovering something actionable. The
woman replied with a flow of what the Master afterwards
described as ' disgraceful language '.[2] But it was the
Master of the Stationers' Company, and not the woman,
who was arrested. Eeles came to the help of his wife, and

---

[1] *Eeles' petition* (*Hist. MSS. Comm.*, Pt. 6, p. 154).

[2] *Hist. MSS. Comm.*, Pt. 6, p. 154.

the Master was taken into custody. The Lords, however, procured his release.[1]

When even the Master of the Stationers' Company was not free from the risk of imprisonment whilst engaged in searching for unlawful books, it is not surprising that the beadle did not escape. The charges against the beadle, however, appear to have been not ill-founded.

[1] *H.L.J.*, Jan., 1647.

CHAPTER IV

1647

THE ARMY AND THE CONTROL OF THE PRESS

ALL the charges which had been brought against the former prelatical censorship of the press (except that of being biassed in favour of popish books) could with justification be levelled against the system of licensing evolved by the Long Parliament. Chiefly was it a source of complaint that Parliament's method of governing by Committees was but a recrudescence of Star Chamber tyranny under a new name. Before the end of the year 1647 the term ' committee-man ' suggested all that was most oppressive and odious. The proceedings taken against Lilburne and Overton show how little there was to choose between the old tyranny and the new.

Lilburne, with a gift for the most pungent invective, conferred upon the committee-men the title of ' their Prerogative Lordships '. The implication was plain and damned them in the eyes of those who had suffered in the long struggle against prerogatives. The title stuck. The author of *England's Remembrancer*[1] repeats all the familiar charges :—

' . . . But now instead of a few unlimited Courts, that did oppress, there is started up many hundreds which are called Committees, and they exercise an absolute arbitrary power within themselves, playing *Rex*, amongst the

[1] Feb., 1647.

people ; yea, every Committee is as a Star Chamber, a High-Commission, a Court of Honour, &c. where they assess men beyond what they are able to pay, and then fine and imprison their fellow Subjects at their will and pleasure. . . .'

The country was in a political ferment and every political event of importance produced its crop of unlicensed pamphlets—for example, the Presbyterian leaders' attempt to gather the fruits of the victory won by the army, which was already out of sympathy with Presbyterianism, and their attempted reaffirmation of the Solemn League and Covenant which was rapidly losing its popularity except with Parliament and the Scots : the rise of the Adjutators, their remonstrance to Fairfax against (*inter alios*) divers persons who ' have laboured by evil aspersions and false calumnies ' to alienate the kingdom's affections from them, in order to ' which they have many books, *viz.*, Ma. *Edwards* his *Gan-* ' *graena* '[1]: the conversion of the army under Fairfax into a political party : the rapid decline of Parliament's power and prestige : the negotiations of Charles, first with the Parliament and then with the army, and the unfavourable opinion of his honesty with which he inspired them both : his removal from Holmby to Carisbrooke Castle : the scene at Westminster in which the Commons played an undignified, and the London apprentices a disorderly, part : the rise and alarming expansion of the Levelling party in the army, with Lilburne the spokesman of its left wing. Each of these events produced a sheaf of unauthorised pamphlets which Parliament, though it left the matter in the hands of the sternly efficient committee-men, was powerless to prevent.

[1] *The Armys Grievances*, May, 1647.

The solid mass of Presbyterianism which for so long had been most emphatically the government was fast dissolving. Power was passing into the hands of the army. Fairfax, supported by his council of officers, who were at least as enterprising and as determined as himself, sent a letter to Parliament in July, 1647, vindicating the army from the charges brought against them by anonymous pamphleteers. From the tone of his letter it is evident that he suspected Parliament of not having used the utmost of its power and ability to suppress such publications, and it may be that members of Parliament were neglecting their duty for the sake of their devotion to the Presbyterian cause.

Even after the occupation of London by the army, the same grievance continued to exercise the army officers, some of whom attributed the authorship of the offensive pamphlets to ' certain Journeymen printers '.[1]

Accordingly Parliament was directed to prepare an ordinance for the suppression of such abuse.[2]

The Army and the Publication of News

In July, 1647, Fairfax had written to Parliament to complain of scandalous pamphleteers. In September he complained about the news-books and ' suggested ' to Parliament a new policy with regard to the publication of news.

[1] *Perfect Occurrences*, August, 1647.

[2] The ordinance fixed the following penalties for unlicensed printing :— the author to pay 40 shillings or be imprisoned for 40 days : the printer 20 shillings or 20 days, also to have his printing press and materials broken : the stationer 10 shillings or 10 days, and the hawker, Pedler or Ballad-singer to be whipt as a common rogue and to lose his stock of books.

The following is a summary of the events that led to the army's intervention in the matter of the publication of news.

The publication of false news continued to disturb Parliament and defy all efforts to prevent it. Feigned declarations by Fairfax and the king which were the concoctions of enterprising and unscrupulous printers were published with every appearance of having been licensed. For example, in May at Chelmsford Assizes a copy of a forged Act of Parliament was produced in defence of a certain prisoner, which, if true, would have procured his discharge. Unfortunately for him, it was not true, although printed on it were the words ' licensed by the Clerk of the Parliament '. John Browne, Clerk of Parliament, decided to prosecute the authors of the Act forged in his name. Six people were arrested, found guilty and fined in all 2,000 l. to the king, and 500 l. to John Browne, bound over to good behaviour for the rest of their lives and also sentenced to a term of imprisonment.[1]

The Multiplication of Royalist News-Books

The increase in the number of news-books in 1647 added to the confusion. They were printed and published in London. Formerly Oxford had been a safe refuge for the solitary *Aulicus*. With the collapse of Charles' army, it was so no longer. London provided a safer hiding-place, partly because of its greater size, and partly because the king's enemies had begun to quarrel violently amongst

[1] *H.L.J.*, May and Sept., 1647.

themselves. The mercuries, *Melancholicus*, *Pragmaticus* and *Elencticus*, the first of which came out in September and the last in October, unfurled an unexpected flag in the cause of the king right in the very centre of the enemy's stronghold, London. They were the king's most subtle allies during a critical period. They were popular and evidently sold well. They were written by abler men than wrote the Parliamentary news-books—John Cleaveland, Samuel Sheppard and the ubiquitous John Berkenhead, all of them poets and men of imagination with a turn for practical affairs. Their weekly relations of current events, if they achieved nothing else, afforded a welcome relief after the monotonous fare provided by the parliamentary news-books.

The royalists were not the only people who objected to the parliamentary news-books. Plain blunt citizens, of the sort that has been writing letters to the editors of news-books since their inception, wrote pamphlets to protest against the persistent libelling of private and public persons by the regular and approved news-writers. The plain John Blunts disclaimed all interest in parties and professed to belong to the moderate middle classes, whose distinguishing trait was a passion for the *status quo*, whatever it might be. It may be doubted whether the said John Blunts were as free from political bias as they pretended. Sometimes they are indistinguishable from royalists.

The anonymous author of *Looke about you* evidently belonged to this class. This tract,[1] and the two that it

[1] 16 July, 1647 : unlicensed.

121

called forth, since they have so far escaped the attention of writers on the subject, are worthy of a short notice here.[1]

The author protested against personal attacks in the mercuries, inscribing at the head of his tract the words,

Licuit semperque licebit

Parcere personis, dicere de vitiis.

After professing himself unmoved by the controversies of his day and devoting an uninspired paragraph to each of the several parties to which he does not belong, he concludes : ' Many will wonder at these few lines ; what then ; ' can they charge the Author with the crimes of *Berkenhead*, ' *Leburne* or *Overton* ? if not, let them wonder how ' the Author could treat of so various subjects, with so ' little losse of his owne and others credits.' *Mercurius Britanicus* did not escape. He was the object of a much more violent attack in *Brittanicus his welcome in Hell*,[2] which, for the same reason as *Looke about you*, deserves a short description here. In it the Devil is represented as giving his blessing to *Britanicus*, ' the greatest libeller of his day '. *Britanicus* replied with a wealth of classical allusions displaying an intimate knowledge of the topographical features of Hell. If he for his part was accused of libel, *Aulicus*, it was certain, had emptied Hell to fill his sheets. The reply was written in verse. It provoked a retort in prose from the royalists, *Match me these two* : or

[1] None of these tracts is mentioned in Mr. J. B. Williams' *History of English Journalism.*

[2] March, 1647.

the Conviction and Arraignment of Britannicus and Lil-burne.[1] Again the charge is one of libel and the spreading of false reports. The court had no hesitation in condemning both of them, Britanicus to be suspended from the triple tree (i.e. Tyburn) and to be slowly roasted over a fire while two persons in the guise of Furies pricked his imposthumated flesh with sharp bodkins, thus giving him as complete a foretaste of the pains of hell as the most medieval of his persecutors could devise : while Lilburne was condemned to be confined in a high turret where his ambition could be left to burn itself out, to be girt with a wooden sword and to be fed on the ' carkasses of Ravens because ' he had made such fatal music and was still croaking ' against his superiors '. The penalties devised (which are here not given in full) rival the ingenuity of Aristophanes.

The Collapse of the Licensing System

The Stationers' Register for the period reveals that Gilbert Mabbott[2] ceased to license news-books after 15 March, and William Newhouse, deputy to Sir Nathaniel Brent, official licenser of general books of philosophy, history, etc., took his place. The reason for the change is still to seek. It was probably not due to illness, for Mabbott's name reappears on 25 March as licenser of books not diurnals. Also, on the same day certain news-books are entered under the hand of both of them. It may be reasonably conjectured that Mabbott had fallen into some slight

[1] 29 July, 1647 : unlicensed.

[2] See p. 91. Mabbott began licensing as Rushworth's deputy, March, 1645.

disfavour, probably through his close connection with the army which was not on good terms with Parliament. But however that may be, it is certain that the whole system of licensing was breaking down. Few books were entered in the Stationers' Register, and between 17 April and 28 June no news-books at all. On 28 June certain news-books were entered, but under whose hand is not specified. A succession of dots (. . . . . .) indicates the absence of any record of the name of the licenser, if any.

The army then interposed. Fairfax sent a letter to the House of Lords in September :

'I have sent inclosed some Printed Pamphlets, that are not only very scandalous and abusive to this Army in particular, but indeed to the whole kingdom in general. My Desire is, That these and all of the like Nature may be suppressed for the future ; and yet, that the Kingdom's Expectation may be satisfied in relation to Intelligence, till a firm Peace be settled, considering the Mischiefs that will follow by the poisonous Writings of evil Men, sent abroad daily to abuse and deceive the People, That (if the House shall see it fit) some Two or Three Sheets may be permitted to come out Weekly which may be licensed, and have some Stamp of Authority with them ; and in respect the former Licenser Mr. *Mabbott* hath approved himself faithful in that Service of Licence, and likewise in the Service of the House and of this Army, I humbly desire that he may be restored and continued in the said Place of Licenser.'[1]

Fairfax's 'humble desire' was speedily satisfied. Within nine days of the writing of this letter an ordinance was prepared in accordance with the Lord General's wishes and passed by both Houses of Parliament. Mabbott was appointed licenser of 'such weekly pamphlets as should be printed'.

Thereafter an official weekly news-bulletin was to be issued by Parliament to prevent misunderstanding.

[1] *H.L.J.*

A Remarkable Charge against the Wardens of the Stationers' Company

A remarkable charge against the Wardens of the Stationers' Company in 1647 arose out of the Government's prosecution of an almanac writer, George Wharton, whose unwelcome prognostications had caused Parliament some uneasiness since February. One unsuccessful attempt had been made to silence him. His almanacs consequently had become not less but more popular. There was an unpleasant rumour current to the effect that the Wardens of the Stationers' Company, forgetful of their duty to the Government in their desire for gain, had offered money for the copyright of Wharton's books. A committee of the militia was called upon ' to examine and find out who were the authors, ' Publishers, Vendors and Printers of *No Merlin Nor* ' *Mercury, but a new Almanac* by Captain George Wharton, ' student in Astronomy : *Bellum Hibernicale*, also by G. ' Wharton : and that they do take effectual course to ' seize and suppress the said Pamphlets and to hinder and ' stop the vending and Publishing of them. They are ' further to examine and inquire out the Information given ' to this House, concerning the Wardens of the Company of ' Stationers giving money to one Gyles, to the use of ' George Wharton, for the copy of the said Pamphlets and ' Almanack '.[1]

In the absence of evidence in support of the charge, the Stationers' Company should have the benefit of the doubt.

[1] *H.C.J.*, Sept., 1647.

THE ORDINANCE OF SEPTEMBER, 1647

Fairfax's plan, which obtained legal expression in the new Ordinance, had distinct advantages, and though the official supervision of news published might promise only a duller diurnal there was much in its favour if the reader could be certain that the diurnal, though dull, would be honest and of good report. Unfortunately the man who more than any other seems to have merited the title of official scribe to Parliament, Henry Walker, did not inspire confidence in either royalist or parliamentarian. His *Perfect Occurrences* was indisputably dull : it was less certain that it was honest. The dullness of Henry Walker, however, could not be impugned and was the occasion of much liveliness of wit amongst his opponents and rivals.

Some of the parliamentary writers were not content to leave it to Walker to prevent the misinformation of the public by royalist writers. Soon there was hardly a royalist mercury that did not have its counter-mercury, existing solely in order to contradict it at every point : for instance, immediately on the appearance of *Pragmaticus* came forth *Anti-Pragmaticus*. The royalist reader presumably believed the royalist version of the week's news, the presbyterian the parliamentarian version, while secretly neither would know where truth ended and party prejudice began. And Henry Walker was soon found to be a not too reliable guide.

Parliament did not delay putting the Ordinance of September, 1647, into effect. On 7 October the Stationers' Company were ordered to use every endeavour to find out the author and printer of *Mercurius Pragmaticus* ' that so they may be persecuted according to the Ordinance '.[1] Other royalist news-books of less importance, *Clericus* and *Diabolicus*, were swept away without much difficulty. *Mercurius Anti-Pragmaticus*, whose *raison d'etre* depended on *Pragmaticus's* ability to evade Joseph Hunscot and his tall pale-faced fellow-searcher, explained in his issue of 19 October :—' The new broom (the late Ordinance against ' Printing) which purged the Exchange of those dusty ' cobwebs, *Melancholicus*,[2] *Clericus* and *Diabolicus*, has ' left *Pragmaticus* in some odd corner as a trap for flies '.

The Government made a thorough attempt to suppress *Pragmaticus* and *Elencticus*, the only extant royalist news-books. The Commons appointed a special committee to undertake their suppression.[3] *Pragmaticus* reviewed the situation not very dispassionately in his next issue :

' What's here ? *A large debate about Pragmaticus and Melancholicus* : Doe ye winch ye gall-back'd spittles, now ye have jaded the whole Kingdome into universall slavery : Doe but you take away the *cause*, and the *effect* will cease ; leave your juggling, and be honest men, *Prag* has done with you, but so long as you continue your Oppressions, *Pragmaticus* will proceed, and bid *the Devill doe his worst*. In despite of all Westminster ban-Doggs, *Walker, Mabbott,* and the rest . . .'

The chase, nevertheless, was hot.[4] Miles Corbet and Mr.

[1] *H.L.J.*, Oct., 1647.

[2] Henry Walker in *Perfect Occurrences*, 15-22 Oct., says that Melancholicus was brought before the Militia on 19 October and was fined 20 shillings with the loss of his printing press.

[3] *H.C.J.*, 27 Nov., 1647.

[4] *Elencticus, Bellicus* and *Melancholicus* soon after succeeded in rousing some of their opponents to surprising fury, e.g., *Mercurio Mastix Hibernicus* prophesied against them—' that if you bee once catcht out of you lurking holes, and *Cacus* dens, where you securely croake (as all Schismaticall frogs) in corners, we have state storkes would catch you by the crags, and Lionized Cats would clapper-claw you till you squeaked '. (*A Muzzle for Cerberus*, 1648.)

Challoner, who held the place of chief authority on the committee entrusted to suppress the royalist news-writers, were the foremost of the pack that hunted them. *Elencticus* sneered at their efforts :—' there's not one right ' Bloodhound amongst them : surely they ought to be ' ashamed, having spent so much time to so little purpose, ' not yet having suppressed this one poore *Penny-worth* of ' *Truth* ! '

While the committee combed London for *Pragmaticus* and *Elencticus,* Mabbott was at his wit's end to know how to combat the subterfuges of more subtle and dangerous opponents of the licensing system. An attempt was being made to undermine his position with Parliament, which had not been assured till Fairfax had appealed on his behalf. Readers of the *Perfect Diurnal* for 22-29 November were desired to take notice that

' the Licencer, Mr. Gilbert Mabbott, notwithstanding his case against Malignant sheets, hath his name forged to many of them of purpose to make him odious to the Parliament and Kingdome. . . . and he hopes to have vindication and reparation against such as have so abused him, and this abuse to be taken off for the future.'

On 21 December Mabbott was called before the Committee for Printing to explain by what authority he had licensed a book entitled *His Majesty's Declaration.*[1] His *imprimatur* had been forged. He was guiltless.

[1] *H.C.J.,* Dec., 1647.

CHAPTER V

1648

The Recrudescence of Royalist News-Books

IT is difficult at first sight to account for the recrudescence,
and the sudden increase in the number, of royalist news-
books during the year 1648.[1] The cynic might attribute it
to the simple fact that they sold for two pence a copy,
whereas the vendor could not hope to get more than the
regulation penny for the parliamentary mercury. There
are other explanations possible—for instance, the royalist
news-books, so long as they remained under the licenser's
ban, would naturally continue to attract more attention
than the regular, orthodox diurnals, which were suspected
of being dull because they were orthodox.

Pragmaticus, Melancholicus and Elencticus, the trium-
virate of the royalist press, wrote their sheets at considerable
risk to themselves, and the printers printed and the vendors
circulated them at no less hazard to their personal liberty.
Of course, nothing could have been better for their sales :
a large circulation was already assured them. It is, however,
only just to add that the royalist mercuries were in themselves more interesting and written with greater literary
skill than were those of the opposite party.

[1] *Mercurius Dogmaticus, M. Academicus, M. Urbanus, Parliament Kite,
M. Anglicus, Colchester Spie, Parliament Porter,* are the chief of these.

The enterprise shown by the royalist scribes may be partly explained as one result of the inability of their enemies to agree amongst themselves. Parliament, whose business it was to regulate the press, was ceasing to be the chief power in the land—a position which the army had come to occupy. So far, Parliament operated the licensing system : the army merely interfered occasionally, as for example, when Fairfax recommended Mabbott to be licenser. But the personnel of the board of licensers which Parliament had elected in 1643 had remained otherwise unchanged, though the army officers had already discovered that there was too strong a flavour of presbyterianism on the board for their Independent stomachs. In their opposition to the royalist mercuries, however, Presbyterians and Independents united forces.

The risk attached to producing royalist news-books increased, though Elencticus was exaggerating when he said that it would mean hanging for him if he were caught.[1]

He *was* caught—within a week—but he was not hanged. He was reserved for a milder form of correction. Few of his fellow news-writers escaped the avenging humour of the state-beagles. Elencticus proved a victim to the ' spight of Bostock, Hunscot and the rest ',[2] while Pragmaticus, also a victim, threatened a neat revenge—to set forth a volume of the lives of the searchers ' as large as Plutarch . . . I ' say once againe (*Gentlemen*) forbeare medling ; one would ' think men of your *guilt* and *gravity* should take fair

[1] *Elencticus*, 1-8 March, 1648.
[2] *Ibid.*, 19-26 April, 1648.

' warning, and not provoke a concealed *Mercury* too far,
' lest . . .'[1] Parliament offered ' good rewards for the
discovery of *Melancholicus, Pragmaticus* and others ',[2] with
the result that the printer of *Mercurius Pragmaticus*, and
Parson Hackluyt, the author of *Mercurius Melancholicus*,
were both taken, and, with some others, ' tryed at the
Gaole delivery at *Newgate*, the next Sessions '.[3]

Conditions of Prison Life

Whilst the writers of the royalist mercuries were in
prison, their journalistic labours were undertaken and
performed by their friends, so that *Melancholicus* came forth
on Saturdays (later on Mondays) as usual, though Melancholicus was under lock and key in Peter House. Escaped
from prison, he returned to the writing of his news :

' . . . *Melanchollicus* hath got his foot out of the springe at *Peterhouse*
and hath made an escape (because he was neere starv'd by that murdering
villane *Symball*), he is in very good health at the writing hereof, and sends
commendations to his friends there, Mr. Sheppheard, John Harrison, and
the rest ; intending not to see them for a while.'[4]

His intention not to see them again for a while is under-
standable in view of the condition of prison life. Prisoners
were exposed to infection from diseases which the dirty,
verminous state of the prisons encouraged and their own
bodies, enfeebled through lack of proper food, could ill

[1] *M. Pragmaticus*, 7-14 March.

[2] *Perfect Occurrences*, 18-25 Feb.

[3] *Ibid.*, 10-17 March. Hackluyt escaped but was recaptured in Grayes
Inne Lane.

[4] *M. Melancholicus*, 19-26 June : it is worth noting that a certain *Mercurius Melancholicus*, 17-24 July, which complains of a false namesake
' printed by a deaf Schismatical Round-head ', denies that Melancholicus
twice broke prison, and calls Henry Walker a liar for having said so.

resist. Here is an illuminating reference to prison life printed by Henry Walker in his *Perfect Occurrences* for 9-16 June. Within recent time Walker had begun to regard prisons no longer exclusively from the prisoners' point of view.

'. . . There was this last night a great hubbub in the *Gatehouse* at *Westminster*, The prisoners were very unruly, and (as some say) it was said amongst them, that they would either breake out, or fire the house, and that they would spare neither man, woman, nor child that should oppose them, The Keepers son put the end of a musket (charged) through one of the holes of the grate, requiring them to be quiet, one of the prisoners got hold of it, and would have pulled it in ; whereupon he discharged it and shot the prisoner (who is said to be a Cavalier Souldier) and killed him.'

The Kingdomes Weekly Intelligencer[1] supplements this with an account of the escape of fifteen condemned prisoners from Newgate on the eve of execution. A friend knocked at the door of the prison till it was at length cautiously opened, and he, admitted. Once inside, he drew his sword, and made a way for the escape of his friends.

Thus, though the prisons were dirty and the prisoners at the mercy of infectious diseases and cruel gaolers, escapes seem to have been frequent.

Popularity of Royalist Mercuries

Meanwhile, the popularity of *Pragmaticus* gained rather than suffered by the attempts of Hunscot, Bostock and the pale-faced fellow to suppress it : witness the numerous attempts to counterfeit it :

'. . . What, another *three-half-penny Counterfeit* ! Once a *quarter* it is my luck to be troubled with one *vermin* or other, that usurps my *name* and *Title-page* to face out his *Nonsence* for a week or two, and then he vanishes.'[2]

Pragmaticus (and probably his fellow writers of the

[1] 19-26 December.

[2] *M. Pragmaticus*, 19-26 December.

royalist persuasion were in like case) had further to contend with the arrogance of his printers, who, because there was a price on his head, had a certain hold over him. It is what one might, from a knowledge of human nature, expect, though there is evidence of another kind to attest it. In his issue for the week ending on 7 March, he complained of the careless way in which his previous number had been printed and confided to his readers that the printers were ' a generation so lost in *Ale* and *Smoake*, that they will neither take, nor give due *Correction* '.

At least once during the year Pragmaticus complained that the text of his relation of news for the week had been tampered with after it had left his hands :

' . . . Mention was made in the close of last weeks *Pragmaticus*, of a certaine meeting lately of *Wharton, Say*, and *Cromwell*, in the House of Mr. *Dillingham* at *Barnet* ; which story (indeed) was put in at the end of all, by him who carried it to the Presse, without my privity or consent and though the circumstances in the Relation I suppose be false ; . . .'[1]

Among the true Pragmaticus and the true Melancholicus and the true Elencticus and the true Aulicus (*Aulicus* recommenced in January and seems to have been written by Samuel Sheppard[2]) good feeling existed. They were united in the cause of Charles : they were fighting for him rather than for a living. Thus they differed from the modern journalist who no more scruples to contribute articles to papers of opposite political faction than the barrister at law to plead the cause of a prisoner whom he knows to be guilty. But the royalist news-writers were

[1] *M. Pragmaticus*, 25 July-1 Aug. Note, also, reports of this supposed Conference of Cromwell, Wharton and Say were repeated by *The Royal Diurnal* before Pragmaticus could contradict them.

[2] J. B. Williams' *Hist. of Journalism.*

first of all royalists, then news-writers. They might regret
the decrease in their income which the increase in the
number of royalist news-books probably entailed, but they
could not fail to welcome every such new mercury as another
ally in the cause of the king. Thus :

'. . . . In this just *Cause*, *Aulicus* values not Life, nor fears death,
much lesse regards the barking of your *Curres* ; or of being taken in your
Parliament *Mousetrapps* : for admit you should noose him, (as lately you
did Captaine Burley) when *Aulicus* is dead *Melancholicus* is alive, *Elencticus*
and *Pragmaticus* too. . . .'[1]

It was less than the truth to say that *Melancholicus* was
alive. There were several *Melancholicuses* alive, kicking one
against the other. *Pragmaticus*, too, existed in duplicate,
and sometimes even in triplicate. It is almost impossible
to decide which speaks with the authentic voice of the
original : for the authentic and the spurious mercuries both
complain of counterfeits.

The Scottish Commissioners again

Fairfax, the previous year, had come to the conclusion
that only by issuing an official news-gazette of its own could
the Government hope to ' prevent the misinformation of
the public '. Others had come over to his way of thinking.
False news, which was true enough to make the refutation
of it a matter of great difficulty, appeared daily in print.
Parliament objected, not only to the false, but to the
inconvenient and inopportune reports as well. Under the
latter designation must be included the printed reports of
the secret meetings of the English Parliament with the
Scottish commissioners. There had already been friction

[1] *M. Aulicus*, 2-30 March.

with the Scottish commissioners on the same score, and one of them, Mr. Buchanan, had allowed information which the English Parliament vainly hoped would be treated as confidential, to be published in defiance of the licensing system :

'The House complained to the Parliament of Scotland regarding the Scots Commissioners in London who printed reports of secret meeting, with the English House of Parliament, although they had agreed that nothing should be published as yet. The Printer, being questioned, produced a warrant under the hand of the Lord Chancellor of Scotland.'

His pamphlet was suppressed, but it reappeared with the title ' Printed at Edenburgh ', when ' (besides that it was ' published wet from the Press) there was not time, by a ' Continual Post, to have sent it to Edenburgh, and bring ' it back '.[1]

The English commissioners in Scotland had the same complaint to make ' of diurnals printing all their doings ' and a good deal else that they had never done : ' gross mistakes ' in these relations of news induced them to advise that an official report be published by Parliament. A special ordinance was passed to prevent the printing of parliamentary proceedings.[2]

It is clear that the leakage of parliamentary news was to be looked for in the House itself. Parliament's attempts to play the plumber to it were unsuccessful. From whom, if not from some member or members of Parliament, did the royalist mercuries obtain their news ? The House of Lords lay under suspicion. *Mercurius Anti-Mercurius* on 2 October warned the Commons :

[1] *H.C.J.*, March,⅜1648.
[2] *H.L.J.*, March, 1648.

' Looke about you Gentlemen of the lower House, there is another *Story*[1] behind your arras, a poysonous spider hangs in the Cobwebs, with Basiliskes eyes killing by reflection, a Snake in your bosome, feeding on your secret councells and vomits them up again in gall, when that incarnate Fury puts into his Inke, and so betraies your actions to the publique ; it will not be labor lost to make inquisition for the *Impostor*, and having found him kicke him to the devill.'

The Change in the News-Books, 1645 and 1648

A change had come over the news-books since 1645. In 1645 an unsigned pamphlet (since attributed to George Wither) entitled *The Great Assizes Holden in Parnassus by Apollo*[2] had analysed royalist and parliamentary diurnals impartially and meted out poetic justice to each of them in turn. It was an amusing pamphlet and gives the best description that we have of the 1645 news-books.

Apollo presided at the Court, Sir Philip Sidney appeared as High Constable of Parnassus ; Julius Caesar, Erasmus, Grotius and Lord Verulam had a seat on the bench : among the jurors were Wither, Davenant, Shakespeare, Tom May. Ben Jonson came in virtue of his office as keeper of the Trophonian Denne, John Taylor the Water poet made a shrill Cryer of the Court, though Edmund Spenser, clerk of the Assizes, was not entrusted with a speaking part. The malefactors were charged with having misused the Press :

' This instrument of Art, is now possest
By some, who have in Art no interest ;
For it is now imploy'd by Paper-wasters,
By mercenary souls, and Poetasters,
Who weekly utter, slanders, libells, lies,
Under the name of specious novelties : '

[1] i.e., The Upper Storey—the Lords.

[2] *Thomason Tracts*, E. 269, 11. The neglect of this pamphlet by writers on the subject is, I hope, a sufficient reason for describing it here in some detail.

Chief of the parliamentary diurnals, *Britanicus* was called first to answer a charge of contempt of Apollo in printing scandal :

> ' Hee likewise was accus'd, to have purloin'd
> Some drachmes of wit, with a felonious mind,
> From *Helicon*, which hee in Satyrs mixt,
> To make some laugh, and others deepely vext.'

Aulicus, sole representative of the royalist faction, was charged :

> '. . . that he with slanders false,
> With forged fictions, calumnies and tales,
> Had sought the *Spartane Ephori* to shame,
> And added fewell to the direfull flame
> Of civill discord, and domesticke blowes,
> By the incentives of malicious prose.'

There is no great variety in the nature of the offences with which the mercuries are charged. They are all accused of lying and of detracting from the reputation of the famous and the glorious. The *Citties Weekly Post* ran his eye in surprise over the jury-men, then strongly protested against being tried by mere ' histrionic poets '.

> ' Justice (sayd he) and no sinister fury,
> Diswades me from a tryall by a jury,
> That of worse misdemeanours guilty bee,
> Than those which are objected against mee ;
> These mercenary pen-men of the Stage,
> That foster the grand vises of this age. . . .'

Shakespeare's neck reddened, Beaumont and Fletcher were observed to grow uneasy ; from the public gallery came loud mutters from Plautus and Terence and a deadly volley of picturesque abuse from Aristophanes, who was ' galled shrewdly, to see Dramatick Poets tax'd so lewdly '.

But Apollo snatched away the apple of discord which the *Citties Weekly Post* had so cunningly thrown into the

137

midst of the jury-box, and after a prolonged but interesting examination of the prisoners at the bar, found them all guilty, and delivered judgment with a passion for *le mot juste* and a gift for devising elaborate and ingenious punishments, and a highly cultivated artistic sense of the fitness of punishment and crime which he has not shown since the seventeenth century. *Britanicus* was condemned to be tied to a post among porcupines who would assuredly jag him to death : *Aulicus* to go to the Den of Vipers from which Parnassus Treacle, made by Apollo himself for sick poets whom the world had scorned, was confected : the *Intelligencer* was to start at once as scullion in Apollo's Kitchen where he would find a use for his papers as pie-wrappers : *Civicus* to angle frogs out of the stinking lake in Lerna : the *Diurnal* to be music-master to the apes : *True Accounts* appointed to the Stygian gallery, there to keep a true record of the arrivals and departures of Ghosts ; *Perfect Passages* to go to a gloomy cave and by glow-worm light to write a full account of the battle between the weasels and the noisome rats, in which the weasels were victorious—a matter in which no one was interested : and the *Scottish Dove*, an Anglo-Scot, collapsed when he heard that he had been sentenced to go back to Scotland. Whereat the heart of Apollo softened, and with great difficulty was he restrained from granting a free pardon to all—so much had he enjoyed his own jokes. He abated the edge of all their punishments.

The Great Assizes had given no offence to the authorities, who permitted it to be licensed and regularly entered in the Stationers' Register. Nor, apparently, did it offend the public taste by treating the news-books with gentle though not unkindly disdain : for the diurnals were generally despised, even outside Parnassus, although they were still tolerated. Yet the parliamentary news-writers objected. *Britanicus* contemptuously classed the pamphlet as ' malignant ', refused to believe that it had really been licensed at all and proclaimed that the author's attack on *Aulicus* was but a blind drawn over his real intent, which was to attack him, *Britanicus*. And who could doubt, he added, but that Apollo was meant to represent King Charles ?

' That gallant man, George Wither ' (as Lilburne described him in 1645, though he afterwards revised his opinion), or whoever was the author of the *Great Assizes*, had no such intention. He had not confused Apollo with Charles the First, nor had he beaten *Britanicus* with more stripes than he gave to *Aulicus*. None had 'scaped whipping, for all had received their deserts. Nevertheless Apollo, who now begins strangely to resemble George Wither, washed the stripes that his own hands had made. Perhaps he *had* been too severe ; for after all, though the diurnals were despised by all right-thinking people, they did little harm and provided a good deal of fun.

By 1648 the *Great Assizes* already belonged to a long-passed state of innocence and gaiety. Civil wars are not as a rule conducted with good humour on both sides. The parliamentary forces were fighting with dreadful and well-directed determination, the royalists with a bitter despair

139

and unshaken tenacity of purpose. The news-books reflect the two tempers—the parliamentary writer marshals his news-items with military precision : like a soldier conserving his breath through the fierceness of the struggle, he wastes no words in needless comment, he speaks grimly and to the point. The royalist, however, peppers the enemy with small-shot, flings a thousand barbs that are more irritating than wounding, and flies like a trackless and tireless mosquito through the enemy's ranks, reducing them to a distracted, undignified condition.

No one had a good word to say for the news-books of 1648. The parliamentary were short-tempered, sharp-tongued and blind to the merits of the enemy : the royalist, denied access to the official sources of information and therefore more dependent on hearsay evidence, became frankly indecent. Elencticus kept his head above dirty water, but Melancholicus promptly sank to a very low level. Ballad stanzas made their first appearance on the front sheet under the title-piece—not a good sign.[1] Scandalous charges against the leaders of Parliament and the army were made every week and related by the royalist journalist with evident relish : the more lascivious the charge, the greater the relish. It was not long before *Melancholicus* became indecent for indecency's sake alone—perhaps, also, there was a ready market for impure literature. Meanwhile, the parliamentary news-books remained clean, if

[1] *cf. Merc. Prag.*, April, 1648 :—' Not that I am a whit opinionated of this way of *Riming* ' (i.e., of ballad-stanza) ' constantly, but only to tickle and charme the more vulgar *Phant'sies*, who little regard *Truths* in a grave and serious garb, have I hitherto been thus light and *Phantastick*, both in *Verse* and *Prose*. And so I must still continue ; but yet I would have you know, in the midst of *jest* I am much in *earnest* '.

dull. The only charitable explanation of this difference is that the royalist news-writer found it increasingly difficult to obtain sufficient news to fill his sheets, and was accordingly compelled to draw upon his imagination. Now and again the parliamentary diurnalists showed themselves capable of making coarse comments, but the deliberate cultivation of the obscene and filthy was almost exclusively left to the royalist scribbler, who was no doubt despised even by men of his own party.

Public contempt for news-books spread rapidly during the year. Contemporary pamphlets abound with scornful references to them. *Mercurius Anti-Mercurius*[1] in April undertook to ' communicate all humours, conditions, forgeries and lyes of Mydas-eard Newsmongers ', in return for a penny. It was no doubt a penny well spent ; the average reader was told just what he had been thinking for a long time, namely, that there was not much to choose between the rival mercuries : if one was filthy and scurrilous, the other was dull and induced sleep. *Mercurius Anti-Mercurius* began with a parody of the ballad-stanzas without which no popular news-book was complete :

> ' *Facit indignatio versum.*
>
> For all those persons, that to tell,
> And write much Newes do love,
> May Charon ferry them to hell,
> And may they ne're remove.
> May all the Colds that on the Hill
> Of Caucasus do meet,
> May Scythian frosts palsie and chill
> Eternally their feet. . . .

[1] If the author be, as J. B. Williams suggests, John Harris, then what he has to say about the parliamentary news-books is surely all the more valuable as evidence of the general disrepute into which the diurnals had fallen. The style, however, suggests Sam Butler rather than Jack Harris. See *Metropolitan Nuncio*, June, 1649.

THE FREEDOM OF THE PRESS

I wonder this world is so bewitched to the *Hydra-headed* monsters, this adle-headed multitude, this filthy Aviary, this moth eating crew of News-mongers, as to let them have a being in the world amongst us.

Every Jack-sprat that hath but a pen in his ink-horn is ready to gather up the Excrements of the Kingdom, purged forth by the glister of distraction, by the suppository of dissention ; and to put them into a curranto, mixt with innumerable lyes of their own making, in the fashion of Newes, to gull the credulous world. . . .

. . . paper-blurring, weekly-teeming pamphleteers : this croaking fry, this indenominable Quacmalry of nudiustertian Mercury-mongers. . . .

The whole Bevy of New-lye-writers may be divided into two sections : First, *Cavaliers*, and they may be sub-divided into :

    Mercurius 1. Pragmaticus
           2. Elencticus

Secondly, *Parliamenteers*, and they may be sub-divided into

    1. The perfect Diurnall-writer.
    2. The moderate Intelligencer.

But first for the Cavaliers.

First, *Mercurius Pragmaticus* is a fellow witty enough, but he hath more wit than honesty ; he is the wittiest knave of the whole crew : (give the Devil his due,) he is the Court-jester, the Cavaliers fool, the chief squib-crack, arch pamphlet-puppy ; if his Brethren (in iniquity) get him, the fools hug him, as the Papists doe a Dispensation, to eat flesh Fridayes ; wherewith they are furnished with jests and jeers for a long time after.

This same *Pragmaticus* (alias *J. Cleveland*) was formerly an University-chitton, but now he is a chief press-whelp; I took him at first for a Chilver-cavalier, because he vented such loud feminine scouldings : he had right a female Dialect, as if he would have unquaifed the Parliament : His motto is, *Nemo me impune lacessit*, None provokes me without punishment. Great gun-powder words, but who fears it ? *Nemo, hercule, nemo. Aut deo, aut nemo.* He spews poyson in every ones face he meets, and snaps at all, as if (like a Cannibal) he meant to bite off their noses ; but shrewd Cowes have short horns : His chief subject of jeering is Religion ; he thinks he doth great matters to cull some Divinity-dragooneers, or the like : But, sirrah *Pragmaticus*, whats become of your religious Ballad-singers, your devout Bellows-blowers, your divine Fidlers, your godly Pipers, together with your heavenly Bawdy-court ? . . .

Secondly, *Mercurius Elencticus* is the silliest fellow of the whole red-nosed tribe of Mercury-mongers, . . . and makes so many vinegar-faces to the wringing of a lame line out, it would grieve one to see it. . . .

2. *Nunc de Parliamenteers.*

First, the Perfect Diurnall-writer is an old standing Pool, and therefore must needs gather much filth ; he is the arch-sedition-monger, he may fib by authority, and lye stoutly (as no doubt but he doth) *Cum publico privilegio, imprimatur G. Mabbott* : He cannot write a jest but at second hand, and seldome rails but at Presbytery, which he doth scouldingly, with much waspishnesse : he takes occasion to speak of the eleven Members in every Diurnall, least happly we should forget them. . . .

Secondly, the Moderate Intelligencer is the epitome of nothing, the gizard of a trifle : This fellow is Liar-royall, and can out-lye a sheet every week ; he tels outlandish, beyond-sea lyes, besides English, and his ears are ubiquitary ; he knowes what ere is done in France, Spain, Holland, Germany. . . .

There are many other silly fellows of this profession, who are not worth the castigating distinctly ; they are all the excrements of humanity, the hemrods of wit, the firebrands of contention, the chafen dishes of hell, (or as the *American* Cobler speaks of fashion-loving women) the gyblets of vanity, the petti-toes of infirmity ; fitter to be kickt, if they were of a kickable substance, than either honoured or humoured.

I wish our noble Senators would be pleased, either to banish these whiflers out of the Kingdom, or to send these gipsies home from tithing to tithing with whip and passe, or bung up the mouthes[1] of these brawling curres with a pension (as *Charillus*[2] was served) that they may no longer corrupt the world with their forgeries : I would willingly allow them Newgate pension, bread and water, on condition they work hard, or a general assessment *per mensem*, for their relief : but if not, may they be hated of all, (or as *Dorcas* in Sir P. S. his malady) may the taste of them be worse than musty cheese, and their sight more odible than a Toad in ones pottage.

> *That henceforth we may live in peace,*
> *And our divisions surcease.*'

George Wharton, perhaps smarting under the injury done him by the anonymous pamphleteer who had so successfully counterfeited his almanac, regretted the licentiousness of the press, and thus sums up the complaints of a growing number of people :

' . . . That the Pulpit and the Presse are in themselves truely Excellent, no man (not possessed with a spirit of Madnesse) will deny ; but that from thence have issued the ruines both of King and people, and his Majesties Subjects been Poysoned with Principles of Heresie, Schisme, Faction, Sedition, Blasphemy, Apostacie, Rebellion, Treason, Sacriledge, Murther, Rapine, Robbery, and all other the enormous Crimes, and detestable Villanies, with which this Kingdome hath of later times swarmed ; and experience hath given us too perfect a sense.'[3]

The Stationers' Company and News-Books

In particular, the licensing machinery was not working

[1] Phrase used by Sam Butler. See page 93.
[2] Alexander gave him a pension to stop writing verse.
[3] *Merc. Impartialis,* 5-12 Dec., 1648.

smoothly. Like an underfed and overworked engine, it made more noise than progress.

Since the ordinance of September, 1647, the *Moderate Intelligencer* was the only news-book to be entered in the Stationers' Register. Then in April, 1648, occurs the first entry of *Weekly Accompts* since 25 March, 1647. It would be wrong, however, to suppose that these were the only diurnals that were officially licensed. The parliamentary mercuries were all licensed, and, according to a law which had not been rescinded, they should all have been duly entered every week in the Stationers' Register. Why they were not entered is not easy to say ; for the Stationers' Company thereby suffered the loss of their fee, sixpence, which was charged for each news-book entry. The stationers as a Company were not the men to forgo without question any fee to which they were legally entitled. It cannot be that the fees were handed over privately to the Company : else, there would have remained some record of the transaction. Nor were the diurnalists likely to pay the fees demanded of them and then to forgo the privilege of having their books entered on the Register. It was not sufficient simply to enter a news-book once, when it first appeared. Each issue was regarded as a new book, which indeed it was, for it differed from the previous week's issue in everything but name : and it was customary for the better-established diurnals to be regularly entered every week.

Supported thus by both law and custom, the stationers, had they protested against the disregard of the diurnalists

144

for their Register, would surely not have protested in vain. Why did they let it pass without protest—unless it be because matters of greater weight and importance took up their attention ? Their own internal affairs, as a Company, probably kept them fully occupied.

The Quarrel between Mabbott and Dillingham

There are several points of different interest raised by the quarrel between Dillingham, author of the weekly *Moderate Intelligencer*, and Mabbott, the official licenser. The cause of the dispute was the refusal of Mabbott to license the *Moderate Intelligencer* in June, 1648 :

' (Mabbott) says that about the 8 of May last, John Dillingham, the pretended writer of the book, malignantly and to the dishonour of Parliament wrote this passage of French therein, " Dieu nous donne les Parlyaments briefe, Rois de vie longue " and did not send the sheet as usual for petitioner's perusal, fearing lest he should correct it ; complaint was made by many members of the House of Commons (in whose esteem petitioner much suffered, his name being printed on the copy as if he had really licensed it), and petitioner thereupon wrote to Dillingham requiring him in his next book to vindicate the honour of Parliament, and crave pardon for that malignant expression, but he has ever since refused so to do ; petitioner therefore prays that Dillingham may be left to be punished under the ordinance of the 28th of Sept. 1647, and enjoy no privilege from the House.' (*Remonstrance and petition of Gilbert Mabbott*, 23 June.)[1]

Dillingham's printer, Robert White, was on the side of law and order. It was the side on which his bread was buttered. He therefore petitioned the Lords in support of his claim to sole rights in the *Moderate Intelligencer*. The rights and customs of the Stationers' Company formed the basis of his claim. Under the ordinance of Sept., 1647, the news-book in question had been ' licensed, printed, and ' registered by the Company as his proper copy and he

---

[1] *Hist. MSS. Comm.*, Pt. 7, p. 33.

' prayed the House to be tender of any violation of the
' custom and ancient privileges of the Company of Sta-
' tioners, and to restore to him his title of Moderate Intelli-
' gencer, as he ought to have free liberty to write the sheet
' himself, or to employ whom he shall think fit to write it
' for him.'[1]

Henry Walley, clerk of the Stationers' Company, vouched
for the truth of all that White had affirmed. Therefore in
view of the official attitude of the Stationers' Company it is
surprising to find judgment given by the Lords in favour of
Dillingham. White lost his rights in the news-book
although it was registered as his proper copy, and Dillingham found another printer, R. Leybourn, and continued
to publish the news-book on Thursdays as usual.

But White was not so easily defeated. He continued to
bring out his own version of the *Moderate Intelligencer* and
when the Lords interfered he merely changed the name to
the *Moderate* and the day of publication from Thursday to
Tuesday.

The new diurnal is first entered in the Register on
28 June, 1648. Mabbott licensed both *Moderate* and
Moderate Intelligencer, and, to complete the anomaly,
became author of the *Moderate*.

Henry Walker now enters the story. His *Perfect Occurrences*, begun in January, 1647, had at first been entered
in the Stationers' Register under the hand of Mabbott, and
thereafter not entered again till March, when William Newhouse had temporarily undertaken the duties of licenser.

[1] *Ibid.*, Pt. 7.

On 28 June, 1647, the diurnal was again entered, but under whose hand is not specified. Then, till 28 July, 1648, entries cease.

Obviously Walker had some motive for suddenly deciding, as he did, to resume the old habit of entering the book in the Stationers' Register. He wished to legalise his own position, which was not possible so long as *Perfect Occurrences* remained unentered : also to establish his claim to his own diurnal as White had established his claim to the *Moderate Intelligencer*. True, White had been unfortunate, but the misfortune was rightly to be understood as due, not to a claim which he could not substantiate, but to a lack of sympathy between Mabbott, who belonged to that section of the Independent party which wished to bring the king to trial, and the Lords, who wanted the king to enjoy his own again. In plain point of law White had clearly established his right of copy in his diurnal, and if other motives had not intervened the Lords would probably have entered judgment accordingly. What White had done, Walker might do ; and Walker had powerful friends that White had not.

On 28 July, 1648, were entered in the Stationers' Register ' under the hand of Mabbott six pamphlets called, *The* ' *Perfect Occurrences*, printed formerly by the said Robte ' Ibitson '. On 16 August Walker preferred his petition to the Lords : further material for which was provided by personal injuries received from the unpopular Mabbott :

' petitioner thanks the House for their order of the 30th June last, granting him license to publish Fridays' occurrences, in contempt of which order Gilbert Mabbott, who has no authority but under order from the

House, has not only threatened petitioner, but has disturbed the printers and sent men to break their presses, scorning their Lordships' order, and telling the men that he would bear them out ; Mabbott, besides his licensing, which is alone worth nearly 100 *l.* per annum, collects the intelligence of Monday's Journal and other sheets of news, which is worth much more ; and being both writer and licenser he has liberty to make use of what he pleases to advance his own writing, and to leave out to disparage others ; for these reasons, when he licensed under his master John Rushworth, the House of Commons put him out ; petitioner prays their Lordships to call Mabbott to account for his contempt of their order, to consider whether it is fit to continue his license, he being a writer, and that the order of the 30th of June last may be confirmed.'[1]

The Lords ordered that Mabbott should see the petition and return his answer within a week.[2] Walker's motive may be gathered from a petition presented by him to the Lords on 22 March, 1648, by which he had sought to obtain a monopoly of the printing of news. He prayed that none of the transactions of Parliament be published without order from one or both Houses, and that provision be made for giving allowance to such as shall discover and take the authors, printers, and publishers of scandalous and seditious papers.[3] He resented the authority which Mabbott had (lawfully obtained or not, he seemed to have it) to poach on what he had come to regard as his proper preserves. He accused Mabbott of erecting what may be called a news-bureau, to which the news-writers applied every week for news already prepared in a form suitable for publication. There are dark hints of corruption—that Mabbott kept the most interesting news-items for exclusive publication in his own diurnal and was generous enough in doling out the dull, more hackneyed items to his rivals.

[1] *Ibid.*, Pt. 7.

[2] *H.L.J.*, 16 Aug., 1648.

[3] *Hist. MSS. Comm.*, Pt. 7.

Walker said as much as he dared in his petition to the Lords, but he hinted at much that the fear of the law restrained him from saying openly.[1]

Henry Walker and Gilbert Mabbott were both of them important personages ; Walker the more versatile in his talents, but of questionable honesty. It is usual to assign unpleasant and mercenary motives to his deeds, and to assume that he was often merely the tool in larger, more magnificent, but anonymous hands. If in this particular affair he was but a tool in somebody's hands, it is improbable that the hands belonged to Oliver Cromwell. *Per contra*, it is less unlikely that the lieutenant-general or some other political or military leader may have been behind Mabbott, instigating him to gain complete personal control over the news-books[2]: for Mabbott was against making peace with the king. It is impossible at present to say more than this, that, while there is evidence disproving the assertion that any of the more aggressive Independents were behind Walker in his fight with Mabbott, there is no apparent justification for supposing that Mabbott was acting for anyone but himself.

A Woman's Protest against Parliament's Tyranny

If Parliament were determined to keep the printing-presses closed against all who disagreed with their policy,

---

[1] Walker's activity in the cause of the Government may be gauged by the repeated references in the royalist news-books to ' Walker and his blood-hounds '. He seems to have shown great eagerness for the chase.

[2] Walker made no such accusation against him. He confined the charge to one of ' Covetousness ' (*Hist. MSS. Comm.*, Pt. 7, 8 Sept.).

they were met with a no less determined resistance : though the woman who sent a messenger along to the House with copies of an unlicensed and seditious book, which she had just published, for distribution among the members probably deserved to be prosecuted. The book was entitled *A Treatise of Magistracy*, and the bearer was committed to Newgate. *Mercurius Elencticus* in his issue for 5-12 January referred to the incident :

> . . . 'their' (i.e. Parliament's) '*Tyranny* is growne to such a height, as that the very *Women* take up the *Cudgells* against them, and resolve to *swaddle* them out of their *absurdities* for (amongst the rest) one *Mistris Pope* (I fear she must fare the worse for her Name) a *Salters* Widdow, caused a Book to be delivered to the Houses concerning the power of *Civill Magistrates*, . . ., wherein she gives his *Majesty* the *Titles* of *Bishop*, *Elder*, and *Stuard*, &c as well as *King* (and yet they say she *miscalls* him) and upon examination⁰of *part* of it, the *whole* was adjudged to be very *Popish*, full of *Salt*, and *Faeminine-Malignancy* : in so much as he that presented it was committed ; and the *Good Soule* and *Printer* Ordered to be enquired after, for the same purpose.'

The Impotence of Parliament

Parliament was baffled. The gentlemen of the county of Bucks came forward with a petition to Parliament inquiring whether nothing could be done to punish the authors, printers and publishers of ' all wicked and scandalous ' pamphlets, who privily instill into the breasts of many a ' sinister conceit and misinterpretation of all your noble actions.'[1] The gentlemen of Bucks meant well, though their question betrays in them a gift for the obvious. Parliament had for long been trying to answer that very question. How to restrain the general lawlessness of the time baffled them. They were prepared to do anything—short of resigning.

[1] *Perfect Diurnal*, 6-13 March, 1648.

They, too, could ask questions. What, for instance, was John Lilburne doing at Watford, when at the same time he was supposed to be confined in the Tower ? The lieutenant of the Tower was invited to explain. It appears that Lilburne, whose effrontery is so cool and on such a grand scale as to compel admiration, was canvassing his *Agreement of the People* at Watford.

Then, again, why did scandalous pamphlets multiply despite the laws against them ? There were not lacking willing and active agents to put those laws in execution. Why so few books entered in the Stationers' Register— and of news-books no more than one or two—when the law demanded that they should all be entered, and the Stationers' Company had the fierce Hunscot, fiercest and most inexhaustible of beadles, the ' pale-faced fellow ' who clung like a limpet, the knowing George Lewis, and all the swift blood-hounds of searchers, to make the way of the transgressor well nigh impassable ? The gentlemen from Bucks must wait for their answer.

A little more vigour was put into prosecuting offenders. As much as 100 *l.* was offered for information leading to the discovery of the author of *The New Testament of the Lords and Saviours at Westminster*, *The Parliaments Ten Commandments*, and other scurrilous attacks on parliament.[1] Two months later the news-books report the arrest and imprisonment of the author : nothing is said about the 100 *l.*

[1] i.e., April, 1648.

151

Then at the end of February, according to Henry Walker
in his *Perfect Occurrences*,[1]

'. . . one *Thompson*, who printed scandalous Pamphlets, some Months
since, against the Parliament, and the Army was tried by a Councell of
warre, who being called in, was obstinate, and the second time, was carried
in by the Marshals. And lying down, was carried out again, saying he
would not be tried by them, reproaching them by wilde and scandalous
aspersions, and despising their authority ; the Councill of Warre passed
sentence against him to be shot to death : '

Clement Walker's *History of Independency*

Desperate efforts were made by Parliament to gain
control over the press. The Lords' and Commons' Journals
were locked away and not to be looked at without special
leave. ' How unjust ' (exclaimed Clement Walker in his
History of Independency)[2] ' to keep records of the House
' from the view and knowledge of any man, and yet to
' expect obedience to them ! ' Walker elaborated the
charges against Parliament and accused them of publishing ' counterfeit news and letters of great victories and
' successes gotten by their party in parts so remote that
' they cannot in a short time be confuted : this serves to
' credit and animate their party . . . and to dishearten
' their opponents '.[3]

Cromwell is accused of being the man responsible for
this policy :

'. . . he oversways the Council of War, over-awes the House of Commons, and is Chairman and Ring-leader of the Council of State : so that he
hath engrossed all the power of *England* into his own hands, and is become
the Triple King, or Lord Paramount over all the Tyrants of England.'[4]

[1] For 25 Feb.-3 March, 1648.
[2] Part I, 1648.
[3] *Ibid.*, Pt. 2.
[4] *Ibid.*

The same charges are re-iterated in the royalist news-books. The Government became alarmed and there was a hue and cry after Clement Walker. There is a note in the minute-book of the Stationers' Court[1] which shows that the Government earnestly desired the help of the Stationers' Company in the hunt for Walker. George Wither replied unofficially for the Government in his *Respublica Anglicana* (the British Museum copy of which bears the date 1650)[2] :

'. . . there is a sort of men that nothing can content, unlesse they may tread on truth's heels, and trample upon the present Governours, nay and this sort, should another but term such Kings Tyrants, will flie in his face, whilst themselves will reproach the present Governors with Tyranny, and what not, because they may not have licence to abuse them, and Truth too, in their scurrillous Pamphlets : yet such is the wisdome of our times, that such as these are the only vendible and cryed up writers, as if Liberty consisted in crying up Tyranny, and defaming those that resist it. . . .

' The *History of Independency*, though it may appear to have been stifled in the Birth, the greatest part of the First Impression being supprest by publike Authority, and together with it's Author prohibited a publike walk ; yet much of it in parcels having been before vented (the crafty Enemy skirmishing in small parties before he would bring on his main body, & by getting off without personall loss growing more daring, but one subtiller than He owed Him a shame) and many of the last escaping the seizure, which were secretly disperst, and covertly reprinted by the Book-sellers, of whom too many are more than enough prone to disserve the State, and these being greedily sought, and at high prices bought, by that sort of men who, *audax omnium perpeti ruit in vetitum nefas*, will hazard a Paradice to partake of forbidden fruit, it came in fine into most hands ; thus being divulg'd, and not to be thought altogether inconsiderable, in regard of the politick composure, and crafty couching of it's Calumnies, backt much by the repute of the Author, lately a Member of the House, and before a seeming zealot in the Parliamentary Cause. . . .'

PARLIAMENT AND THE STATIONERS' COMPANY

It may be reasonably assumed that Parliament was at this time soliciting the support of the Stationers' Company,

[1] I am indebted to Mr. R. Rivington, Clerk of the Stationers' Company, for permission to examine the Court Book for the year 1648.

[2] The book was advertised in the *Perfect Diurnal*, 21-28 Oct., 1650, as being then already published.

but how far the Company yielded to its tender soliciting will remain a matter of speculation so long as important documents of the Company's proceedings remain unpublished and undivulged. There is, however, evidence of Parliament's attitude. The Stationers' Company were frequently during the year called in to help in the discovery of offending printers and authors, and to supply searchers.

Notice also was taken of the good endeavours of the printing trade ; George Thomason,[1] whose sympathies were unmistakably royalist, was nevertheless warmly thanked and generously remunerated by the Commons for securing for the nation ' the library of choice and valuable books in the Eastern language brought out of Italy '. The Commons expressed themselves grateful that the ' kingdom ' had not been deprived of so great a Treasure, and Learning ' deprived of so great an encouragement '.[2] The services of Edward Husbands in printing declarations for Parliament were handsomely recognised in a grant to him of 617 *l.* from the treasury.[3] And all this, ten months before the trial and execution of the king. It was not all chaos in the book trade.

Internal Affairs of the Stationers' Company

Meanwhile, the Stationers' Court decided, in view of the ' present distractions '[4], not to hold their customary annual

---

[1] Who bequeathed to posterity the infinite riches of the collection of Tracts that now bears his name. He died poor.

[2] *H.C.J.*, 24 March, 1648.

[3] Though he was kept waiting for his money.

[4] *Court Minute Book*, 1 July, 1648.

dinner. By ' present distractions ' may be meant no more than the political situation. On the other hand, it may be a reference to internal distractions of the Company's affairs. Parker, master of the Company, was probably ill at the time—he died on the 30th of the same month[1]—and his condition may have been the cause of the said distractions. There may have been tributary causes. For example, the Court order of 8 June, 1648, ' that the books in the Warden's room be examined ' may or may not refer to the normal yearly audit of accounts.[2] There certainly was trouble over a financial account drawn up, and submitted to the Court, by Thomas Whitaker, brother to the former master of the Company. On examination it was found that Whitaker (and another freeman) had charged for a dinner which they had not given, the defalcation involving the sum of twelve pounds, which they had to refund.[3] President of the Court and master of the Company, till his death in July, 1648, was John Parker, who was friend enough to Thomas Whitaker to remember him in his will. The connection between Whitaker and Parker is interesting in view of the dispute in which Whitaker was involved with a son of Lord Herbert of Cherbury in September, 1648.

A Dispute about Copyright

Apart from the main issue of our argument, but by no means irrelevant to it, is this dispute about copyright in October, 1648. The dispute did not come to a head until

[1] Smyth's *Obituary*.
[2] 8 June, 1648. I think it does.
[3] *Court Book*, 7 August, 1648.

the end of the year, by which time Parliament had altered the machinery for controlling the press. But before that alteration took place the dispute about the right of copy in Lord Herbert's books had already begun ; and, if for no other reason than that it was one of the ' distractions ' of the Stationers' Company at the time, it is worth noticing here.

On the death of Lord Herbert his son applied to the Lords for a fourteen years' monopoly to print his father's books, which was granted him on 5 September. On 11 September Whitaker entered Lord Herbert's books in the Stationers' Register as his own copy, and petitioned the Lords against their decision to grant to the son a privilege which the father had already made over to petitioner. Whitaker appeared to answer the charge of pirating. The new Lord Herbert produced a copy of the book in question which was, he said, an altered and revised version prepared by the late earl just before his death. A debate followed ; and the matter was considered by *Mercurius Elencticus*[1] to be of sufficient interest to merit the ensuing paragraph :

' A debate was had in the house of *Lords* concerning the *Earll* of *Cherburies* History of *Henry* the 8 which of right belongeth to Mr. *Whitaker* (the *Stationer*) who had it from the Author's hands, with leave to Publish it, which he was about to do, having yet it *Licens'd* and *Entered* in the *Hall-book*, according to Order. But in the *Interim*, a son of this *Earles* (who laies claim not so much to the *Wit*, as the Profit) produces another *Copy* ; which he saies is the last corrected by his Father : and because the *Copy* ought to be pat for their purpose ; It is referred to the *Lord North*, and he is to referre it to his Crop-ear'd *Chaplain*, to *Review* and *compare* the *Copies* : That is, he is to take speciall care, there passe nothing that may any waies intrench on the Members *Copyhold* and where he see a fit occasion, to insert such things as may approve the wickedness of that *King* in robbing the *Church* of her rights, and by demollishing of *Abbeys* and other *Religious*

[1] 18-25 October.

156

Houses ; the better to justifie their own *Sacrilegious* Acts, now against the honest *Bishops* and their *Revenues.* But if Mr. *Whitaker* intends to doe the deceased Author Right ; he can in nothing more, than by preserving his Book (whatever it be) from Corruption : which will not easily be avoided if once it come in their clutches.'

Elencticus did not disguise his distrust of the men responsible for the censorship of the press, nor his strong suspicion that even so well-connected a stationer as Whitaker would not get justice at their hands. In this case he was mistaken. Whitaker benefited by a very fair arrangement by which he shared equally with Herbert the profits of the book.[1]

THE MILITIA CALLED IN TO CONTROL
THE PRESS

By the end of 1648 it must have seemed to Parliament that the Press was uncontrollable—royalist mercuries had increased in number and vitality : let the writers of them be cast into prison, yet would they make their escape or else find their friends willing to carry on their diurnals for them whilst imprisonment lasted : indecent mercuries, like a running sore, could not be stopped : even amongst the parliamentary news-writers there was disharmony and friction : the licensing of the approved news-books was not the simple matter that it should have been : the Stationers' Company, distracted by its own internal affairs, supported Parliament only half-heartedly ; Parliament was on the one side assailed for its tyranny and on the other reproached for its failure to exercise control over the press.

[1] *H.L.J.*, 6 November, 1648.

On 31 August Mabbott submitted to the Commons certain proposals for the better regulation of the press and for the suppression of seditious news-books and the more numerous pamphlets of occasional interest which were more harmful and more difficult to trace back to their source. Mabbott proffered advice how best to give effect to the moribund press-regulations. It was said by the news-writers afterwards that he proposed himself as the best man to undertake the work. The Commons thanked him for his advice, voted him forty pounds—and called in the Stationers' Company to advise them. The matter was agitated in Parliament. ' Ned Ash the clothier ' (*Mercurius Pragmaticus* reported) told the House that it was high time something was done,

'. . . *Considering the Impudence and boldness of* Pragmaticus, *and that if the State did allow* 600 *or* 1000 *l.* per annum, *to some one faithfull man to Suppresse such things, it would prove money well and wisely bestowed.* O excellent *State-wisard* ! . . . In the meane time, the work goes on a pace, and the *Master* and *Wardens* of the loyall Company of Stationers are brought in to advise with the Committee about it. But I am confident they will appeare men of more *Loyalty* and wisdom, than to foule their Fingers in so unworthy and ridiculous an *Imployment.*'

The stationers, however, did not justify the special confidence which *Pragmaticus* reposed in them.

The first result of Parliament's deliberations was the appointment of Francis Bethan to be ' Provost Marshall for the Safeguarding of Parliament, with power to apprehend and surprise all such persons as sell, sing or publish Ballads or Books, scandalous to the Parliament or their Proceedings. . . . Such to be handed over to the militia '.

For his services Bethan was given five shillings a day, his deputy three shillings and four pence, and each of his

'flying squad' (of twenty[1]) eighteenpence a day. It was
not good pay : perhaps Ned Ashe shook his head, thinking
it poor economy to pay so little. Besides, it was a thankless
task. Elencticus warned Bethan what would happen if he
undertook it—' I'le rip thee and thy whole Generation up
' to the very Backs and throw the *Guts* in thy Face to blind
' thy pursuit'.[2] The State-beagles were now red-coats
and more like blood-hounds than they had been.

The royalist news-writers, for whose discovery handsome
rewards were promised, gloried in their elusiveness and
filled their sheets with mocking taunts against the clumsy
Bethan and his stupid assistants. ' The more they enquire
after me ' (said Elencticus) ' the further am I from them :
' yet still have I a Presse thundering under their Noses '.[3]
But the methods of Bethan were not unsuccessful. None
but the most intrepid continued to print in defiance of the
law.

The Stationers demand more Licensers

This forceful attempt by the Government to control the
press encouraged the Stationers' Company to adopt an
attitude which the instinct of self-preservation had already
counselled. Whatever their private convictions may have
been, they came out on the side of law and order as represented by Parliament. The officials of the Company were

[1] Melancholicus in his *New Marriage between Mr. King and Mrs. Parliament*, Nov., 1648, says that Bethan had ' 40 blood-hounds, informers,
setters, peepers, sneakers, false accusers. . . .'

[2] *Merc. Elen.*, 13-20 September, 1648.

[3] *Ibid.*, 14-21 November.

on friendly terms with the Government, to whose good will they were indebted for the continuance of their privileges and monopolies : but it is less certain that the large body of freemen endorsed the action of their officials.

Subdued mutterings against the master and wardens, echoing faintly after the lapse of nearly three centuries, may still be heard. For instance, one would like to hear more about the ' opprobrious language of Thomas Walkly against the Master and Wardens of the Company ' mentioned in the Court minute-book : the Court decided that he should be ' advised with '.[1]

The Stationers proposed to Parliament that the number of licensers should be increased. This was in the interest of law and order, as well as to the advantage of the Company. A complaint from Thomas Walkly to the Master and Wardens was the occasion of the proposal, and perhaps also of the ' opprobrious language '.

Walkly had six years before bought for forty pounds a piece of Ben Johnson's poetry which he had printed at a cost to himself of three hundred pounds : since which time a new licensing board had been appointed. In order to obtain permission to re-issue the poem, application had to be made to Sir Nathaniel Brent, licenser of such books, or else to Mr. Langley, schoolmaster of Paul's. Walkly complained of the negligence of both of them—Sir Nathaniel Brent was never at home, and Mr. Langley was too busy with his scholastic duties to have time for licensing.

The Stationers' Company petitioned the Government to

[1] 22 December, 1648.

appoint different licensers :—' Sir Nathaniel Brent is
' employed in greater business, Mr. Farnaby is dead and
' Mr. Langley cannot spare time in regard of his school, so
' that divers books that would be beneficial to the Common-
' wealth lie unprinted, and trade is much hindered.'[1]

Dissatisfaction with the licensers had become general
since 1646, when Edwards in his *Gangraena* had drawn
attention to the dangerous tolerance of one of the licencers,
Mr. Bachiler :—

> ' I am afraid that, if the Devil himself should make a book and give it
> the title *A Plea for Liberty of Conscience*. . . . and bring it to Mr. Bachiler,
> he would license it, and not only with a bare *imprimatur*, but set before it
> the commendations of " a useful treatise " of " a sweet and excellent
> book ".'

With Farnaby dead, Brent absent on business and Langley otherwise engaged, there was sufficient to justify the
Stationers' demand for ' some additional licensers '. There
may have been other reasons.

[1] *Hist. MSS. Comm.*, Pt. 7.

CHAPTER VI

THE REVOLT OF THE LICENSERS

The Stationers' Company supports the Government

THERE can be no doubt as to what part the Stationers'
Company played in the struggle for the freedom of the
press at this time. The Company was on the side of the
Government. The men who had been appointed under the
Ordinance of 1642 to search for law-breakers were now,
in 1649, in control of the Company. Those[1] in charge of
the Company's affairs had considerable power in their
hands. The intervention of the City Common Council on
their behalf in 1645 had given them further power and their
position had been made thoroughly secure by an order of
Parliament in 1648 which interfered with the ancient right
of the freemen of the city companies to elect whomsoever
they pleased to be their officials. The freemen objected,
naturally, to this interference with their rights, and thousands of ' well-affected citizens ' petitioned the Commons
' to rectify the election of Publike Officers of the Citie of
' London, and of every particular Company therein, restor-
' ing the Communalty thereof to their just Rights, most
' unjustly with-held from them, to the producing and

[1] *i.e.* Felix Kingston, Samuel Man, George Miller, John Bellamy, William
Lee junior, John Partridge, Christopher Meredith, Robert Dawlman,
Matthew Walbench, Richard Cotes, Joseph Hunscot, John Reworth
(*Thomason Tracts*, E.538, Jan., 1649).

' maintaining of corrupt interest, opposite to common
' Freedom, and exceedingly prejudicial to the Trade and
' Manufacture of this Nation '.[1]

To make certain that none but their friends should control
the city companies, Parliament ordered on 20 December,
1648, that ' no person whatever that subscribed, promoted
' or abetted any engagement in the Yeare 1648 relating to a
' personell Treaty with the King at London ' should be
' elected, chosen or put into any of the Offices ' of any of
the Companies or of the Common Council of the City.[2]
Thereafter, the political opinions professed by masters and
wardens of the Stationers' Company were guaranteed to
cause the Government little anxiety. The vicar of Bray had
gone into livery.

The deference shown in 1649 by the Government to the
Stationers' Company now becomes explicable. At every
turn the Government advised with the Stationers' Company. In January the Stationers' Company petitioned the
Government to enforce its Ordinances for regulating the
Press: and at once Fairfax was authorised to issue a warrant
to the Marshall-General of the Army ' to put in execution
' the former ordinances of parliament for the regulating of
' printing '.[3] The summoning of military power to aid in
enforcing the Ordinances was just what the officials of the
Stationers' Company desired. The warrant was a direct
answer to their prayers. Lawrence, the Marshall-General,

[1] *Petition to Commons,* 11 Sept., 1648 (*Thomason Tracts,* 669 *f.*13 (16)).

[2] *Ordinance of Parliament,* 20 Dec., 1648 (*Thomason Tracts,* 669 *f.*13 (59)).

[3] *Warrant of Fairfax to the Marshall Generall of the Army* (*Thomason Tracts*) 11 Jan.

was further required to take special pains to redress the stationers' grievances against all who pirated books in their privilege, and to carry the printing presses, instruments of piracy, to Stationers' Hall, there to be (surely most thoroughly) defaced : all of which might be done on the oath of one credible witness. Lawrence, according to the terms of the warrant, was to expect the ready assistance of soldiers, mayors, constables, Mr. Mabbott and the Stationers' Company.

Here is what *Elencticus* had to say about it :—

'. . . a warrant is given to the *Marshall-General* to *Mount* all the Rusty *Ordinances*, that ever were *Pounded* since the first houre of the *Rebellion* (for Paper-service) upon new *Carriages*, and to *levell* them *Point-blank* against all Malignant Books and Pamphlets, particularly this harmless *Rag of Loyalty* : so that (in the first place) I have for enemies this stincking Marshall (*Lawrence* by name) : I have also *Bethen* (my old *Antagonist*) I have *Moore* (that *Lancashire Horne pipe*) and all his *shake-rags* : the *City Lubbard*, and his *Whelps*. But above all the worthy Company of *Stationers* amongst whom John *Partridge* is not the least, (but him I do not greatly feare of all men, because he carries a *Beacon* on his face ready *fir'd* at all times, which gives me faire warning when ever they *invade* my *Territories*. . . .'[1]

A Plea for the Abolition of the Licensing System.

On 18 January Walley, judge advocate of the army, and Mr. Jennings were added to Mr. Mabbott, for licensing of pamphlets.[2] Simultaneously the Levellers, the moderate promoters of the large petition of 11 September, 1648, presented a paper petitioning Parliament to sweep away the entire licensing system :

' A short time after the beginning of this Parliament, upon pretense of publike good, and at the solicitation of the Company of Stationers (who in all times have bin officiously instrumental unto Tyrannie) the Press again (notwithstanding the good service it immediately before had done)

[1] 6-13 Feb., 1649.

[2] *H.L.J.*

164

was most ungratefully committed to the custody of Licensers, when through scandalous Books from or in behalf of the Enemy then at *Oxford* was the pretended occasion ; yet the first that suffered was M. *Lawrence Sanders*, for Printing without license, a book intituled, *Gods Love to Mankind* ; and not long after, M. *John Lilburne*, M. *William Larner*, and M. *Richard Overton*, and others, about books discovering the then approaching Tyrannie ; whilst scandalous Pamphlets nevertheless abounded, and did the greater mischief, in that Licensers have never bin so free to pass, as good men have bin forward to compile proper and effectual answers to such books and pamphlets : And whether Tyrannie did soon follow thereupon, the courses you were forced unto in opposition, and the necessities you were put upon for your preservation, will most clearly demonstrate. And if you, and your Army shall be pleased to look a little back upon affairs, you will find you have bin very much strengthened all along by unlicensed Printing ; yea, that it hath done (with greatest danger to the doers) what it could to preserve you, when licensed did its utmost to destroy you ; and we are very confident, those very excellent and necessary Votes of yours fore-mentioned, had made you a multitude of enemies, if unlicensed printing had not prepared and smoothed your way for them, whereas now they are received with great content and satisfaction.

And generally, as to the whole course of printing, as justly in our apprehensions, may Licensers be put over all publike or private Teachings, and Discourses in Divine, Moral, Natural, Civil, or Political things, as over the Press ; the liberty whereof appears so essential unto Freedom, as that without it, its impossible to preserve any Nation from being liable to the worst of bondage : for what may not be done to that people who may not speak or write, but at the pleasure of Licensers ?

As for any prejudice to Government thereby, if Government be just in its Constitution, and equal in its distributions, it will be good, if not absolutely necessary for them, to hear all voices and judgements, which they can never do, but by giving freedom to the Press ; and in case any abuse their authority by scandalous Pamphlets, they will never want Advocates to vindicate their innocency. And therefore all things being duly weighed, to refer all Books and Pamphlets to the judgement, discretion, or affection of Licensers, or to put the least restraint upon the Press, seems altogether inconsistent with the good of the Common-wealth, and expressly opposite and dangerous to the liberties of the people, and to be carefully avoided, as any other exorbitancy or prejudice in Government.'[1]

The Freedom of the Press and the Execution
of Charles

In the general uproar in Parliament no heed was paid for the moment to this petition of Levellers who had evidently been reading the *Areopagitica*. The Commons for their own

[1] *Thomason Tracts*, 669 *f*.13 (75), 19 Jan.

safety were driven to desperate expedients. The king was on trial for his life, and it was obvious to Pragmaticus and the rest of the royalist scribes that public discussion of the king's trial was not going to be tolerated by Parliament, at least not in print. So long as the matter remained *sub judice* it could not safely be broached by any but the antimonarchical. The press was closed to all who objected to regicide :

' . . . Pamphlets are daily scattered abroad, as Preambles to that said conclusion ; to prepare the Peoples eares for that Doleful Sentence ; as that railing Fool call'd the *Moderate*, weekly stuff'd with a fardle of Fictitious tales, to bring if possible his Masters Rebellions into President : and another of the same Quality sirnam'd *Intelligencer* sworne to write nothing but the justification of the Army, and their present Proceedings . . .'[1]

Neither of these news-books, however, openly advocated the execution of the king, though there can be little doubt as to which side Mabbott, licenser of both diurnals, favoured. He could be relied upon to write in his *Moderate*, and to license what was written in the other news-books for which his *imprimatur* was asked, in ' justification of the army and their present proceedings '.

The king was executed, and immediately began to regain the popularity which in his latter years his methods of diplomacy had cost him. The Commons ousted the Lords from Westminster, the upper House was abolished. By special ordinance public preaching, or the printing of anything, against the proceedings of the now truncated Parliament or the recent proceedings of the High Court of Justice was forbidden. Kingship was abolished, England became a republic ; and for the preservation of domestic

[1] *M. Pragmaticus*, 9-16 Jan., 1649.

tranquility, chiefly, a new tyranny, the Council of State, was set up, of which Bradshaw, the man who had presided at the trial of the king and signed his death-warrant, was the ruling power. Cromwell as yet was not supreme : his objections, for example, to the abolition of the House of Lords had been over-ridden.

It is Bradshaw who is responsible for the new tyranny over the press. *Pragmaticus* held him responsible :

'. . . That *Scarlet Cutthrot*, and *Scelestick Regicid Bradshaw*, I here [i.e. hear] hath desired to have the managing of that businesse [i.e. the control of the press] and will take some such new course as was never taken yet. . . .'[1]

It was on Bradshaw's warrant that Pragmaticus and other persistent defiers of the licensing laws were imprisoned.

Joseph Caryll, Licenser

Joseph Caryll was the first of the licensers to rebel against Parliament. His sympathies were with the royalists. The condemned king on the last night of his life received a visit from Caryll, who ' presented his duty to the king, with ' the humble desire to pray with him, and perform other ' offices of service if his majesty would please to accept ' of them '. The king returned thanks for his love[2] and, had he not already chosen Dr. Juxon to administer ghostly comfort to his soul, it is not unlikely that a divine who was also a parliamentary licenser would have stood by his side on the scaffold.

There is so much to prove the intolerance of the regicides

[1] *M. Pragmaticus*, 3-10 April, 1649.
[2] *Athenae Oxonienses*, Vol. IV., col. 29.

that their neglect to expel Caryll from the office of licenser cannot feasibly be attributed to any policy of toleration on their part. It was more probably an oversight—a disastrous one, for according to an entry in the Stationers' Register for 16 March, deleted in 1651, Caryll licensed the *Eikon Basilike*, thus conferring an *imprimatur* on a book which more than any other proved distasteful to the Government. The *imprimatur* opened the way for the early circulation of the book, which would otherwise have had no place in the shops and on the stalls of law-abiding stationers.

Too late the Government tried to stop the circulation of the book. The sergeant-at-arms did his best to stop it. *Pragmaticus* (27 Feb.-5 March) reported the violence of the searchers :

'. . . They make daily search and inquiry at all *Book-sellers* and *Printing houses*, and with all diligence that may bee, endeavour that none bee dispierc't abroad, using more than ordinary violence where they find *any*, either *Imprisoning, plundering*, or *wounding* any one that shall sell or dispierce them *abroad*. As may appeare by one *Mumford*, a poore man living in St. *Pulchers* Parish, who according to his Trade and profession had taken some of the Bookes to bind, thinking to get some money towards the *maintenance* of his wife and *charge*, but Information being given (by a base Sychophanticall jade who lived neare by him) a crew of *Sectarian Ragamuffin* Souldiers came into his house, his *Wife* being great with Child,[1] wounding the poore man in foure or five places, cut his bookes to pieces and tooke what they lik't of his *goods* away with them.'

Pragmaticus knew how to work up his effects, but even if the too obvious appeal to the reader's pity be discounted there is enough to prove the violence of the Government searchers.

[1] It is a coincidence that the wives of Mumford, Lilburne, Larner and Overton should all have been in the same physical condition when their husbands were summoned for breaking the Press-Laws. The condition of the wife was calculated to plead for the release of the husband.

Downham, Licenser

Downham's use of his power to license was equally displeasing to Bradshaw and his Council. The Commons protested in June because he had licensed a versified edition of part of the *Eikon Basilike*. Yet, like Caryll, he benefited by an oversight on the part of the authorities, although he had already embarrassed them by licensing the Koran in March. There were many protests that the ' heathenish ' Koran should have passed the licenser, whilst the writings of good Protestants of unimpeachable orthodoxy were restrained from publication if their political flavour was unpalatable to the licensers. This was to exalt politics above religion, it was said, and the news-books promptly chronicled the inconsistency : among them was the *Moderate*, written by Mabbott the licenser, whose conduct was surely unprofessional. Here is Mabbott's comment :

' . . . the Printer of the *Turkish Alcoran* (translated into English) to be taken into safe custody,[1] and his presse seized, though the Printer had a license according to Ordinance of Parliament, for the Printing thereof : *This is to punish the Innocent for the Nocent.* The Council of State were to take cognisance of this book, and (*saies one*) proceed therein as they see cause : *I deny that, unless it be according to Justice.*[2]

The Commons reversed Downham's judgment.

The Revolt of the Licensers

Cranford, the licenser, was less fortunate : he was dismissed and his power of licensing revoked[3] on 16 March.

[1] *H.C.J.*, 22 March, 1649.

[2] *The Moderate*, 20-27 March. The usual printed notice that the book had been licensed is absent, though according to an entry in the Stationers' Register the book was licensed.

[3] *H.C.J.*, 16 March, 1649.

That did not prevent a book being entered in the Stationers' Register on 2 April under his hand, and two on 15 April, and several being printed by Robert Bostock in August, '*imprimatur J. Cranford*'.[1]

With the exception of Mabbott, the licensers were showing a readiness to permit the publication of doubtful books, which did not commend itself to the Commons. Richard Royston, the royalist printer who must surely have been 'wanted' for many an offence against the law, had no difficulty in obtaining a license for *Papers that passed between His Sacred Majesty and Mr. Henderson regarding the change of Clerical Government*. Had Royston applied to Mabbott instead of to Downham for an *imprimatur* for his book, the title-reference to his Majesty, whom Mabbott certainly did not hold sacred, would have been sufficient to damn the book, if the mere fact that Royston sponsored it had not been enough in itself. Shelton, the astronomer, protested against the carelessness of the licensers and requested them not to license his books without his consent. It appears that unauthorised persons had been acting on his behalf.[2]

---

[1] J. Playford, stationer, entered *Four Prayers used by his late Majesty* in the Register on 2 April under the hand of Cranford with a note subjoined to the effect that Cranford had given his *imprimatur* on 23 February. There are several other instances of the same delay in registering books after they had been licensed, and Playford's name occurs more than once in this connection (e.g. *Lovelace's Poems* are thus entered by Harper, who was Playford's printer). The nature of the book entered on 2 April and Playford's known sympathies with the royalist cause justify suspicion. On 19 November Playford was arrested for publishing without license *Charles' Trial*. (C.S.P.D.)

[2] See entries in Stationers' Register on 7 June, 1649 and 25 January, 1649-50.

Lilburne's Protests

Mabbott's disaffection was alone required to complete the revolt of the licensers, and this came about through his sympathy with the Levellers who, with John Lilburne as their most truculent spokesman, were clamouring for a free press—for themselves, at any rate.

In *Englands New Chains* (1st Part, 26 Feb., 2nd Part, 24 March) Lilburne demanded :

' (5) That you will open the Press, whereby all trecherous and tyranical designes may be the easier discovered, and so prevented, which is a liberty of greatest concernment to the Commonwealth, and which such only as intend a tyrannie are engaged to prohibit : The mouths of Adversaries being best stopped, by the sensible good which the people receive from the actions of such as are in Authority.'

A sentiment with which the Latin Secretary to the Council of State, Milton, could not fail to agree !

The popularity of Lilburne added potency to his protest against the policy of the Government that closed the press to him and his friends. Petitions from the Levellers demanding the release of their champion from the Tower poured into the House of Commons in a steady stream, until, the patience of the House being at length exhausted, ' a sharp reprehension ' was administered to the petitioners, and ' Mr. Lysle, Ireton and Martyn were ordered to pen an answer to the petitions '.[1] For some time past it had been a popular method of evading the press restrictions to promote petitions, print and circulate them, and to present copies to Parliament. The keenness with which they were circulated justifies a suspicion that their presentation to Parliament was a matter of but secondary importance—like

[1] *H.C.J.*, 18 April, 1649.

presenting the empty cartridge case after the gunpowder had been exploded elsewhere and the lead discharged in another direction. The Commons forbade the practice.

Lilburne and his associates, Thomas Price, Richard Overton and William Walwin, experienced little difficulty in getting their own protests printed and circulated : they did not depend on petitioners to state their case for them. That they could do for themselves, and when they pleased they could even persuade Mabbott to license their publications. He licensed Lilburne's *Agreement of the People* in May. Lilburne at the time was confined in the Tower, taking an enforced rest from pamphleteering, but he would not allow imprisonment to interfere with his habit of defying the law. And Mabbott the leveller proved too strong for Mabbott the licenser.

Curious to relate, W. Kiffin's reply[1] to Lilburne and the rest of the Levellers in the Tower was not entered in the Stationers' Register.

Mabbott's Resignation

Overburdened with Levelling principles, Mabbott retired from licensing at the end of May. In coming to this decision he may have been influenced by Milton. As Latin Secretary to the Council of State Milton had an opportunity of regarding unlicensed printing from a new standpoint. He had even been ordered as an official of the State to examine Pragmaticus,[2] persistent defier of the licensing system.

[1] *Walwin's Wiles* (B.M., E.554).
[2] *C.S.P.D.*, 1649-50.

172

The author of the *Areopagitica* cannot have reported favourably of Pragmaticus, for two months later Pragmaticus found himself again in prison. Not that this convicts Milton of inconsistency. It will be remembered that in his plea for unlicensed printing he had not mentioned news-books nor suggested that chronicles of news needed no supervision.[1]

In the course of his duty Milton must often have met Mabbott—the author of the first reasoned plea for unlicensed printing meets the hitherto most active of the licensers. It is not difficult to predict what they will talk about.

On 7 May Mabbott resigned, setting forth reasons which have a strong Miltonic flavour. It is a pity that he did not publish his reasons until 28 May, that is, three weeks after Parliament had called him to account for the kind of books he was allowing to be printed : for the reasons which he gave for withdrawing from the licensing board bear the imprimatur of truth and do not appear merely to have been adduced because his own interest had been interfered with by a decision of the Council of State on 7 May to suppress the *Moderate*, which he both wrote and licensed. By special request the *Perfect Diurnal* for 21-28 May published the following statement from Mabbott :—

' Mr. *Mabbot* hath long desired severall Members of the house and lately the Councell of State to move the House that he might be discharged of Lycensing Books for the future, upon these reasons following *viz* :

1. Because many thousands of scandalous and Malignant Pamphlets have been published with his name thereunto, as if he had licensed the same, (though he never saw them) on purpose (as he conceives) to prejudice him in his reputation amongst the honest party of this Nation :

[1] See p. 79, *supra*.

2. Because that Imployment (as he conceives) is unjust and Ilegall as to the end of its first Institution, *viz.* to stop the Presse for publishing any thing that might discover the Corruption of Church or State in the time of Popery, Episcopacy, and Tyranny, the better to keep the People in Ignorance, and carry on their Popish, Factious, Trayterous and Tyrannicall designes for the enslaving and distruction both of the bodies and soules of all the free people of this Nation.

3. Because Licensing is as great a Monopoly as ever was in this Nation, in that all mens Judgements, Reasons &c. are to be bound up in the Licencers (as to Lycenceing) for if the Author of any Sheet Book or Treatise writ not to please the fancie, and come within the compasse of the Lycencers Judgement, then he is not to receive any stamp of authority for publishing thereof.

4. Because it is lawfull (in his Judgement) to print any Book sheet, &c. without Lycenceing, so as the Authors and Printers do subscribe their true names thereunto, that so they may be lyable to answer the contents thereof, and if they offend therein, then to be punished by such Lawes as are or shall be for those cases provided.'[1]

'The Councell of State' (added the *Perfect Diurnal*) 'were satisfied with these and other Reasons of Mr. Mabbot 'concerning Lycenceing', and by order of the House he was discharged.

No one can fail to be satisfied with the justness of his complaint and the truth of his four points. Certainly his *imprimatur* had been freely and fraudulently used by the unscrupulous. Even one of the *Pragmaticuses* (which both appear bearing the same device, *Nemo me impune lacessit*, so that the original can hardly be distinguished from its counterfeit) took to printing the legend ' *Imprimatur, Gilbert Mabbot* '—' for the better sale of it ' (added the other *Pragmaticus*). A similar motive may have induced the author of the *Kingdomes Weekly Intelligencer* to inform readers of his issue of 4-11 September that it had been licensed by Gilbert Mabbott, but the author's habitually conscientious regard for truth makes it probable that in this matter he

[1] *Burney*, C. 38.g.10.

was right and that Mabbott, in despite of his own views on licensing and his resignation as licenser, had indeed granted a quite illegal *imprimatur*. The author's desire to impart the whole truth triumphed over modesty :

> ' It seems the Prince (for all his Agents) is much straightened in his Intelligence, And I believe it to be the reason why he reads all our weekly Books of news amongst which, that which he gives most credit too (if I heare the truth) is this.'

Thereafter Jennings replaced Mabbott as licenser of the *Kingdomes Weekly Intelligencer*. That Mabbott should have continued till September as licenser even of this one newsbook, after his public renunciation of licensing in May, and after the acceptance of his resignation, argues a quite surprising laxity on the part of the authorities whose business it was to see that the law was obeyed, and on Mabbott's part, probably, a determination not to let his principles interfere with his habits.

EVENTS LEADING UP TO THE ACT OF SEPTEMBER, 1649

Cromwell and the Man in the Moon

The *Man in the Moon* seems to have been responsible for the story that Cromwell authorized the granting of an *imprimatur* to certain papistical and regicidal books. There is no doubt that they were licensed : one of them, ' Doleman's book ', had the sanction of the Government, though it was not entered in the Stationers' Register. The *Man in the Moon's* evidence is here given in full :

' . . . 'Tis even so ; *Cromwel* and his *Holiness* of Rome are agreed :
Mark you not what *Amity* there is betwixt those two brethren in *iniquity*,
Owen Roe and he ; the one a *Papist*, and the other a *Jesuite* : Nay, more
than this, I heard his *Holiness* the *Pope* hath sent his beloved Son *Iron-
sides* the First, a *Dispensation* for all *Oaths* and *Covenants* whatsoever
already made, or to be made, the better to unburden his Conscience ; and
a *Pardon* for his breach of *Faith* and *Trust* to his *King* and *Country*, and
destroying of the very image of *God* in his *Soveraign* : but because he would
dawbe over his Villanies with pretended *Justice* and *seeming Zeal*, he hath
hired that *Factotum* of villanous Imposturisme *Walker* with 30*l*. to Re-print
a Book of one *Dolemans* a Jesuite, (that was formerly hang'd, drawn, and
quartered for the same) to justifie that unparallel'd and inhuman Murder
of butchering the King : The said Book is new Dipped by our *blest reformers*,
and intituled, *Several Speeches delivered at a Conference concerning the
Power of Parliaments* : and these *Coppies* were cunningly conveyed into
the hands of *Bradshaw* and the *Regicides* as a *Catechisme* to instruct them in
the *Devils-horn-book*, writ in bloudy Characters of the Murder'd Saints and
Servants of God ; and the seeds of this Crop of villany was by perjur'd
Noll committed to the care of that *Saffron-bearded Judas*, *Walker* ; a
villain sold to work mischief, tell lyes, and print and divulge their Rogueries;
one, (I am perswaded) that for all parts in the *science* of *schisme*, cannot be
match'd in the three Kingdoms ; nay not in Christendome, or Europe.
This piece of *Impostorisme* was divulged for Speeches made by some
Members of the Commons House, at a Conference, to cry up their *People-
power*, the better to Divest his Majesty, and usurpe and place the *Supreame
Authority* on themselves : Though this was as high an affront put upon
their pretended Parliament as could be, to have the Book and Doctrine of
Jesuites fathered upon the holy Self-denying Saints ; yet some that complained to the Juncto thereof out of Conscience, to vindicate their Honors,
were by *Cromwel* and his disciples sharply reproved, and threatened if
they stirred any more in that *Discovery*, dearly to suffer : After this, they
published another Book, entituled, *Royal Tyrannies Discovered* ; on very
purpose to Depose and Execute the King : and still other Papists and
Jesuites Works are by their Commands printed and published, as Dr.
Caryes Book, Bishop *Sales* Book, a Book entituled, *The Key of paradice* ;
and a Book printed for *Francis Ash* at *Westminster*, and others newly
printed by the Authority of Almightly *Noll*, and to be sold in Saint *Pauls*
Church-yard, *Cum privilegio*. I forgot the *Turkish Alkoran* ; but these
may suffice to unblind the Nation, and let them see into what Trusty
hands, and religious Saints they have committed the keeping of their
Religion, King, Priviledge of Parliament, Liberties and Lawes.'[1]

The *Man in the Moon*, by attacking Cromwell for his
supposed devotion to Popery, has revealed his own intent,
which was to check the growing popularity of Cromwell.
There was no swifter means to that end than the one he

[1] *Man in the Moon*, 27 June-4 July, 1649.

chose—that of persuading the country that their idol secretly leaned towards Rome. Therefore, Doleman's book and the rest were fathered upon him. *The Man in the Moon's* attempt failed : it was a self-evident untruth to assert that Cromwell was a papist : but his innocence of the other charge could not be so easily refuted, particularly when it was broadly whispered that the author of last year's *Brittanicus*, John Hall, was a ' creature ' of Cromwell's.[1] Whether or not the accusation was founded in fact—and in the absence of more reliable evidence than that advanced by the *Man in the Moon* and his friends, the critical historian will reserve his judgment—it must be admitted that the Government's policy of closing the press to their enemies came to the same thing in the end, namely, that they employed the press for their own purposes : it became in their hands an instrument reserved for their exclusive trumpetings.

New Searchers

One, Bishop, became provost-marshal in June, bringing a new enthusiasm to the attack on unlicensed publications and receiving 100 *l. per annum* in return. He was not to

[1] *C.S.P.D.*, 1654, p. 163 : ' Petition of John Hall to the Protector, for continuance of a pension of 100 *l.* a year, having no other subsistence, and for the 25 *l.* now due. I have been a constant servant of the several Councils, being brought in by your Highness, and always discharged my duty, especially in attending on you in Scotland, and since your assumption of the government, by my book " Confusion confounded ". With order thereon for payment of the arrear. Continuance of the pension, to be paid quarterly from the Council's contingencies, and a warrant to be prepared accordingly.' *Confusion Confounded* was published on 18 Jan., 1654 (E.726.11).

be restricted in the number of his searchers, who, being better supported than Hunscot formerly had been, became particularly offensive. With less authority behind him to back him up, Hunscot had succeeded in making himself unpopular by his own unaided, rampant, officious efforts. The new searchers, however, could afford to be intrepid with so energetic a provost-marshal at their back ; yet it was possible even for a searcher at this period to go beyond his duty and to suffer for his presumption. Both[1] Wright, who is often reviled in the royalist diurnals for his vigorous searchings, and ' parliament Joan ', later known as Mrs. Stroffe, were taken to task by the authorities :

 . . . 'The House was informed that one *Joan* (a clamerous Woman whose Husband was hanged at *Oxford* for a spye and she sometimes imployed in finding out the presses of scandalous Pamphlets) had shewed great incivilities to Sir *James Harrington*, (one of their Members) as he was this day coming to the house, . . . she was taken into custody, and sent to the house of correction.'[2]

News-Books—the Anomalies of Licensing

Since 30 June, 1648, Henry Walker had enjoyed the legal sanction of the House of Lords for publishing (i.e. writing) his *Perfect Occurrences*, and had thereby been protected from Mabbott's genius for interference. Walker had inter-

[1] William Wright and Joan are reviled by *Elencticus* (21-28 Feb., 1649) for being both of them ' curres ' i.e. beagles. That William Wright was a searcher is confirmed by an entry in the *C.S.P.D.*, 1649-1650, p. 528. On 16 April the Council of State issued a warrant for the arrest of ' William Wright, the printer of *Elencticus* '. (*C.S.P.D.*). If these two William Wrights are, and they seem to be, one and the same person, then here is an interesting case of a searcher being paid by the Council of State to search for himself, while Elencticus keeps up the pretence by reproaching him for the thoroughness of his searches.

[2] *Perfect Diurnal*, 2-9 July, 1649.

preted this privilege to publish as carrying with it the power to license, and for six months his book had not been entered in the Stationers' Register. The Stationers' Company protested that the ordinance of September, 1648, made no exception in favour of Henry Walker. Walker replied with a petition to Parliament to renew his rights in the *Perfect Occurrences*, and annexed a copy of a certificate of colonels and other general officers of Fairfax's army approving of the book.[1]

Walker was forced to come into line with the other news-writers. Accordingly his *Perfect Occurrences* was licensed by Mabbott on 18 January, and thereafter by Walley.

The history of the licensing of news-books during 1649 is full of such anomalies : for example, not all of the parliamentary diurnals were entered in the Stationers' Register, and of those that were, only the *Perfect Diurnal* was duly entered every week. To mention only one of many curious examples, the *Kingdomes Weekly Intelligencer*, though it was undoubtedly licensed, was not entered at all.

The *Kingdomes Faithfull Scout* and *Perfect Occurrences* in the course of a violent quarrel in June betrayed certain pieces of information which are invaluable to the student of the licensing system. The *Kingdomes Faithfull Scout*, it appears, was ' collected by R. Wood ', as the *Moderate Intelligencer* had been collected by R. White, and in both cases the stationer and printer, and not the author, was the real

[1] *Hist. MSS. Comm.*, Pt. 1.

owner of the copyright.[1] As White, the stationer, had asserted his right to the *Moderate Intelligencer* by entering it
as his copy in the Stationers' Register, so Wood had safeguarded his interest in the *Scout*, and when he quarrelled with
Border who had been writing the diurnal for him, he dismissed
him and proceeded to write it himself. One of his complaints against Walker was ' that the Licenser doth not
' constantly peruse all *Walkers Occurrences*, and hath
' affirmed that part thereof (containing matters of great
' Malignancy) hath been inserted without his knowledge :
' yet is there to the whole sheet, Imprimatur Theodore
' Jennings '.[2]

The general carelessness of the licensers of news-books
contrasts with the activity of the Government in legislating
for complete control of the press. The beagles at least were
doing their duty, earning unpopularity by performing their
unpleasant tasks with a right good will, whilst the royalist
mercuries reviled them as ' rat-catchers with state-ferrets,
' setting-dogs, bitches,[3] blood-hounds who hunt dry-foot
' day and night '. Pragmaticus was ' routed out of his
' lodgings and acquaintance by Parliament beagles and
' whole squadrons of rebellious Mermidons, & forc't to build
' his nest in another angle '.[4] Levellers as well as royalists

[1] *cf.* the case of the *Moderate Intelligencer* (printed for R. White, 4-11
September) which refused to state the grievances of the miners, though
specially requested to do so. The author of the news-book for the following
week disclaimed responsibility for the refusal, on the ground that ' he had
gone into the country and had left others to write the diurnal '.

[2] *Kingdomes Faithfull and Impartiall Scout*, 22-29 June, 1649.

[3] An uncomplimentary reference to ' Parliament Joan '.

[4] *M. Pragmaticus*, 20-27 Feb., 1649.

bore testimony that the beagles were an even worse set of men than those who had hunted for unlawful books in High Commission and Star Chamber days.[1]

The state-ferrets, by burrowing down every hole where an illicit press was suspected of being hidden, did their best to stop the printing of unlawful news-books. They returned in April with Elencticus, who was discovered to be Samuel Sheppard,[2] and his printer William Wright, and with Nedham, author of *Pragmaticus*, whose printers were identified as being Francis Heldersham, Martha Harrison and William Ellis.[3]

It is impossible to follow the fortunes, or misfortunes, of the delinquent diurnalists and their printers at this time, and it is not the purpose of this volume to attempt it. Warrants were issued for the arrest of all of them, the beagles pursued them unwearyingly, the chief of them served various terms of imprisonment during the year. Nevertheless the diurnals for which they were responsible continued to appear.

The Trials and Quarrels of Diurnalists

The trials and quarrels of the diurnalists (from the January Warrant of Fairfax to the new Act of September) are worth more than a passing notice.

The public thirst for news was not easily slaked, and the supply kept pace with the demand during this period.

[1] e.g. *vide The Soldiers Standards*, April, 1649 (*Thomason Tracts*).
[2] *C.S.P.D.*, 1649-50, and *Impartial Intelligencer*, 18-25 April, 1649.
[3] *C.S.P.D.*, 1649-50.

Additional mercuries were begun, notably *Britannicus* for the Parliament and the *Man in the Moon* for the royalists. The *Man in the Moon* fell far below the standard of purity that *Elencticus* was striving with but indifferent success to impose on his fellow diurnalists. The *Man in the Moon* set out to retail tap-room indecencies under the mistaken impression that his readers after taking in the coarse story would be more in the mood to appreciate the *moralitas* (as it happened, a royalistic one) which the story could be made to illustrate. *Elencticus*, on the other hand, did not fight with a dirty sword, and his weekly plea for unlicensed printing was wholly admirable.

In the midst of his troubles *Elencticus*, foremost of the royalist diurnals, probably realised that something would have to be done to correct the false reporting of news. False reports appeared frequently in the parliamentary news-books and at least as frequently in the royalist. Elencticus went so far as to protest against the false reports current in the mercuries of his own faction.[1] The habit of falsifying the news, though a well-intentioned effort on the part of the royalist to nonplus the enemy, unfortunately mystified friend as much as foe.

Both sides had similar troubles. *Pragmaticus* suffered from the attacks of pirates, who appropriated the Latin tags, distinguishing mottoes, as well as the titles[2]: and *Perfect*

---

[1] *M. Elencticus*, 17-24 September, 1649.

[2] For instance, two different news-books appeared, the first entitled *Pragmaticus For King Charles II.*, 17-24 Sept., and the other *Pragmaticus*, Pt. 2, No. 23, 18-25 Sept., both bearing the same device that was formerly a safe guide to the identity of the author—*nemo me impune lacessit*.

Occurrences also complained of counterfeits. The royalists, of course, found the printers more difficult to deal with than did the parliamentary news-writers. *Elencticus* humorously referred to the tyranny of the printers to which he had to submit—he could not even write what he liked in his own diurnal, but the printer must first be consulted :

   . . . ' I would have told you last weeke (but his *worship* the *Printer* would not let me). . . .'[1]

The *Man in the Moon*, making an unambitious start in journalism, informed readers that he would be satisfied if he made enough money by the sale of his pamphlet to pay the printer.

In spite of all these difficulties the news-books appeared in undiminished volume. John Hackluyt, D.D., well known as the author of *Melancholicus*, changed sides in May and started *Mercurius Militaris* in the interests of Parliament. He issued his first number in jaunty disregard of the licensing system, going out of his way to draw attention to the fact in a footnote.

   ' The Author desires (because he could not meet with his friend Mr. *Jennings* to procure his *Imprimatur,* and the Presse requiring haste) that he may passe the streets this weeke without offence, and the next weeke you shall see him in state, strutting by authority.'[2]

Hackluyt had disregarded the licensing system for so long that he could not be expected all at once to treat it with the high seriousness and careful respect which it demanded. He spiritedly attacked the news-books, not sparing the licensed :

   ' I cannot but looke upon our weekly Tel-tales as the greatest enemies the Nation hath, who by their lyes and forgeries abuse both Parliament and

   [1] *M. Elencticus*, 29 January, 1648-9.
   [2] *Mercurius Militaris*, 22-29 May, 1649.

people, telling them pretty tales whilst they pick their pockets; but chiefly in that they lye by Authority, making the Parliament both Authors and protectors of their falsehoods; for the future I request them into truths, and that they straine not so far for fables to fill up their illiterate sheets else I vow to strip them naked, and set them at the publique ring for all to hisse at.'[1]

Henry Walker, ' Luke the liar, perpetually sick of the yellow jaundice ', was mercilessly lashed for his inconsistencies; and important personages such as Hugh Peters were so frankly and freely criticised that it seems more reasonable to assume that Hackluyt was speaking *in propria persona* than to regard him, as his enemies did, as merely expressing the opinions of the parliamentarians who paid him. *Pragmaticus* (John Cleaveland), *Elencticus* (Samuel Sheppard) and *Melancholicus* (John Taylor) all came under his lash. John Taylor[2] retorted by calling him a lascivious turn-coat and by saying that he had written *Militaris* and *Anti-Mercurius* in order to curry favour with Parliament. Taylor reprinted a petition which he professed to have found behind Hackluyt's bed when they were both in Peter House, by which it appears that ' meere povertie at first, together with the wicked enticements of the Printer, enforced him to write ', but that now, cooped up in jail and compelled to listen to ' the horrid blasphemies of Cavaliers that infected the prison air ', he had revolted from the royalists and offered his services to Parliament.

Elencticus[3] replied with a sharp *argumentum ad hominem*,

[1] *Ibid.*

[2] *M. Melancholicus for K. Charles II.*, 31 May-7 June.

[3] 18-25 June, 1649.

accused Hackluyt of having six wives, and further objected to the laxity of his views on divorce. Perhaps he had been reading both the *Areopagitica* and the *Divorce Tracts*, and had, no less than Mabbott, felt the influence of Milton.

That the news-books were by this time generally despised and that the large majority thereof deserved their ill reputation is clear : but it does not follow that they were less eagerly read on that account. *Pragmaticus*[1] has left on record a memorable description of a typical scene in the London streets when a new mercury came out :

' When the Hawkers come roaring along the streets, like the religious ballad singers of *Bartholemew* fayre, the high Crownd Citizen pricks up his ears, and Cranes his neck over the bulk, till he looks as blew under the gills as an Eelskin to hear whether there be any news of the *Publique* faith, which was eaten up at a break-fast by the *Solemn League and Covenant* in *Turne*-again lane ; but failing of his expectation, he shrinks in his lanthorn soule again, with a pittiful riveling up of the nose, and a *Synodical* Hem. Then traversing *Fleet-street* (the Lawyers Exchange) out comes a Petty-fogger of the threes with his profession in his eare and his Tar-Box at his side, keeping touch with his pocket like *Hopkins* and *Sternhold* in martyring the Psalmes and looking as big as a bag pudding farmer of the long twelves, if his Clerical gizzard be not with him, he calls out Sirrah, books, what Act's on foot ? no gingle to demurr ? to deceive ? to detract ? away you noisemonger. Alas good gentleman his buckeram pouch is never at peace longer than his lunges are bellowing down the sides of Westminster Hall. At last comes by the Country Parson with his canonicall breeches, run up the seames with a figure of a statute lace, like the Anatomy of the old Letany, interloyned with a *libera nos Domine* ; who never attempted to preach above once in his life time, and that was on the *Wake* day, for which he was sequestred ; and he rubs his Elbows, and Winks at the *Mercury* to convey him a pennyworth of Wit into his Hawking Bagg, and so goes tripping along, to show it to his Worshipful Patron, to bespeak him a Sunday Collation.'

Bradshaw and the Press

The press had been captured for the Council of State, and the royalist news-writers unanimously blamed Jack Bradshaw, the president, for the policy which had closed the

[1] 15-22 June.

press to them. By May Bradshaw had realised that a new Act was required for regulating the press, and a conference of the new licensers, Walley and Jennings, with the Stationers' Company was arranged. In August, when the new Act was almost ready to be passed, *Pragmaticus*[1] spoke out against Bradshaw :

'. . . But now I know beforehand the gentleman [i.e. Bradshaw] is highly enraged against all such as dare Print or Publish any thing which tells him and the rest of their *Usurpation* and *Tyranny* ; and uses all meanes possible to suppress them : to which purpose (before they finished the intended knack or Treason-trap, which so long the Committee have beene a licking) it was *Bradshawes* Designe (upon the advise of that hypo-criticall Levite *Nye*, and some else I could name) to treate with and engage the *Printers* of *London* to assist them with the promise of any Acts of Grace and favour they could doe them, for advancement of their Mistery in defyance of the *Stationers* (who had ever failed them in this service) whereupon a generall meeting of the *Printers* was appointed at the *Mouth* neare *Aldersgate*, where only some of the principall did mete, such as *Symmons*, *White*, *Brudenell* and the rest of that gang, out of whom they choose foure to treat with *Bradshaw*, who accordingly repaired to *White-Hall*, but what they did I have not as yet, nor is the knack finished.'

Prison Reform

There was another reason for reform, quite apart from all that has been said above : namely, that the Government's earnest endeavours to put contraveners of the press-laws into prison were being partially cancelled out by the ease with which the offenders managed to escape from prison. In January, 1649, the Commons had found it necessary to order an inquiry to be made into ' the business of escapes from Peter House '[2]; yet by the end of the year it was apparently no more difficult to escape.[3] On the

[1] *M. Pragmaticus* (*For King Charles II.*), 14-21 August, 1649.

[2] *H.C.J.*, 6 Jan.

[3] *Perfect Occurrences*, 1-8 Sept., 1649.

other hand (lest it be assumed that prison life was comfortable), George Wharton[1] pointed out that 90,000 *l.* *per annum* were 'raised by the profit of imprisoning prisoners in the Fleet ', and what ' extorted over and above ' by gaolers, the serjeant of the mace, in corporations and ' by clerks ' he knew not. James Frese, in *Why Not ? being 8 Queries made to Parliament*, 3 September, spoke corroboratively of ' corrupt judges, mercenary lawyers and cruel murthering gaolers '.

THE ACT OF 20 SEPTEMBER, 1649

The Act, which had been so long in preparation, ' against ' unlicensed and scandalous books and pamphlets, and for ' better regulating of Printing ' was passed on 20 September. It began with a reference to the mischiefs arising from ' weekly Pamphlets ' :

' Whereas divers Scandalous, Seditious and Libellous Pamphlets, Papers and Books are daily contrived, printed, vended and dispersed, with officious care and industry by the Malignant party at home and abroad, for the better compassing of their wicked ends, the subversion of the Parliament and present Government, which they well know cannot with more ease be attempted, than by lies and false suggestions, cunningly insinuated, and spread amongst the people, and by malicious mis-representation of things acted and done, to take off and divide their affections from that just Authority[2] which is set over them for their good and safety, and to bring a low and mean esteem upon the persons, and a suspition and hatred upon the courses and intentions of the faithful Members of the Peoples Representative in Parliament, . . . especially such who are most constant and conscientious in discharge of their Trust, and are therefore become the utmost object of their wretched spleen and malice. And whereas a great occasion of these mischiefs and scandals, and dissatisfaction of many, hath

[1] *Abuses Discovered*, 15 June, 1649 (B.M., 669 *f.*14) : signed W. G. The inversion of author's initials was common.

[2] An Act of 17 July, 1649, thus defined the Government's idea of Treason :—' If any person shall maliciously or advisedly publish by writing, printing, or open declaring, That the said Government is Tyrannical, usurped, or Unlawful, and that the Commons assembled in Parliament, are not the Supream Authority of this Nation. . . . every such offence shall be adjudged to be High Treason '.

been as well the ignorance and assumed boldness of the weekly Pamph-leteers, without leave or due information, taking upon them to publish, and at pleasure to censure the Proceedings of Parliament and Army, and other Affairs of State, as also the irregularity and licentiousness of Printing, the Art whereof in this Commonwealth, and in all Forein parts, hath been and ought to be restrained from too arbitrary and general an exercise : To prevent the many mischiefs inevitably following thereupon, . . .'[1]

The clauses of the Act may thus be summarised :—

1. Former laws against spreaders of false news to be put to execution.
2. The penalty for making, printing or uttering scandalous Books, Papers or Pictures—the author ten pounds, the printer five pounds, and the bookseller two pounds.
3. The buyer to forfeit one pound, if he conceal such book bought.
4. All books and pamphlets to be licensed.
5. Former licenses for printing news-books made null.
6. Clerk of the Parliament to license news-books : Army news to be licensed by the Secretary of the Army : all news-books to be entered in the Stationers' Register, ' according to ancient custom '.[2]
7. Treasonable matter liable to further punishment.
8. Master and Wardens to search for unallowed presses and books.
9. No seditious books to be sent by post or carrier.
10. No printing or rolling-press to be used, but in London and the two Universities.
11. Exception for press at York and Finsbury now used for the printing of Bibles and Psalms.
12. Printers to enter into bond of 300 *l.*
13. Authors' or Licensers' names to be prefixed to every publication.
14. No house or room to be let to a printer, without notice given to the Master and Wardens and entry made in the Stationers' Register.
15. Nor any implements to be made, press imported, or letters founded without such notice.
16. Importers of seditious books to forfeit 5 *l.*
17. No imported book to be landed, but at London.
18. Imported books to be viewed by the Master and Wardens.
19. No Bibles, Psalms, &c., to be imported.
20. Books entered in the Stationers' Register not to be printed by others : penalty, forfeiture of the same and a fine of six shillings and eight pence for every copy.
21. Any two magistrates may upon just cause of suspicion grant warrants to search packs and packets.
22. All unlicensed books seized, to be delivered to the Secretary of the Council.
23. Hawkers and ballad-singers to be sent to the House of Correction.
24. Lord Mayor to see the laws against hawkers put in execution.
25. Offenders must be prosecuted within six months.

[1] Quoted from *Acts and Ordinances of the Interregnum* (C. H. Firth and R. S. Rait), Vol. II., p. 245.

[2] More honoured in the breach than in the observance.

How the Act Worked

Thus Parliament took over the press. Forty printers paid 300 *l.* each : Richard Royston, whose chances of keeping on the right side of the law for any lengthy period were but small, was asked to pay 500 *l.* : new diurnals appeared, *A Briefe Relation* written and licensed by Frost, secretary to the Council of State, *Severall Proceedings in Parliament* for which Scobell, clerk to the Parliament, was wholly responsible, and *A Perfect Diurnall of some Passages and Proceedings of and in Relation to the Armies* by Rushworth, secretary of the Army under Fairfax. These were official gazettes rather than diurnals of the sort that had been in vogue since 1640. The old diurnals disappeared.

The change of tone in the official news-books as compared with their licensed precursors was immediately apparent. The licensed news-books had been written by men with a conscious pride in displaying and elaborating their items of news for the week. The more news there was to relate and the more startling its nature, the better they were pleased. To them the attitude adopted by writers of the official gazettes towards ' news ' was inconceivable. No one of the old school of journalists, for example, would have dreamed of beginning his diurnal as Frost began his third number of *A Briefe Relation :*—

Through the goodnesse of *God* wee *still* can say we have not *much Newes at home.*'

A scarcity of news would not have been regarded as a Godsend. News good or bad was always ' copy ', and the diurnalist of the old school could have found it in his heart to be grateful for a murder or a witch-hunt—whatever improved the marketable quality of his book. Nor would he have left a blank page at the end as Frost did, saying that he had reserved it for news which had not come, and that rather than fill it up with what signified nothing, ' which hath been the usual custom till now ', he had preferred to leave it blank. This is one of the most eloquent blank pages in the history of journalism.

The new licensing system threatened to collapse by its own weight. The *Moderate* drew attention to the complexity which was its weakness :

' All business of the Army to be Licenced by a Member thereof. The proceedings of the House to be Licenced by such as the Clerk thereof shall appoint. And Foreign Affairs concerning the State to be Licenced, by such as the Council of State shall think fit. *And must every Pamphlet that hath something of all these, go to three Licencers for its stamp of Authority* ? '[1]

There was no reply given to that question : and there are other questions to which an answer is difficult to discover. Why, for instance, between the end of September and 24 December were there only three entries of the *Perfect Diurnal* in the Stationers' Register, when according to the new Act every book had to be entered ? If it was not necessary to register a news-book more than once, why should it have been entered thrice in three months ? and, more particularly, why should Frost's *Briefe Relation* have been entered only twice, while Scobell's *Severall Proceedings* was regularly entered every week ? The licensers, it is true, had been enjoined by law to keep a record of every book to which they gave their *imprimatur*, but such a

[1] 18-25 Sept., 1649.

record was not intended to supplant the more important
Register of the Stationers' Company. It was the Government's firm desire to strengthen the Company's position—
as the royalist news-writers immediately observed :

. . . ' The Company of *Stationers* are impowred in their old Trade of
breaking open Doors, plundering, and taking away Presses, Letters, or
Books, that shall Print any thing against them, though never so true :
this is *Liberty* ! where be the *Bishops* now ? who stops the Mouth of the
Press now ? this is no Tyranny, no Persecution, no Freedom, Liberty,
Mercy, Propriety, Justice ! '[1]

In other respects the new regulations were enforced with
rigour. As usual, the privileged stationers made reliable
searchers. The Council of State did not fail to add new
ones, among them John Harris, the converted play-actor.
Hunscot was given encouragement (he was more in
need of restraining) : an illicit printing-press which he
had seized and dragged triumphantly to Stationers' Hall
was presented to him for his personal use by a grateful
Government. Warrants were punctually issued for the
arrest of Pragmaticus and the rest, whose long experience
at the game of hide-and-seek enabled them to elude capture
for several months after the passing of the new Act. ' Let
them do their worst ', said the *Man in the Moon* defiantly,
while *Pragmaticus* exclaimed ' Would you have thought
' the State-Rampant could have been so sensible of a little
' Malignant Inke, as should make them thunder out
' Anathema's against the societies of Hawkers and Ballad-
' singers ? ' No longer would the hawkers come roaring
along the streets like the religious ballad-singers of Bar-
tholomew fair.

[1] *Man in Moon,* 19-26 Sept., 1649.

An immediate result of the institution of *official* gazettes, in place of the licensed diurnals which had been maintained by private enterprise, was that the Government dispensed for public consumption only those items of news which it considered fit.

The Press and the News of Drogheda and Wexford

The assertion, put forward by Mr. J. B. Williams in his *History of Journalism* and elaborated by him in *Fresh Light on Cromwell at Drogheda*,[1] that the Council of State took unfair advantage of the new Act in order to suppress the news of the massacres at Drogheda and Wexford is not founded in fact.

Mr. Williams, noting that the suppression of the licensed news-books took place a few days after the news of Drogheda reached London, has come to the conclusion that the one was caused by the other. ' For very obvious reasons the Council of State ', he says, ' decided to suppress the whole of the licensed press '. This interpretation, however, is based on a palpable *post hoc, ergo propter hoc* argument and on a misreading both of the Act for the regulating of printing, 20 September, 1649, and of the conditions of licensing from 20 September to 12 October. Mr. Williams states, without giving any evidence in support of his statement, that the suppression of the licensed news-books had not been contemplated by the Act. But the Act not only appointed three new licensers but also nullified all former

[1] *Nineteenth Century*, 1912. Vol. lxxii, p. 471-490 : See also Vol. lxxiii, p. 812-828. I have dealt with the whole matter in a volume which will shortly be published.

licences for printing news-books. In the provisions of the Act not one exception was made to this rule, nor was any assurance given that any licenses would be renewed.

It happened that a few days before the date fixed for the new Act to come into force, 1 October, the news of Drogheda reached London. The date of the suppression of the licensed newsbooks had been settled some time before the news of Drogheda was received in London. Thus the true reason for the suppression cannot have been, as Mr. Williams affirms, the desire to suppress the truth of the Drogheda massacre : it was, instead, a genuine desire, quite independent of any event in the Irish Campaign, to prevent the misinformation of the people.

Lilburne's Acquittal

Lilburne was brought to trial for having written and published ' treasonable venemous books '. He had ' not ' dreamed that only books should have been laid to his ' charge ', and was therefore unprepared with his defence. The trial took place in the Guildhall before as lordly and distinguished a set of judges as Parliament could command, and before ' a multitude of people ' plainly in sympathy with ' freeborn John '. The judges did not show themselves particularly just, one of them taking it upon himself to advise the intrepid John thus :—' Your distemper will ' break out, your heart is so full of boiling malice and ' venom, you cannot contain yourself '.[1] The prisoner defended himself with great dexterity, and though there

[1] *State Trials*, Vol. 4, col. 1313.

could have been little doubt of his guilt, he was found not guilty by a sympathetic jury :

'Immediately the whole multitude of people in the Hall, for joy of the Prisoner's acquittal, gave such a loud and unanimous shout, as is believed was never heard in Guildhall, which lasted for about half an-hour without intermission ; which made the Judges for fear turn pale, and hang down their heads ; but the Prisoner stood silent at the bar, rather more sad in his countenance than he was before.'[1]

His acquittal was a blow to the Government. Nevertheless it was some time before he was permitted to leave the Tower.

A Year of Forgeries

The year 1649 was a year of forgeries, and it was chiefly in order to prevent their recurrence that the new Act was passed. As Cromwell had been freely charged with responsibility for 'Doleman's book', *Royal Tyrannies Discovered*, Dr. Caryes' book, Bishop Sales' book, *The key of paradice*, the book printed by Francis Ash, together with numerous 'papists and jesuites works'—so the child of another man's brains was laid on the royal door-step ; the *Eikon Basilike* was issued as being the work of the dead king, though it was almost certainly written not by Charles at all but by Dr. Gauden.[2] *The Impartial Intelligencer* for 21-28 March reported 'Mr. *Thomas Goodwin* was angry that Mr. *Playford* 'fathered Mr. *Braynes* visions upon him to countinance ' that forgery ',[3] James Howell was likewise indignant that *A Perfect Description of the People and Country of Scotland*

[1] *Ibid., col.* 1405.

[2] Here I am indebted to the researches of Professor J. W. Williams of St Andrews University.

[3] B.M., 669 f.14 (5)—*A Vision which one Mr. Brayne, one of the Ministers of Winchester, had in Sept.* 1647. (MS. note by Thomason : ' Said to be made by Mr. Hugh Peeters, and made in February '.) *Printed* for *John Playford.* For further particulars regarding the career of Playford see *supra*, page 170.

should have been published as his when it was none of his composition. A less important person, T. Broad, the York printer, denied having printed certain papers of doubtful loyalty which were popularly supposed to have come from his printing-press.[1]

In every case a note from the injured party disclaiming responsibility was permitted to appear in one or more of the official news-books : but with regard to the *Eikon Basilike* the Government deemed it expedient to reply at greater length. The following paragraph was inserted in the *Briefe Relation* for 6 November :

' *From Paris of the same Date* [i.e. 27 October].
There is newly come out in Print here a French Booke, the Title whereof is, Memories of Charles the First, King of great Brittaine Written with his owne hand during his Imprisonment, whereby it appeareth that the Booke intituled, The Royall Portrait, is falsely Fathered upon him : At which Booke the Protestant Royallists here are greatly troubled, perswading themselves that the Queen her selfe and *Germine* have a hand in it, the rather because that *Mercier*, whose name is put to that Booke as of the Author of it is a creature of Jermin, who hath made use of him for to teach the Prince and the Duke of Yorke French, and it is thought, that they have done this for to gratifie the Papists, who are very much out upon that other Booke, because of some passages in it against their Religion. . . .

Concerning that reverend Idoll, the Booke fostered upon the late King, to which there hath been such Idolatrous veneration given, the World will be shortly informed whose Brat it was, or at least, that it was not his ; and so these Idolators will find that they worshipped the Painters Mistresse, for our Lady.'

George Walker had already done his best to prove that the King's book was a forgery. *Elencticus* scoffed at his efforts :—

' George Walker, quondam gentleman of Lincolne Inne, formerly pretended to be a Royallist, now shows himself traitor and apostate by endeavouring to prove that unparalleled book of the king's, none of his, but a doctor's which he neither knows nor names, nor yet inserteth his own name to justifie the cursed pamphlet.'[2]

[1] *A Modest Narrative of Intelligence*, 4-11 August, 1649.

[2] *M. Elencticus*, 10-17 Sept., 1649.

195

But something more than the best that George Walker could do was required. John Milton, whose views on the freedom of the press and on divorce had been no bar to his appointment as Latin Secretary to the Council of State, was invited to supply the final answer to the *Eikon Basilike* : which he did with his *Eikonoklastes*. It was advertised in the official news-books, the writers of which claimed that ' it removed the gold from that Idol, and sufficiently and ' clearly laid open that gross hypocrisie, and incongruity ' between those specious professions and the late king's ' constant practise '.[1]

Thus it may be seen what use the Government was prepared to make of the press. Had anyone been bold enough to risk conclusions with Milton in a further battle of wits, he would, most probably, have found the press closed against him and the new set of licensers adamant.

There is no doubt that by the end of the year printers were showing a quite unusual unwillingness to print unlicensed books. The new Act made the printers and stationers more careful, for each of them had been compelled to deposit 300 *l.* with the Government in surety of good behaviour, and for a while good behaviour was maintained by a natural fear of forfeiting the deposit. This sudden respect for the law was with many of them quite a new thing. It is reflected in the Stationers' Register in the increase of entries after September. No more than 6 books (news-books apart) were entered for August, only 5 for September, while 25 were entered for October, 15 for November and 18 for December.

[1] *Briefe Relation*, 13-20 Nov., 1649.

CHAPTER VII

1650-1651

News-Books Suppressed

THE old licensed news-books disappeared, not immediately but gradually : Robert Ibbitson and John
Clowes, for instance, did not cease printing *Perfect Occurrences* till February, 1650, when a warrant was issued for
their arrest.[1] There seemed to be a general reluctance to
disband, which was only removed by the tact of the Government in appointing several of the former news-writers to
the staff of the official gazettes. The hardier (i.e. royalist)
diurnals offered a more stubborn resistance. *The Man
in the Moon* retreated fighting till June, then at last gave
up the unequal struggle, having outlived *Pragmaticus* by
one week.

News-Books Re-Sanctioned

Strange to record, no sooner had the Government
suppressed the old licensed news-books than it permitted
them to be revived. Samuel Pecke the bald reappeared in
July, 1650, with a *Perfect Diurnall of Some Passages of
Parliament* (but whether or not Pecke had the Government's sanction, it is impossible at present to say), Border
with the *Perfect Weekly Account*, and R. Wood with the

[1] *C.S.P.D.*, 1650, Vol. 8, p. 16.

Impartial Scout (a venture inspired apparently by ' Parliament Joan ', the female beagle). These news-books seem to have had at least unofficial sanction for their revival, else the printers and writers thereof, whose names there was no attempt to conceal, would certainly have been prosecuted. On the other hand, none of them was entered in the Stationers' Register ; which makes it fairly certain that, though allowed to be printed, they had not the same official standing as the *Perfect Diurnal, Severall Proceedings* and *Mercurius Politicus*, all of which were duly entered. *Mercurius Politicus* was at first written by Marchamont Nedham[1] ' in defence of the Commonwealth, and for Information of the People '. His motto—' Ita vertere Seria Ludo '—would lead the reader to expect something more explicit and commodious than the brief relations with which (for example) Frost in his *Briefe Relation* was evidently quite satisfied. And Nedham supplied what Frost's exact and bare narrations left unsaid. For his services he was well remunerated, the Council of State voting him 100 *l.* a year as a pension ' whereby he may subsist while en-
' deavouring to serve the Commonwealth : this to be
' done for one year, by way of probation ', and a further
50 *l.* ' as a gift for service already done '. His services[2] did not end with ' making sport of serious things ' in his diurnal : he stated the case of the commonwealth in print[3]—anonymously for the better sale of his work among

[1] See *Merc. Politicus*, No. 31, 2-9 January, 1650-1, in *Burney Collection* (B.M.) : also numerous references in *Thomason Tracts* of same date.

[2] *C.S.P.D.*, May, 1650, Vol. 9, p. 174.

[3] See *infra*, p. 211.

those who had been prejudiced by his journalistic career—
and the Government rewarded his good offices with a
pension and a gratuity. It cannot be that he was popular
when B. Alsop the stationer, who was on friendly terms
with the ruling authorities, put his own name, as printer,
to a pamphlet in which Nedham was held up to contempt
and classed with ' those rambling protonotaries of the
' times, *Elencticus, Britanicus, Melancholicus* and *Aulicus* ' :

' Those counter-currs : which when men most shall Need 'um
Will bark on any side to shark their freedome.'[1]

The author of this tract exulted over the silencing of the
mercuries and from his undisguised reference to Nedham
it is likely enough that he would have rejoiced also in the
suppression of *Politicus*.

Distrust of Diurnals

Opposition to the news-books did not come solely from
the parliamentary side. During the last two years it came
equally from the royalists. No one trusted the diurnalist—
least of all those who were in the trade themselves and who
knew from personal experience how much ingenuity of
wit and how little regard for the truth went to the concoc-
tion of the average news-book every week. John Taylor,
the royalist water-poet, himself formerly a writer of news,
came forward with a pamphlet entitled *Mercurius Pacificus*,
which revealed him as a lover of concord and an opponent
of mercuries : he attacked them as one of the causes of
the country's disorders, finding parliamentary and royalist
equally reprehensible :

[1] *Hue and Cry after Elencticus,* etc., Feb., 1650-1, E.623.

199

' . . . the most of these Mercuries have been interwoven and mingled with truths, and falsityes, jeers, mocks, frumps, flatteries, scoffes, and fooleries, the spume, fume, scum, and froath of wit, and the very dregs of folly, not any of them but have exasperated War, Contention, Plunder, Bloodshed, and perplexities ; very few, or none, endeavouring or enciting to the Restauration of Peace, Tranquility, and Concord, for what end I have made bold to set Pen to Paper. . . .'[1]

Both sides admitted the existence of the evil. It was an age of false rumours. For instance, there were frequent reports that Cromwell had been defeated by the Scots and slain : premature thanksgiving services being held at Rotterdam, where the royalist ambassador McDowell (whose broad Scotch accent made his speech unintelligible to all but Scotsmen and Dutchmen), and Brown the ' Arminian book-seller in the Hague ', were not averse from propagating rumours of that sort. Charles, king of Scots, was at regular intervals reported as having set up his standard in England, and all the parliamentary leaders were knowingly rumoured by their enemies to have been unfaithful to their wives.

The Searchers

Repressive measures against the printers and publishers of false and unlicensed news were aggressively carried out by ' beagles fleshed by Mr. Scott ' of the Council of State. Best known among the searchers were Parliament Joan, ' a fat woman aged about fifty ' ; Smith a printer, ' a tall thin chapt knave ' ; Holt, ' with a thin payre of scratch'd chaps ' ; Matthewes, ' a cheat ' ; Jack Rudd, ' a figger-flinger ', and John Harris, who in his time had been an

[1] *Mercurius Pacificus*, 7 July, 1650 (E.607, *Thomason Tracts*), not being a mercury in the usual sense, is not included in the list of news-books given by J. B. Williams in his *History of Journalism* (Appendix).

actor and a printer. None of these descriptions need be taken for solemn statement of fact. There were times when the dreaded ' fat woman aged about fifty ' proved herself good-natured and kind.

The searcher had an ill-paid and dangerous task, as may be seen from the fate of the three messengers—' pursuivants'—who were sent to arrest Captain Marston the Leveller at his dwelling. Marston resisted arrest and slew the three men. He did it in self-defence, for (he said) the men had rushed boldly into his room and threatened him with their weapons. Now (admonished the *Man in the Moon* in his next issue) let that be a good warning for Holt, Matthewes, Rudd and the other idle knaves that forsake their callings to hunt after a poor diurnal.

The Growing Power and Self-Importance of the Printers

The printers of this time seem to have become more and more conscious of their own importance. They assumed an increasing measure of independence. Even Frost's printer, the printer of the *Briefe Relation*, was not content to take orders : he must needs better his instructions. Frost complained in his next number :

' . . . There was in the last a very great omission on the Printers behalfe, a broken story for a continued Relation ; an abuse not so much reflecting upon the Relator, as the eminency of that Person to whom it is related. The great merit of Lieut. Generall *Jones* had drawne from me last weeke, a very few Lines, extremealy short of his just commendation. The Printers Servant thought it too much, & therefore would needs leave out very near the one half, which the change of letter into a smaller Character, would have given him sufficient place for. I have for his fault imposed him this penance, in the beginning of this Sheet, and beg the Readers patience. . . .'[1]

[1] *Briefe Relation*, 8-15 January, 1649-50.

Again, it was not stupidity that made John Harris the printer alter the title of John Fry's book to which the House of Commons took exception in February, 1651. On his own admission, he did it ' to make the book more vendible '.[1]

The rise of William Dugard in the printing trade also illustrates the growing importance and independence of the printers. Schoolmaster of Merchant Taylors' School, he had erected a private printing-press from which had come impressions of the *Eikon Basilike* and Salmasius' *Defensio Regia*.[2] Hunscot was ordered to seize his press, and the governors of the school to dismiss him as a person ' unfit to have charge of the education of youths '.[3] Milton, it seems, was interested in the schoolmaster and through his influence in September, 1650, Dugard became printer to the Council of State and printed, *inter alia*, the *Briefe Relation*. Despite his manifest services rendered to the royalist cause, Dugard suffered nothing at the hands of the Government. Even his printing-press was restored to him (though perhaps Hunscot resigned it none too willingly), and no more was expected of him than that he should ' pay those who were employed in taking it from him '[4], and that he should conform with the press-regulations and, like all other printers, enter into a bond in surety of good behaviour. Like Royston, he was asked to pay 500 *l.* instead of the usual 300 *l.*

[1] *H.C.J.*, Feb., 1651.
[2] Plomer's *Dict. of Printers and Book-sellers*, 1641-67.
[3] *C.S.P.D.*, 1649-50, p. 568.
[4] *Ibid.*, April, 1650, p. 76.

Peter Cole further exemplifies the recalcitrance of the printers. He pirated a book in the privilege of Dugard in March, 1651. Milton complained, and Cole was called before the Committee of Examinations. There was no improvement in Cole after this warning, as the following entry in the Council of State papers for October shows :

' Council being informed that Peter Cole has a copy of a sermon which, if printed, would be of advantage to the State, and which he will neither print himself nor deliver to those who would, order that the Committee for Examinations, send for Cole, and examine him as to detaining the sermon in his hands.'[1]

That the printers were impatient of interference and not prepared to brook it is shown by an important tract published in November, 1651, and entitled *A Briefe Treatise concerning the Regulating of Printing* : *By William Ball*[2] ; from which it appears that, ' the multitude of printers being greatly increased ', the printers petitioned the Honourable Committee for regulating of Printing, that they would be pleased to report to the ' High Representative of ' this Nation, that the said Printers might be made a ' Fraternity, or Company distinct from the Stationers. . . .' Ball concluded with the hope that the printers might be willing to be ' subject to the good Orders and Constitutions of the Company of Stationers '. Philemon Stephens, Warden of the Stationers' Company, had petitioned the Council of State to ' prevent certain evils '.[3] What those evils were may be gathered from a study of Ball's tract on printing and printers.[4]

[1] *C.S.P.D.*, Oct., 1651.

[2] The importance of this tract has, I believe, been overlooked, and the tract itself is almost unknown. *Thomason Tracts* (E.1295). See Appendix B.

[3] *C.S.P.D.*, June, 1651, p. 267.

[4] See Appendix, B.

The Success of the September, 1649, *Act in London*

Although the risk of discovery was gradually increasing, printers could nevertheless be prevailed on to print unlawfully if there was a sufficient inducement to do so, as the post-script to the *Rebells Warning-Piece*[1] (February, 1649-50) will show :

‘ This foregoing Paper came to my hands by his Servant [i.e. the servant of Hoyle whose suicide the author of the pamphlet hoped might act as a warning to rebels], which I seriously perusing, thought it worthy the revealing in print ; to dehort others from the like, yet finding great difficulty in the Presse (which is ty’d up from delivering *Truths* in this nature) I at last prevailed with the Printer, (notwithstanding any Act to the contrary,) to Print and publish the same. . . .’

At the beginning of the year (1650) the determination of the leaders of the army, Fairfax excepted, to invade Scotland, revived the now almost forgotten question of the Solemn League and Covenant and raked the warm embers of the old presbyterianism into a sullen flame. Enemies of the Government’s policy had cause to regret the passing of the recent press laws. The author of *A Pack of Old Puritans,* surreptitiously printed ‘ by the Company of Covenant-keepers dwelling in Great Brittain ’, commented :

‘ . . . Be pleased also (Courteous Reader) to take notice, that had there been as free a passage for *Truth* as there is for *error,* and that the *Men* of this *Generation* exceeded not the *Prelates* for their strict *suppression* of the *presse* ; we had not onely followed him at the *heels of his first Edition,*[2] but many more able *Combatants* had got through the Presse into the *field* against him, and long since laid him flat on his back, and broke the neck of his *Printing pride.*’

But there were others who complained of the laxity of Parliament in dealing with the scurrilous pamphleteer.

[1] B.M., E.593.

[2] *i.e.,* John Dury’s *Considerations and Reproposals.*

One writer[1] could so interpret the situation as to utter a lament for the good old days when pamphleteers were soundly lashed for lashing others. Alas, those Nectar years had passed—' O Times, O Manners ! ' Existing records show that during the period 1650-1 there were not a great many prosecutions under the press act, too few to satisfy the author of *New news from the Old Exchange*. The truth is that in London the new Act was working fairly successfully.

Unlicensed Pamphlets in the Provinces

The mayor of Sarum sent a letter to the Commons on the first of March, 1650, with a book enclosed, *The Doctrine of the Fourth Commandmant deformed by Popery, reformed and restored to its primitive Purity*. The mayor was thanked for his care in seizing copies of the said book, and within a week Gertrude Dawson the printer, and John Hide the author, were involved in trouble with the authorities, while copies of the book were burnt at the Exchange in Cheapside. It was only to be expected that resistance to the press laws would come from the provinces as well as from London. In June a warrant from the Council of State was given to William Thompson, stationer of Harborough in Leicestershire, to search for and deface unlicensed presses, ' he having ' complained of abuses and of inconveniences ensuing by ' hawkers and criers of books '. Justices of peace, mayors and constables were commanded to assist him in the work. By an afterthought of the Council of State he was six days

[1] See *New News from the Old Exchange*, March, 1650 (*Thomason Tracts*).

later enjoined ' not to make any undue use of the warrant,' and two stationers were found willing to pay 300 *l.* each in surety for the good demeanour of the said William Thompson.

The Ranters and the Press

The Ranters, no less than the Levellers, found the press closed to them, and Lawrence Clarkson was banished out of the Commonwealth for venting his ranting principles in an unlicensed book, *A Single Eye.* The Commons expressed their gratitude to the person who had discovered Clarkson as the author of the ranting book by rewarding him with the sum of ' twenty marks out of the Box '. Another ranter, Abiezer Coppe, ignoring the laws for the regulation of the press, published *The Fiery Flying Roll.* The godly were outraged by the heresies it contained. Coppe was sent for, and the Committee of Examinations interviewed him. The interview is thus described in the *Weekly Intelligencer :*[1]

'. . . I had almost forgot to acquaint you with the arrogant and wild deportment of Mr. *Copp* the great Ranter, who made the *Fiery Roll*, who being lately brought before the Committee of Examinations, refused to be uncovered, and disguised himself into a madnesse, flinging Apples and Pears about the roome, whereupon the Committee returned him to Newgate from whence he came.'

No doubt Mr. Coppe returned to Newgate well satisfied that he had registered a strong and memorable, if unusual, protest against the refusal of the Government to grant the freedom of the press to himself and his fellow ranters. He had no difficulty in getting his next book published. Indeed

[1] 1-8 October, 1650.

it was advertised in *Mercurius Politicus* (10-17 July, 1651) as ' a peece very worthy of observation '. It was entitled *Copp's Return to the Way of Truth written by Abiezer Coppe, recanting all errors*. The licensers were satisfied that Coppe had merited their *imprimatur*, the godly that the back-slider was fully restored.

In the matter of John Fry's *The Clergy in their True Colours* and *The Accuser Shamed*, it was once again the godly rather than the executors of the press laws who were disturbed. The Committee of Plundered Ministers, called upon by the Commons to ' state the Exceptions against the first book ', stated that there were two ; namely, that Fry ' had published in print an accusation made *viva voce* ' only, in the House by a member of parliament, naming ' and reproaching the said member ', which was an intoler-able breach of custom and good form ; he had also denied the Holy Trinity, which was blasphemy. He denied the second and admitted the first of these charges. John Harris, the printer of the *Accuser Shamed*, was sent for, and his evidence is interesting. Asked to produce a copy of the book, he said that it was not usual for printers to retain copies of books they had printed ' unless the copies ' they print be matter of controversy, and licensed, and ' that business of this nature, as pamphlets, they never ' keep '. He knew not how many of them he had printed, but ' the ordinary number of such things as they print was one thousand '.[1] John Fry lost his seat in the House, and Harris fell into temporary disfavour.

[1] *H.C.J.*, Feb., 1650-1.

This surely cannot have been ignorance on the part of John Harris, whose periodic incursions upon the authors and printers of small unlicensed pamphlets, such as news-books, imply some slight acquaintance at least with the laws governing the press. It was unlawful for *any* pamphlet, uncontroversial or controversial, not to be licensed and approved before publication. There is a certain naivety in his confession that he did not retain copies of unlicensed books in his shop.

Buyers of Unlawful Books Prosecuted

Severall Proceedings (8-15 May, 1651) records the prosecution under the Act of September, 1649, of buyers as well as vendors of unlicensed books :

'. . . Some persons were apprehended for buying and selling unlicensed Bookes and Pamphlets, and divers have payed their Fines 40 *s.* a peece. A faire warning to all to take heede how they buy any unlicensed Bookes or Pamphlets : every person that buyes any unlicensed Booke or Pamphlet whatsoever ; though but a sheet of Paper of a penny, is by the Act of Parliament to pay his Fine, Those that are licensed have the Imprimatur of the Licenser, with his name.'

It might be added that some that were not licensed at all also bore the *imprimatur* of the licenser with his name ; for instance, the *Last Will and Testament of the Earl of Pembroke*,[1] an amusing satire, had printed on it, ' *Concordat cum originale, Nathaniel Brent*,' although it is certain that Brent had never seen it.

The Printing of Petitions

The most noteworthy of the prosecutions during this period is the one in which the irrepressible John Lilburne played an unfortunate part. A certain Josiah Prymatt, a

[1] In *Burney Collection.*

leather-seller, wrote a petition to Parliament complaining that Sir Arthur Haslerigg had unlawfully sequestered collieries of his in Durham. Newcombe, the printer, so far risked his own position with Parliament as to print the petition without having any authority for so doing. Prymatt presented copies of it to the members of Parliament. He was arrested, and in course of the enquiry it was revealed that Lilburne had been present when the petition was written. Honest John not only admitted having been present, but added that he liked the petition well : far be it from him to find fault with a petition that charged any member of the Government with tyranny and oppression. So pleased was he with it that he had distributed copies to his friends. The Government welcomed an opportunity of recovering some of the dignity which they had lost at the Guildhall in 1649 by the acquittal of the prisoner. *Then*, for very fear the judges had turned pale and hung down their heads :[1] *now*, they had the same prisoner at their mercy. They sentenced him to pay in all 7000 *l.* and banished him out of the country. Josiah Prymatt, though fined an equal sum, was permitted to remain in England—in the Fleet prison.[2]

The Licensers and Plays

While books like the *Fiery Flying Roll*, the *Accuser Shamed*, the *Single Eye*, the *History of Independency*, Prymatt's petition and the royalist news-books were beyond hope of receiving an *imprimatur*, the licensers,

[1] See *supra*, p. 193.
[2] *H.C.J.*, Dec., 1651.

though stage plays had been suppressed, had apparently
no objection to books of plays or poems even when written
by confirmed royalists. *Gondibert*, by Sir William Davenant,
was allowed to be printed. Part of it had been composed
in a Paris prison, the preface at Louvre, and the postscript
in Cowes Castle in the Isle of Wight where the author lay
expecting execution. His life was spared, probably owing
to the influence of Milton, who knew a poet when he saw
one.

> ' But Davenant was releas'd, we know it,
> The man was pardon'd for the Poet.'[1]

The parliamentary news-writers showed great interest in
Gondibert. *Mercurius Politicus* in July, 1650, was apprehen-
sive lest the high Court of Justice, condemning Davenant
to death, should deprive the world of *Gondibert*, then in
preparation, and of a good jest into the bargain. His fears
were unnecessary. Davenant was pardoned, and in
December *Politicus*[2] announced that *Gondibert*, ' commended by Mr. Hobbes ', was at length published.

Salmasius' Defensio Regia

When politics were involved the Government was not so
broadminded. Salmasius' *Defensio Regia* was not allowed
to be printed or copies from abroad to be circulated in this
country. Every net was spread to catch copies of the book
that were being imported from Holland, but, though the
Gravesend searchers exerted their utmost efforts, copies
were smuggled through in large numbers. Unable to

[1] *Certain Verses Written By severall of the Authours Friends* (p. 21 of 3rd
part of *the Loves of Hero and Leander*, 1653).

[2] 19-26 December.

frustrate the smugglers, the Government decided to take the advice laid down in the *Areopagitica* and to destroy the influence of the book, not by burning copies in Smithfield or Cheapside, but by issuing a reply which should demolish its arguments. The suggestion that this should be done came from the Hague in a letter to the *Briefe Relation*.[1] The unknown correspondent observed that the *Defensio Regia* had in January, 1650, already passed into four editions :

' . . . it girds so much at Puritans and Saints. . . . it were to be wish't that one of that Nation [i.e. England] which he calls fanatick would take up the Buckler against him in a Latine Style. . . .'

Obviously the writer had Milton in mind. The Latin Secretary was asked to undertake the task, which he achieved with distinguished success. Salmasius was eclipsed—and copies of Milton's reply were ' burnt at *Thoulose*, by an Arrest of that parliament '.[2]

The counsel of *Areopagitica* was, however, not accepted *in toto*, for, although the Government combated in print the arguments of its enemies, it did not grant its *imprimatur* to their publications, as the Levellers were not slow to observe. The year closed with further complaints from them that ' the liberty of *Printing* was even more restrained ' than ever (except to books maintaining the most tyrannous ' principles) as the Book entitled, *The Case of the Common-* ' *wealth of England stated*,[3] and the like, which to the shame ' of these times were freely licensed '.[4]

[1] 22-29 January, 1650.
[2] *Mercurius Politicus*, 26 June-3 July, 1651.
[3] See *supra*, p. 198.
[4] *Petition to Commons* (by approvers of the Petition of 11 September, 1648), B.M. 669 f.15.(54).

CHAPTER VIII

1652 TO THE BEGINNING OF
THE PROTECTORATE

News-Books and the Stationers' Register

OF the seventeen or eighteen different news-books that
were hawked through the streets of London in 1652
there was not one that was definitely royalist in character,
though several were by no means friendly to the Government. Even these, however, appeared with more or less
authority. *Mercurius Politicus* and the *Perfect Diurnal*
alone fulfilled both the letter and the spirit of the law.
None of the others fulfilled the letter, though they may
have done the spirit, of the law regulating the press, for
nearly all of them were published by authority : *Mercurius
Politicus* and the *Perfect Diurnal* alone obeyed the law
which demanded that all news-books should be entered in
the Stationers' Register ' according to ancient custom '.
The entry of these two was made every week. There was
no entry of any other news-book during the year. The
issue of the *Faithfull Scout* for 30 July to 7 August, printed
by R. Wood for G. Horton, proclaimed itself ' Entred in
the Hall Book of the Stationers' Company ', but no such
entry was made in the Register. Why did the Government
allow its own carefully devised laws to be thus lightly set
on one side ? A likely explanation is that the licensers

themselves did not insist on the stationer visiting Stationers' Hall after the *imprimatur* had been granted. The licenser was satisfied with the book—and the visit to Stationers' Hall which the law enjoined seemed to be a troublesome formality. The licensers must take the blame for this non-compliance with the law, for they could so easily have refused their *imprimatur* to a news-book which the previous week, after being licensed, had not been duly entered at Stationers' Hall.

There are some slight grounds for supposing that the authorities ignored the news-books, deeming them unworthy of notice. The Act of 1649 had officially expired in September, 1651. The Government had hoped that it might set a tradition among the printers—a tradition of printing only what was licensed and approved—which would remain set when the legal mould, which had made it compulsory, was removed two years later. No such hopes were justified. The Stationers' Company was plainly incapable of regulating printing without continued reinforcement from Westminster. This was amply proved after September, 1651. By May, 1652, a new Act was in preparation for the control of the printing trade. In June the publishers of *Mercurius Politicus* and of the *Perfect Diurnal* respectively decided that there was nothing to be gained by the weekly entry in the Stationers' Register, and from that date till a year later news-books ceased to be entered.[1] The Government were evidently in no hurry to revise the

[1] N.B.—Except for two entries of *Severall Proceedings in Parlt* in January, 1653, and one of *Mercurius Politicus* in the same month.

law and to prosecute the law-breakers. The preparation of the new bill proceeded in a leisurely way and was not completed till January of the following year.

The News-Books Attacked

The printer of a slashing attack on current news-books, James Cottrell, was so sure of immunity from prosecution that he printed his name at the end of it. Neither he nor the author, Samuel Sheppard, was prosecuted—perhaps because the Government agreed that the mercuries had been not undeservedly lashed. The flagellation by mercury, however, was not continued. For the time being, James Cottrell decided to take no further risks, but although no further numbers were printed Samuel Sheppard could remain satisfied that the ' Scouts, Mercuries, Posts, Spyes, ' and others who cheated the Commonwealth under the ' name of Intelligence ' had been faithfully and soundly lashed in one number :

' No rest day nor night with these cursed caterpillers, *Perfect Passages*, *Weekly Occurrences*, *Scout*, *Spye*, *Politicus*, *Diurnal*, the devil and his dam. If the States have occasion for Souldiers, they may no doubt press a whole Regiment of these Paper-vermine. . . . Yet if these were the worst inconveniences that arise from these Weekly Juglers, they were something sufferable : but to see men grosly abused in their beliefs, the whole Nation deceiv'd and gull'd out of their money, by a company of impudent snakes, of whom (one onely excepted) I dare aver None of them was ever guilty of writing three lines of sense—They prey upon the Printer or Stationer, the Stationer on the Hawker, and the Hawker upon Every-body. . . .

' It would much refresh a man with laughter, to consider how these Rakeshames piece and patch up that abovesaid account which they weekly diffuse amongst the people ; *News*, and *this weeks news*. For they have more tricks in these relations, than a Cook of a Three-peny Ordinary has with his cold meat : first, he boyls it ; if he miss of good custom, he roasts it ; if that will not serve, he stues it ; and if he miss then too, he minces it ; but if in cases of hot weather he be prevented of performing all his pleasure upon it, he casts it stinking, and full of maggots, into the Prisoners basket, beseeching God to mistake that necessity which he had to rid himself of

214

stinking meat, for pure charity. After the very self-same manner, these cheating talemongers, if they finde any thing that has the least probability of truth, first they give you it at large, and with a solemn preface. Well, it goes merrily down that week, and is authentically dispersed in City and Country : but by your leave, when the Carryer comes up again, he findes nothing but the self-same thing abridged, or in another dress ; and the Parson, when he returns, complains that he is cheated of his money : so that he that buyes them once in three or four weeks, cannot miss of the whole time's Intelligence.

' They thank their stars, and congratulate their own good fortune, if any sad accident fall out, or Fire happen in the City : and if a Witch or Murderer be condemned to die, rather than he shall want a winding-sheet, they'll be so charitable as to lend him half of theirs, and thank him too. . . .'[1]

And much more in the same amusing strain. Samuel Sheppard continued the attack the following week in *The Weepers, Or, The bed of Snakes broken. . . . Six Cupping-Glasses, clapt to the cloven Feet of the six Daemons, who Govern the times by turns from Monday to Saturday Annually.*[2] Thomas Bucknell printed his own name on the title page which announced the author as S. S. Again neither the printer nor the author suffered for his pains. They could not have anticipated trouble, else they would not have printed their names on the pamphlet.

Democritus was the chief object of attack. It had long been a reproach to the Government that it had not suppressed *Democritus* for its deliberate cultivation of the obscene. *Democritus* professed no politics. Instead it retailed filthy stories which were intended to appeal to members of all parties. In August, 1652, *Democritus* gave offence to the authorities ; and John Crouch, the author, and publisher, was taken to task. His mercury continued with the name changed to the *Laughing Mercury*, and to the

[1] *Mercurius Mastix*, 20 Aug.-27 Aug., 1652. Brit. Mus. (E.674.18).
[2] *Brit. Mus.* (E.674.34).

first issue of the rechristened mercury were prefixed the following verses :—

> ' *Democritus* must write no more,
>   since some he doth offend ;
> They'll punish him upon that score ;
>   *Apollo* stand his *Friend*.
>
> Free Mirth is all I aime to write,
>   to laugh down *Lyes* and *Folly* ;
> To tell some *Stories* of the *night*,
>   to cure *Melancholly*.
>
> No *Law*, nor *State* do I offend,
>   in words, Writing or Action,
> No Plot, or evill do intend,
>   my *Muse* hates strife or *faction*.
>
> Now he strikes sayle, and must submit,
>   his *Quibbles* end in *sadness*,
> But yet perhaps hee'l study *Wit*,
>   to orecome *woes* with gladness.

Exit poor *Democritus* as dead as a dround Mouse ; and Enter *The Merry Mercury* his onely Son and Heir, that intends nothing more than Mirth, to please all, and to offend none. . . .'

A mock *Last Will and Testament* of Democritus was anonymously published, by which all his effects were appropriately disposed : his wit he bequeathed to ' him that never knew misery, or would fain see the inside of a prison ' ; which suggests that Democritus was imprisoned for his sins. *The Laughing Mercury*, 8-16 September, to show how little ill feeling there was, on his side at least, reported that *Democritus* read the *Weepers* ' with so much affectation ' that he had like to have overstrain'd himself with laughing ' at the ingenious garilitic of that blatant beast, that ' worm that but the other day crope out of a Pillory for ' his Pasquills—an AS.S ', he concluded. There was nothing bad-tempered in this flyting.

216

Counterfeit News-Books

It was clear that the Government was in no hurry to frame new laws for the regulating of the press, and the signs of the times indicated that the discreet production of an unlicensed news-book or two might bring in a large profit at a trifling risk. The revived *Britannicus* was immediately counterfeited, Samuel Sheppard had a hand in the production of several news-books that ran for the briefest time, and there was a counterfeit *Pragmaticus* on sale. A warrant was issued on 18 October for the arrest of the printer and publisher of the *Faithfull Scout*, and order given on 28 December for the ' suppressing of the un- ' licensed Pamphlets and News-Books that are published, ' as *Mercurius Britanicus*, *The Scout*, and others ', and ' instructions passed for the Imprisoning and punishing the Offenders '.[1] There were many who were glad to see the Government firmly handling the situation : among them was, no doubt, the author of *Certain Proposals Humbly presented to the Parliament, In relation to the Common Good of the People of this Nation*, the nineteenth proposal of which had been ' that a severe Law may be made against ' all *obscene, lying*, and *malignant Diurnals*, that are now ' familiarly published to the world, which tend not onely ' to the keeping *unfixed* of the peoples mindes from a ' *quiet obedience* to the Government, but do fearfully ' debauch and corrupt their understandings '.[2]

Even the *Moderate Intelligencer* rose from the dead on

[1] *Severall Proceedings*, 23-30 Dec., 1652.
[2] 3 Dec., 1652 (B.M., E.683.14).

8 December in order to ' castigate the looser transgressions
' of the Presse, which seemes enslaved to the drudgery of
' every Mercenary Relation '. He did not doubt his reception in an age ' which embraced news in any language, or
under any colour '.

A Leveller's Plea for Restraining the Press

The Levellers, champions in the cause of the freedom of
the press, showed no sign of subsiding into acquiescence
with Parliament's interpretation of the rights of free-born
Englishmen when their leader, John Lilburne, was banished
out of the country for life. Lilburne set out on his travels
in January, 1652. His disciples, however, had caught
something of his spirit and protested against the tyranny
which their absent master had lost his liberty in combating.
One of his friends, Samuel Chidley, printed, ' to satisfy all
his friends ', an attack on David Brown, a bookseller who
had informed against Lilburne. Chidley professed his
contempt for Brown and his admiration of Lilburne, and
printed his name on the front page of the pamphlet (obviously unlicensed) to show that he had the courage of his
convictions. And no one seems to have protested in the
name of the licensing laws. Brown's information, which
had been laid against Lilburne at his trial, had been already
published in pamphlet form : ' an idle pamphlet ', said
Chidley, ' presented to parliament to curry favour with
them '. Chidley's *Vindication of Lilburne*[1] from Brown's

[1] *The Dissembling Scot Set forth in his Coulours Or a Vindication of
Lieu. Col. John Lilburn and others. From those Aspersions cast upon them
by David Brown in his idle pamphlet.* . . . *Written by* Samuel Chidley
February, 1652. (Brit. Mus., E.652.13.) Brown was a Scotsman.

218

aspersions contains some important observations on the question of the freedom of the press. He thought Parliament would be well advised to muzzle a pamphleteer like Brown :

> ' . . . So its better for the Parliament to silence such Babblers, than to suffer themselves to be so disgraced, by having their praise set forth in scurrillous Pamphlets, such as this Authours. . . .'

There was one man at least to whom a wise Government would deny the freedom to express his thoughts in print :

> ' . . . As concerning the rest of the persons whom Mr. *Brown* inveighes against, though he name no man, yet I partly guesse whom he meanes, and what it is that distastes him, because that they would not give him money for printing the whimses of his owne braine, and such crotchets as they were ashamed of. Indeed if he had kept to their rules, and directions, and printed nothing, nor no more of a sort than they gave him order to print, nor foysted in his own tedious stuffe to the disparagement of that party of which he was a wise one, in his owne conceit, then he might have expected wages for his work. But when LIEU. COL. LILBURNE had written a matter and delivered it to him to print, and money to discharge the Printers ; he would be stealing and foysting in some mad stuffe or other, of his own, that would make honest *Lilburne* very much vexe an chafe, and then he would put it out againe, and send him againe to undoe what he had inserted. . . .'

To George Wither's character of the dishonest stationer[1] must be added this of the officious stationer. Chidley, pursuing the subject, pronounced woes against the printers :

> ' . . . Whereas the accuser saith, that Printing hath beene our chiefest weapon, and by that occasion, that wee have great correspondency with Printers, and some of us ready to print what we please against them.
>
> ' I answer, that my judgement is not for printing of heresie or blasphemy, or matter of scandall, or a lye but onely the truth, and I hold it one of the greatest abuses of the Commonwealth, that so many lying foolish Pamphlets have been, and are suffered to go abroad ; surely the Printers have much to answer for at the day of judgement, seeing for every idle word which a man shall speak, he must answer for at the day of Judgement, so farre am I from holding a correspondence with them, that I pronounce the judgements of God against them, saying Woe unto you Printers, for you have much to answer for. . . .
>
> ' Now whosoever readeth the last leafe of this our Accusers Pamphlet, will have occasion to think the man not to bee of very deep judgement, for though the Presse is free for all men both knaves and fooles, as well as wise

[1] *Supra*, p. 31.

men, provided they put their names to it, and the Printer his name, which is too large a latitude (as I humbly conceive) Yet our Accuser would have the Parliaments order to print against us, and layeth downe a positive Law, as if he and his family were a high Commission, or Spanish Inquisition, yea and worse ; . . .

'. . . he [i.e. Brown] craveth the equall benefit of the Presse, competent meanes of subsistance, and monies to Printers, but I hope the Parliament will not put, but rather wrest the sword out of such mad mens hands, and will not afford the like benefit to slaves by promise, as to those who have not made any such obligation, nor cast away the Commonwealths money to them, or their Printers, unlesse it were for a better purpose than to propagate that hatefull sinne of sowing strife amongst brethren.'

This is an important piece of evidence. Apparently, even a Leveller at times could feel that too great latitude was being granted to the press, and that it would be better if the licensing system were more rigorously enforced. But among his brethren Chidley could not have found many to agree with him. Nearly every petition of the Levellers to Parliament—and there were frequent petitions—contained a plea for the liberating of the printing-press.[1]

The Printing Trade

The printing trade could not complain of unfair treatment. Only rarely were the printers and stationers interfered with. The stern measures of September, 1649, had been laid aside now since September, 1651, and the Stationers' Company had been left to control its own affairs according to its traditions and privileges based on former Acts of Parliament. In 1652 there was not a single noteworthy prosecution under the press-laws till the month of October. True, the Government searchers were still needed, and on the first of March George Lewis, the beagle,

[1] e.g., *Constant Adherers' Petition*, June, 1652 (Brit. Mus., 669 f.16.50). But it is worth noting that the Levellers' Petition to the Government (July, 1653, E.705.5), which is a complete statement of all their grievances, contains no reference to the freedom of the press.

had rendered services which the Council of State acknowledged by a gift of money. But there is no record of the printers and publishers of the scandalous books, for the discovery of which George Lewis was remunerated, being penalised for their offences. Not a printer or a stationer was in gaol.

Also, the Government showed itself ready to overlook the past sins of penitent printers. William Dugard the printer, in whom Milton had been interested, was examined by Committee for having printed the *Catechisis Ecclesiarum Poloniae*, the Racovian catechism[1] which, according to Parliament, was full of blasphemies. He was found guilty, the book was suppressed and copies were burned at the Old Exchange in April. It might have been supposed that thereafter Dugard would have had to wait long before he was restored to favour, that he would have had to go softly all his days and at the end maybe regain only a little of the former confidence that he had enjoyed. But his indiscretions did not deprive him of any of his privileges. Two months later he was specially invited by the Council of State, whose printer he was, to print the *Mare Clausum*, to reserve two hundred copies for the use of the members of the Council, and he was later asked to accept a hundred pounds for his trouble. There was, it is evident, no ill-feeling on either side.

[1] *A Beacon Set On Fire* (21 Sept.) stated that even after the Racovian book had been banned certain bold stationers reprinted it. The authors of the *Beacon* lamented :—' But alas, there is no standing penal Law (that gives sufficient encouragement to the Prosecutor, and investeth the Master and Wardens of the Company of *Stationers,* or some others, with sufficient Authority) to deter men from Writing Printing and Publishing the like for the future. . . .'

A Powerless Parliament

Nothing that Parliament did availed to prevent the printing and dissemination of scandalous books since September, 1651, when the Act of September, 1649, lapsed. It was a powerless Parliament ; which is not surprising, seeing that it had been purged so often, added to and subtracted from, called, dismissed and recalled so often. It hardly knew its own constitution, what it was or where it stood. It had little authority apart from the sword that hung at Cromwell's side. At any moment this small handful of men sitting at Westminster in the name of the English people might be asked to leave the House. Others before them had had to go. Everything was unsettled ; and a Government unsettled and with an uncertain tenure of office is a Government in name only. It has no power, and there was no real Government till Cromwell became Lord Protector.

With a glut of pamphlets on the market there was work for more and more hawkers. In former days (i.e. before September, 1649) they had come roaring down the streets, and windows above had been opened and heads thrust out to catch the latest buzz of intelligence. Then when the 1649 Act lapsed they returned, and by 1652 they had definitely become a nuisance to householders who liked the streets to be kept quiet. There was no modification of the roaring. *Pragmaticus* said that the only way to silence the hawker was to buy up his stock :

'. . . such is the restless noise of your subsizers through the whole City, that Gentlemen even in their own defence, are constrained to buy up your pamphlets, to prevent the hazard of being struck deafe with the lamentable cries of the paper-mongers.'[1]

[1] 18-25 May, 1652.

The Press Abroad

If there was little control of the press in England there was less abroad : for instance, at the Hague there was a daily production of pamphlets against the English Parliament. English rhymers at the Hague brought out innumerable scurrilous verses in which England was always known as Hell, and the Council of State as a conclave of superior devils. *Mercurius Politicus'* correspondent from the Hague kept English readers well posted with news of this sort. He thought it strange that such seemingly wise men as the Governors were should permit and countenance such stuff to pass the press and streets without control.[1]

A Stationer's Apology to Hugh Peters

The most libelled man in England at the moment was Hugh Peters, Cromwell's chaplain. Anonymous pamphleteers accused him of every kind and degree of wickedness. Many of these squibs exploded in nothing more obnoxious than a merry laugh, and left not a smell behind. The age could appreciate an incongruously coarse jest concerning its dignitaries without believing it to be true or allowing it to lessen its respect for them ; but the charges brought against Peters were so vile and reiterated so often that his reputation was painfully damaged. It is a pity that they should have been anonymous. *The Weekly Intelligencer* (7-14 September) recorded for the thirteenth of September :

'. . . Mr. *Peters* preached yesterday before my Lord Generall at Whitehall. There were none that heard him but cried down the libels spoken and printed against him.'

[1] See *Mercurius Politicus*, 15-22 July, 1652.

More significant was the publication of the following paragraph in the *Perfect Diurnal* (13-20 September) :

'. . . There have been lately such grosse falsehoods raised and published concerning Mr. *Peters* in Print and otherwise, that we cannot do lesse in his Vindication than to publish one of the abusers Recantation as followeth : A *declaration or Recantation by* Robert Eeles, *touching a scandalous Pamphlet lately by him published.*

" Whereas I did lately disperse some malicious base scandalous Pamphlets of an *Hue and Cry* and *Peters Keys*, &c., and in it very filthy and lying scandals, which were brought to me by one *Acton*, by whom I was seduced, and he is now fled out of the way, that I know not where to find him. These are to certifie to the world, that I do acknowledge that I have done Master *Peters* so much wrong that I am ashamed, and confesse I am not able to give him satisfaction ; but do blesse God that hath put it into his heart to passe by so intollerable an injury ".'

The same retraction was published in *Severall Proceedings* as well, and the apology was, of course, accepted.

The Increase of Unlawful Religious Books

Of great interest is the sudden recrudescence of popish literature in this country in 1652. The law of the land was against it on every point and the press regulations should have been sufficient to prevent the printing at home or the importation from abroad of popish books. During the year, however, thousands of such books were not only circulated but even printed and bound in puritan England. There was an influx, too, of cheap and inaccurate foreign editions of the Bible. A warning against them was officially published in *The Weekly Intelligencer*, 6-13 April :

'. . . Whereas there have been, and now are great multitudes of Bibles printed beyond the Seas, and imported into this Common wealth, known to Booksellers by these termes, in *octavo duodecimo*, and *vigessimo quarto*, which Books upon examination have been found to be so extreme false, and so full of grosse errors, that heretofore they have been suppressed, and by authority seized upon, and taken away, yet notwithstanding, there are now great numbers of them bound up under hand, and by stealth, which Bibles are not only basely printed, and imperfect, but also are imperfectly bound up, that they cannot last to do good service, and are sold in **Tavernes,** **Alehouses,** and **Inns,** by **Hawkers,** **Pedlars,** and such like. It is thought fit to give notice to all, that all men may beware of the deceit, and withall to take notice, that being bound they are sold at two shillings a book or under, so that they may be discried as well by the very price, as by the false binding, which, God assisting, will be redressed by the Parliament, and State, and such a course taken, as the Common-wealth may no longer be abused in a very short juncture of time.'

The ' Beacon Firers '

The privileged stationers were, whatever their religion, likely to be profoundly disturbed at this shameless under-cutting of their privileges. But they were even more disturbed by this unauthorised printing and publishing of thousands of popish books. Several of the more important of the stationers found it necessary to protest to Parliament against the consequent shaking of the faith once delivered to the saints and of the privileges once delivered to the Stationers' Company. The protesting stationers were Luke Fawne, Samuel Gellibrand, Joshua Kirton, John Rothwell, Thomas Underhill and Nathaniel Webb, and their printed protest, which ran to sixteen pages, was entitled *A Beacon Set On Fire*[1] and published on 21 September with an *Index Expurgatorius* of popish books specified at the end. The stationers pointed out, quite rightly, that while the people of God in this country, that is to say, the Protestants, were using up their energies in disputing among themselves about lesser points in Divinity or else in destroying one another in civil strife, the common enemy, the Jesuists and Papists, had been indefatigably endeavouring to convert the country to the popish religion, and to that end had

[1] *Brit. Mus.* E.657. 14.

' taken the boldness to publish among the people of this Nation divers Impressions of several sorts of Popish books in the English Tongue, and printed in *England* within these last three years, to the number of (as we guess, reckoning 1500 to an Impression of each Book that hath been in that time printed) Thirty thousand at least : . . .

' . . . And although upon the Titles of most of the Books there be Paris, or other places beyond the Sea, prefixed as if they were printed there ; yet we, and all the Booksellers and Printers in *London*, that have seen or shall see them, do upon such sight know that they are printed in *London* : And the Founders of Printing-letters that live in *London*, do infallibly know, that the letters with which the said Books are printed, were by them cast and made in *London*. . . .'

Parliament was exhorted by all that was sacred in the Protestant religion to suppress such books and to amend, if necessary, the Act then depending, concerning the Company of Stationers and Printing, so that ample provision for the suppression might be made in the premises :

' . . . And to the end so good a work may be accomplished, and effectual means may be applyed, we shall humbly offer our Proposals (if commanded) how it maybe done, without any trouble or charge to the State ; In the mean time begging leave, that without offence we may say, we humbly conceive, that we shall despair of ever seeing a sufficient Redress in this case, unless the way of Licensing Books, by faithful able men that are sound in the faith, be strictly enjoyn'd and an equitable penalty layd upon all that print and publish, or cause to be printed and published, any Book not Licensed, and the said penalty to be recovered by any that shall prosecute the Offender at the Common-Law, with good encouragement to the Prosecutor.'

Parliament ordered the Committee of Plundered Ministers to consider and to report how best to attempt the suppression of popish books ; but the Committee moved slowly. Meanwhile *A Beacon Set On Fire* had created wide-spread interest. *A Second Beacon Fired by Scintilla*[1], a stationer, came out on 4 October corroborating the truth of the declarations made by the six stationers in the former pamphlet, and also ' shewing and setting forth the misery of the whole Company of Stationers '. The author regretted that a

[1] i.e. Michael Sparke.

226

Parliament which had made a greater profession for Reformation than any before had done, and which had formerly shown so much care in demolishing images, pictures in windows, and in burning certain notoriously popish books, should have done so little of late to stop the printing of multitudes of equally notorious and popish books, and that those who vented such books should have been either very slenderly punished or, as more often happened, discharged without any punishment at all.

He did not speak uninformed. He was a stationer himself, with over forty years' experience of the book trade, and he knew what he was talking about. As an apprentice in the first year of James's reign, he had bound popish books in Staffordshire and had learned to abhor Popery for the encouragement it gave to ignorance, and to hate the Papists for their frauds : in Worcester, too, and in Bristol, Gloucester, Shrewsbury and Hereford he had observed the activities of secret agents for the sale of popish books. The Government's tolerance was no less than an act of treachery to the Protestantism it professed to maintain. ' O consider, true ' religion is corrupted, and the misery of poor perishing ' stationers overthrown, and how every pedlar, hawker, ' running mercury, now hath got the trade of bibles, ' popish, blasphemous, conjuring, heretical, impious and ' slanderous books and libels '. God was dishonoured, religion outraged, the Government disgraced. What punish ment had Coppe received for his blasphemous *Fiery Flying Roll* ? No more than a mild reproof ! In Queen Elizabeth's day one was hanged for a book like that.

227

'. . . Have not I of late seen many *Books*, that had they been published in the Bishops dayes, how had a man *suffered* ? I know, and with grief I *speak* it, I heard an *Anabaptist* (as he professeth himself) affirm it to my face, when I told him I marvelled he would *print* such a *Book*, as he had then *printed*, and how he could in *conscience* publish a Book so erroneous : his answer was in these plain *ungodly termes*, he got by it, and well too ; I told him although a man got never so much, yet he should have a care what he printed, his reply was thus, if the *Devill* himself, should give him or bring him a Book that he was sure to get by, he would print it : so I left him to be the *Devils Stationer*. . . .'

The miseries of the poor but honest stationers were feelingly displayed :

'. . . Next look into *Pauls Churchyard*, how many have lived *bravely* kept good *houses*, invited, entertained *Clergy*, *Gentry*, and all *sorts* to their *Tables*, were able to give entertainment to men of *learning*, men of *parts*, *knowing men, travellers, strangers*, of most *Christian Nations*, and able to *entertain* and *welcome* any, and to give liberally to the *poor*, and who so well *respected* in *Court*, *City*, or *Countrey* as *Stationers, knowing men, honest men, pious men, men* in *name* and *fame* of *credit* ; and happy were the *strangers* that *travelled* these *parts* that knew *Stationers*, and now, now, now, *poor honest Stationer*, where's thy *glory* ? where's they *fame* ? where's thy *plenty* ? Alas, alas ! in *penury*, whereas yearly came a hundred, or at least eighty great *Dryfats* from beyond the *seas* with *Books*, now four or five *Dryfats* serves. . . .

' I dare say, and I have heard it, and from honest *Stationers*, that have had *brave plentifull Warehouses*, full *Shops*, *excellently stored*, and able to fit any *Customer*, and these have told me, and I find and know it to be too *true*, that they have not taken 20 *s.* a week, and their *Rent* to be paid was so much without *Firing*, *Beer*, and *Bread*, with much more charges, &c. nay I have heard others that have been excellent well furnished, that they took not above 12 *s.* a week, some not so much ; . . .'

A final exordium to Parliament concluded thus :—

'. . . Come and begin this *Reformation* against *base poysonous Popish Books*, against *Conjuring, horrid Blasphemous Books*, and Disorders in *Church* and *State* : Execute those your *Acts* (upon such horrid *Books*, as hath been Printed) also set out *Licensing and Licensers* : Look to *Pedlers, Hawkers, Running Mercurists* and sellers of *Popish Blasphemous Books* : you can do what you please to them that deny *Assessements* or *Taxes*, and presently *curb* them, and why not so to the abusers of *Printing unlicensed Books* ; and you that can punish for old *Primers* can punish for *Masse Books, lying, scandalous Ranting Books, Blasphemous Scurrillous Books*, for *poysonous Popish Pictures*, and for what you please ; you know a File of *Red Cotes* can command Taxes for you ; let this command your Ordinances. . . .'

There can be no doubt about the truth of all this. Parliament had evolved a licensing system which, had it been enforced, would have put a stop to the output of scandalous books. But it had not been applied with all the rigour of the law. Even the licensers themselves neglected their duty—no wonder the stationers neglected theirs. There would have been no need to talk of red-coats if the licensers had been faithful : or if the committees appointed to examine offenders had less been lenient than the Committee of Examinations was with Coppe, the author of the *Flying Fiery Roll*, who pelted the committee-men with bad fruit and yet managed to escape without a conviction. Truly, the Government had only itself to blame.

The Beacon Quenchers

The conclusions drawn by the six stationers and Scintilla were not allowed to pass unchallenged. The challenge, strange to say, came not from papists or from any who were friendly with them, but from the left wing of the Independent party—from Col. Pride, Lieut.-Col. Gough, Major Bridge, Adjutant-General Merest, Captain Kiffen and Isaac Grey, who on 8 October published *The Beacons Quenched* : Or *The Humble Information of divers Officers of the Army, and other wel-affected persons, to the Parliament and Commonwealth of England ; Concerning the Machivilian design of the Presbyterians, now carrying on by the Stationers of London, To bring an odium upon the Parliament and Army, Introduce the whole body of Presbyterian doctrine and worship ; To seduce the good People of this Common-wealth, unto the Presbyterian slavery, than which nothing can be worse. By Publishing divers Treasonable and most Scandalous Books*

229

(*a Catalogue of many whereof is here inserted*) *against the Honor of the Parliament, the Lord Generall and severall other worthy Members of this Common-wealth.*[1]

That is the title in full, and it gives a clear idea of the contents—neither William Prynne nor John Lilburne was ever more explicit in his titles. The six Independents charged the six stationers with being Presbyterians, and affirmed that it was a zeal for Presbyterianism rather than a purely disinterested anti-papistical passion that had fired the beacon. The sale of popish books was even said to form the greatest part of the trade of some of them ; yet they complained of the laxity of Parliament in dealing with such books. The Independent officers did not complain of the leniency of Parliament :

'. . . We presume not to propose, but we humbly conceive that your late former care of the *Printers name*, and readiness to produce the *Authors*, or *bringers* of their *Copies*, together with some convenient *Regulations*, cannot justly by any just man be complained against.'

Better to pray God to stir up faithful and able writers against Poperies and Blasphemies than to shut the press entirely against them : and if against popish, why not against presbyterian, writings ? The Independents confessed that they had found the prelatical bondage and the presbyterian slavery equally distasteful and thanked God for delivering them from both. Who but the Presbyterians, in the pulpit and at the press, had brought odium on the Government and been responsible for the scandalous besmirching of the character of Hugh Peters ? It was plain that if the Presbyterians returned to power the press would be free

[1] It was printed by Henry Hills and sold by Giles Calvert and William Larner. (Brit. Mus. E.678.3.)

to none but themselves. How different was the policy of
the present Government, who ' have disclaimed all other
' punishment for matters of Religion, and will not permit
' them to be revived under any image or shape whatsoever,
' the weapons of Fasting and Prayer being both more
' available and more Christian in such cases, than those of
' force and violence ! ' The licensing laws (the Quenchers
continued) were meant to be but mildly enforced. Scandalous books and libels against the State and present
Government would not, of course, be permitted, but great
latitude would be given to men of all reasonable opinions
to print what they pleased. ' And if those Books have 19
' parts of good Matter, and the 20th part Popery, it were a
' great pitty the much good should suffer for the little evill,
' as it was excellently said by a Worthy Member of Parlia-
' ment upon occasion of debate concerning the *Racovian*
' *Catechism*, who upon that reason passed his Vote against
' the burning of it '.

Like Milton, these Independents were in advance of their
age. *The Beacon Quenched* concluded with a suggested
index expurgatorius of presbyterian books, in imitation of
the *index expurgatorius* of popish books which the presbyterian stationers had drawn up.

A Fraudulent Use of an Imprimatur

The Beacon Quenched reproached Edmund Calamy, the
presbyterian divine, with having abused the Parliament in
an epistle prefixed to a book of sermons by Dr. Love which
he had licensed for the press. When the charge appeared

in print it led to a further revelation of the methods of contemporary stationers. George Eversden, a conscience-stricken stationer, addressed the following note to the Committee of Plundered Ministers :—

' *The Humble Acknowledgement* of George Eversden
    Stationer, Sheweth,
    That whereas I placed the *Imprimatur* of M. *Edmund Calamy* before the Seventeen Sermons of M. *Love,* which should have been only before M. *Mantons* Sermon preeched at M. *Loves* Funeral ; and whereas I put the Letters E.C. at the later end of the Epistle of the said Book, wherein I gave occasion to the Reader to believe that it was written by M. *Edmund Calamy,* and finde it accordingly charged upon him in a late Book, called *The Beacon quenched* : I do hereby acknowledge that herein I have greatly wronged M. *Calamy,* that he was not the Author of the Epistle, and I added his *Imprimatur* to the whole, and subscribed the Letters E.C. to the Epistle, not out of any malice to him, but meerely and only to make the Book sell the better, and therefore humbly desire this Honourable Committee to pardon this great offence.
                                                    George Eversden.'

The Beacon Re-Fired

This confession came at an opportune moment, for it enabled the six stationers to defend Calamy, the presbyterian licenser, from the charges levelled against him by the Independents. *The Beacon Flameing*[1] was published by way of animadversion upon *The Beacon Quenched.* The damp remains of the beacon were rekindled with fresh fuel. The stationers denied that they were engaged in the sale of popish books :

' . . . let us tell you, that we so little regard increase of Trade by such loathesome ware, as that we were quickned up for fear of that temptation to pray against the publishing and increase thereof.'

They would have it suppressed, and nothing allowed to be printed which had not first been submitted to careful examination by the licensers. The Independents were

[1] Written, according to Thomason, by ' Dr. Chenell of Petworth.' (Brit. Mus E.683.30.) 15 Dec., 1652.

mistaken if they supposed every bookseller and printer to be a competent judge of whatsoever matter should be printed. Nor was it fair to accuse them, as the Quenchers had done, of wanting to screw themselves into some office or monopoly for licensing, printing and selling books :

'. . . nor were we so foolish or presumptuous as to desire or ask the licensing of Books, its a trust too great for such as we or you either.'

The Beacon-firers found themselves in disagreement with the mild gentleman who had pleaded with Parliament to spare the *Racovian Catechism*, though they were guarded in what they said :

'. . . Whether that Gentleman spake excellently in the Parliament House or no, we have learned better than to pass our censure, especially considering that his speech was against the sence of the House. Certainly the time will come, that the secret debates of the Members of the Supreme Councell shall not be commended or censured without the walls of the Senate House by private men in publique print.'

The stationers concluded by reaffirming ' the necessity of ' the Parliament's regulating the exorbitancy of the press, ' as the only way to prevent the publishing of such books as ' tended to the dishonour of God and disturbance of the ' State '.

The Laxity of the Government

It will be seen that, on one point at least, both sides were agreed ; namely, that the Government had dealt leniently with those who broke the press-regulations.

That does not mean that there were no prosecutions of offenders. The authors, publishers and printers of several scandalous but not very important pamphlets were summoned to appear before the Council of State ; but William Lilly, the almanack writer, was the only person of note to be prosecuted during the year 1652. For many years he had printed his prognostications for every new year. His was a long-established and, to judge from the numerous counterfeits, a lucrative business. The political prejudice which coloured his astrological observations had earned him many enemies. Even those who shared his politics—he was a vigorous parliamentarian—were sometimes offended by him, but though there had been many complaints raised against him, he had till then escaped prosecution. Official record of the trial is wanting, but there is no doubt that it took place. On 3 November Robert Eeles printed *Strange Predictions*,[1] which began thus :

> ' *Will Lilly* being taken as Prisoner of late
> Most strange alterations doth Prognosticate.'

An issue of the *Laughing Mercury* for the same day confirms the report.

> ' . . . Mr. *Lil-ly* the Ass-strologician being now Try'd for his *Predictions*, desires but till the end of the next year, 1653, to prove his Writings true ; . . . could he have fore-seen Events to come, he had certainly fore-seen and shunned the *mischiefs* ready to fall on himself.'

And *Severall Proceedings* noted, but did not comment on, the appearance of Lilly before a Committee of Parliament. It seems that the inquiry was conducted at the request of divers London ministers who held that there was a certain impiety in the assumption of Lilly and his fellow astrologers that Providence confided its secrets to the stars, that the mysteries of the future could be read by star-light, and that the Lillys, the Whartons and the Culpepers, by studying the planetary system, knew more about things to come than did divines who studied the Prophets. It was a source of

[1] *Brit. Mus.* 669. f.16.69.

great amusement to Lilly's enemies that he should, at length, have been called to account and it added to the prestige of the Government.

Lilly did not suffer alone. Wharton was examined for ' something prejudicial to the Common wealth ' which appeared in his almanack for the same year, and Culpeper's book was narrowly scrutinised by the Committee of Examinations. The prosecutions, however, were few and, that of Lilly excepted, of little importance and less interest.

THE ACT OF 7 JANUARY, 1653

The new Act for the regulating of printing became law on 7 January, 1653. It had taken a long time preparing. The first draft of it had been submitted to Parliament as far back as June. In October it had to be deferred because the printers knew nothing of its provisions. Said *The Weekly Intelligencer*, 28 Sept.—5 Oct., ' The Act for the ' Regulation of Printing was this Day called upon, but it ' being informed, that many Printers who were interested in ' it, had not the least knowledge of it, it was deferred ' to another Day '. (For the complete text of the Act and a list of rejected amendments, see Appendix, C.)

In the preamble Parliament professed to believe that the Act of 1649 had been a success, and that if it were revived it needed only a few additions to make it effective again. It was accordingly revived, with one important addition to it. The new clause provided that control of the mystery of printing and printers should rest with the Council of State, who were empowered to impose their will on the Stationers'

Company, the Master and Wardens being answerable to them. Thus the Stationers' Company lost its autonomy and became a Government department. It must not be supposed that the stationers objected. Probably that was just what they desired ; for thereafter their privileges and rights were guaranteed by the Council of State.[1]

The new relationship of the Council of State and the Stationers' Company brought about by the Act was in itself a proof of the Government's determination to enforce the press regulations. As the presbyterian stationers had pointed out, it could see that its laws with regard to taxes and assessment were upheld, so why not those concerning the press ? The new Act was the answer to that question. It was not more oppressive than previous Acts. The difference is that there was a more systematic attempt to apply it : for instance, Richard Moon published certain seditious books, and, to his surprise no doubt, found himself in the Gate-house, where he was joined by Richard Moore, John Streater, and others of his fellow stationers who had not supposed that the Government intended its latest press Act to be taken too literally. But that is just what the Government did intend.

With full control over the Stationers' Company, the Council of State were able to set about the task of controlling the

[1] As, for instance, in the dispute with R. White, the printer, who had infringed the Company's copyright by printing almanacks. The officials of the Company, following the provisions of the new Act, seized White's stock. White's protest was at first apparently successful, but when the Council of State learned from *The Remonstrance of the Stationers' Company* (See Appendix, D) the true state of affairs, judgment was given for the Company, whose ancient rights were thus upheld.

press without let or hindrance. Committees appointed to deal with special cases were sub-divided into more committees. A committee of only two members (with, perhaps, a *quorum* of one!) was formed in October to examine offenders. There was work for the committees to do. John Speed was arrested for having written *The Parliament's Catechism*, a scandalous pamphlet, and other pamphleteers were detained on suspicion. But occasional squibs let off in back streets did no one any harm and attracted little attention, and so long as the noise was not heard in Whitehall, the Council of State did not feel called upon to set in motion the heavy machinery by which the press was controlled. *Democritus*, for example, whose sympathies were sometimes, it was feared, not wholly parliamentarian, was allowed to be as coarse as he liked so long as it was not at the expense of state officials.

Another Protest by Lilburne

One night in September hundreds of copies of a libel entitled *A Charge of High-Treason exhibited against Oliver Cromwel* were scattered up and down the streets in London. It was a calculated and forthright attack on Cromwell at the very moment when he seemed assured of the highest position in the State. The author and the publisher of the libel had done their work well, and before morning it had been widely circulated. Every effort was made to stamp it out and to land the contrivers in gaol: every cog in the machinery that controlled the press was set in immediate revolution. Some arrests were made, a few careless vendors, who could tell the authorities nothing, were taken and then released. The author[1] was not discovered at the time, though John Clowes and Robert Austin, the printers, were imprisoned ;[2] and the exertions of Humphrey Robinson and Joseph Hunscot procured damning evidence against James Wayte of Bedfordberry, Robert Hanham of Adling-hill, London, Thomas Lock and Henry Barnes, both of Sea-coale Lane, which proved them to have been the printers of the scandalous and seditious book.[3] They were sent to prison. The Council of State, who had the matter in hand, were not content to leave it at that. A reply to the charge of high treason was published on 20 October with the title, *Sedition Scourg'd, Or A View Of That Rascally & Venemous Paper, Entituled A Charge of High-Treason exhibited against Oliver Cromwel, Esq : for several Treasons by him committed.* The author said that the Government had none but themselves to blame for the inconveniences that they were suffering through the licentiousness of pamphleteers :

'. . . Nor indeed if a man may dare to speak it, are the Governours themselves wholly blameless for such inconveniences. For *Printing* being ever accounted among the *Regalia* of every Government, as well as *Coyning*, &c. it should be looked on with such a jealous and strict eye ; there should be such a circumspect care of prevention, and such painful pursuance of misdemeanours, as would be required against the most dangerous crimes. . . .'[4]

At the end of his first year of exile John Lilburne, who had been banished for life, returned home. He was arrested

[1] i.e. John Lilburne.

[2] *C.S.P.D.*, Vol. 1653-4, p. 436.

[3] *H.C.J.*, 11 Oct.

[4] See *supra*, page 1.

and put in the Tower. The information of several Government spies, namely Isaac Berkenhead, John Tytus and John
Bartlet, was published in July and Lilburne's intentions
disclosed. He had, it was said, poisoned the Duke of
Buckingham's mind against Cromwell and had volunteered,
in return for ten thousand pounds from the Duke and his
royalist brothers in exile, to destroy the Common-wealth
in six months, murder Cromwell and prepare the way for
the restoration of Charles Stuart. Asked how he would
achieve all this, Lilburne had replied :

' My Lord, Ile tell you how : First Ile set my Presse on work (for which
purpose I have bought one with a Letter at *Amsterdam*, which cost me thirty
pounds) and then Ile send my papers over into *England*, which by my
Agents shall be spread all over the Nation . . .'

Two days after the publication of this information
Lilburne, ignoring the laws governing the press, published
a pamphlet, *Malice detected, In Printing certain Informations And Examinations Concerning Lieut. Col. John Lilburn.
The morning of his Tryal* : *And Which were not at all
brought into his Indictment*. The charges against him he
dismissed as being the usual sort of rumours, and Berkenhead, Tytus and Bartlet as the usual sort of liars.

A more powerful defence of the prisoner was the anonymous *A Conference with the Souldiers*,[1] which accused the
Council of State of having published and circulated books
defaming him. The publisher's address to the reader
began thus :—

' Countryman, I pray thee take notice of two things in this place : first
that those lying and false informations lately published against Mr. *Lilburn*
are printed for or by the councel of States-Printers, or Booksellers, *viz.*
H. Hills, *G. Calvert*, and *T. Brewster*, and so in reason may be judged to

[1] 18 July (E.705.25).

239

be Printed by the authority of the Councel of State themselves, or by the
Authority of their Supream Lord, Master, and Creator the General.'

At the trial in August scandalous and seditious papers
derogatory to Parliament were dispersed : which gave the
Council of State further matter for investigation. The
attempt to stop unlicensed printing had failed once more,
and again it was John Lilburne who demonstrated to the
Government that it had failed. He had been the occasion
of much law-breaking on the part of others, and he himself
had completely disregarded the law. The last word, however, was with the Council of State. A full indictment of
Lilburne on every point was ' published by authority '[1] on 22
November, and occupied one hundred and sixty-four pages.
Lilburne was characterised as the greatest libeller of his
time—' honest men hearing of a libel against the state knew
' that Lilburne would have had something to do with it,
' and the more seditious, treacherous and barbarous it was,
' the more Lilburn-like ; that is, the more were they
' persuaded that the action was his '.

But it is possible also to regard him as a champion in the
cause of the freedom of the press.

News-Books and the New Act

As a result of the new Act, 7 Jan., 1653, order was largely
restored in the book-trade, the Stationers' Company vir-
tually became a Government department and control of
stationers and printers passed from the Stationers' Court
to the Council of State. This new orderliness is reflected in

---

[1] Written, according to Thomason, by ' Cann the sectary '. (E.720.2.)

the Stationers' Register. The news-books, *Severall Proceedings in Parliament*, *Mercurius Politicus*, the *Perfect Diurnal*, *Perfect Occurrences*, began to be re-entered in the Register. A committee was appointed to examine all who broke the press laws. James Cottrell spent several days in the Gatehouse for illegally printing *Britannicus*. The Agent for the Army replaced the Secretary of the Army as licenser of military news. Thus Gilbert Mabbott returned as licenser. In July Parliament proclaimed that it reserved to itself a monopoly of its own news, which should be printed by its its own printer John Field and by none other, and licensed by the Clerk of the Parliament.

The majority of twenty-two votes to seventeen by which the Act had been passed was too small to be satisfactory. There was no unanimity even among those thirty-nine members of Parliament who had survived the various purges administered to that representative assembly with the object of making it less and less representative, and who had kept their seats through it all. A bill made law under such conditions was unlikely to be rigorously enforced. The work of enforcement was delegated to committees. And on 6 August the ' Committee for the Poor and Justices of the Peace ' was asked ' to examine the Breach of the ' Privilege of Parliament, by printing the Proceedings of ' Parliament in News-Books or Pamphlets. . . . ', and to propose, if they could, some remedy for the redress of the abuse. The new Act had failed in six months.

There were minor prosecutions of news-writers during the

four months that preceded the setting up of the Protectorate. *The Faithfull Scout*, which had fallen into temporary
disfavour with the authorities in October, 1652, incurred
official displeasure again in September, 1653. It professed
to have been ' Examined by the Original, Licensed and
' Entered into the Hall-book of the Company of Stationers ',
but unless the Scout was referring to a Hall-book other
than the Stationers' Register, his profession was false.
There was no such entry made. A mocking paragraph in
Mercurius Democritus, 5-12 October, makes it probable
that the Scout was sent to prison for his irregularities.
Democritus at regular intervals protested that as for
himself ' he was sure never to intermeddle with State-
' business, he scorned that piece of pye ; no, no, his muse
' was as innocent as the sleep of a sucking-pig '—but in
November he was again in gaol.

In the same month John Cleaveland in his *Character
of a Diurnal-Maker* expressed his complete contempt for
diurnals and those who made them—' vermine ' :

'. . . I know not what *ignis fatuus* adulterates the Press, but it seems
much after the fashion, else how could the Vermine think to be Twin to a
legitimate Writer ? . . .'

The 1649 Act had succeeded, being a good Act, whereas
the 1653 Act, which was equally good, failed. The failure
was due to the weakness of the central government.

In December, 1653, Cromwell became Lord Protector.

CHAPTER IX

THE PROTECTORATE, 1653-1655

CROMWELL'S SOLUTION OF THE NEWS-BOOK PROBLEM

The Problem

THERE seemed at first no reason to suppose that where prelate and presbyterian had failed the Protector would succeed. There was an attempt to print an unlawful edition of his first proclamation, the *Instrument of Government*, but, rumour of the printer's design having reached Parliament's ears, R. Wood was taken in the very act of piracy and his press broken.[1]

The Act of 1653 had already proved itself incapable of controlling the news-books, which failure continued to be demonstrated after Cromwell's accession. About twenty different news-books were being printed regularly every week and of these only *The Perfect Diurnal, Mercurius Politicus, Perfect Occurrences* and *Severall Proceedings* were entered in the Stationers' Register, and even these were entered, not regularly every week as the law had a right to expect, but once a year in batches of fifty-two numbers. The rest of the news-books ignored the Register

[1] *C.S.P.D.*, Vol. 1654, p. 309.

and got on quite as well without it as their more law-abiding contemporaries did with it. Of the several news-books which appeared for the first time in 1654 not one was entered. *The Faithfull Scout* continued to announce every week that it was ' Licensed and Entred into the Hall-book of the Company of Stationers' , thus assuming a virtue that it did not have. It is possible, however, that some record of news-books other than that preserved in the official Register was kept at Stationers' Hall, for other news-books besides *The Faithfull Scout*—for instance, R. Moon's *Observations*, April, 1654[1]—persisted in making the same claim of having been ' entred into the Register-Book of the Company of Stationers ', although no such entries appear.

The Act of January, 1653, had revived the law by which all news-books were to be licensed by the Clerk of the Parliament, Army news to be licensed by the Secretary of the Army, and all news-books to be entered in the Stationers' Register according to ancient custom. Only four news-books complied with this rule of entry, but as those that remained unentered continued to announce the name of the stationer responsible for their publication, it is reasonable to conclude that if the law had really been broken the stationers would not have thus incriminated themselves. But if the Stationers' Register was indeed the only record kept of news-books, then it is plain that out of all the stationers who published and printed diurnals only four

[1] See *Burney Collection* in Brit. Mus. The title in full is *Observations upon Aristotle's Political Government with a Narrative of State Affairs in England.* (No. 1, 4-11 April, 1654.)

paid any attention to the law's demands : the rest continued to ignore the law and still printed their names on every illicit news-book, thus letting the Government know whom to prosecute if it wished.

Mercurius Aulicus, revived in March, 1654, in the interest of the newly settled Government, provides in itself a curious example of the same successful disregard for the licensing laws. The following couplet was inscribed on its front page :—

> ' That Paper that great Cromwel's Name doth bear,
> Ye all will grant need's not a Licenser.'

Under that banner *Aulicus* promised to speak the truth, the whole truth and nothing but the truth every week and not to allow passion or interest to interpose :

> ' Lying is abominated by *Aulicus*. . . . Yet in these Times (wherein the Tongue and Press assume so luxurious a Latitude) He will not presume to interfere with Reason of State, nor the necessary Art of Government : To doubt of his Highness my Lord Protectors doing Justice, is an effeminacy of belief. . . .'[1]

Legally, justice could be satisfied only by the suppression of *Aulicus*, a news-book not licensed by the official licenser, nor entered in the Stationers' Register, nor announcing the name of its printer or licenser ; but justice according to the Act of 1653 was not done. The second number came forth with an arrogant couplet prefixed,

> ' A Licenser ! thou piece of ignorance !
> In my Lord's Name fearles, my Book, advance.'

The Provost Marshal for Middlesex and Westminster, whose duty was to repress scandalous pamphlets as well as to prevent riots, duels and abuses on the Lord's day, was given no encouragement. He was never certain of his pay.

[1] *Merc. Aulicus*, No. 1, 13-20 March, 1654. (*Burney Collection.*)

In May, 1654, he complained of being 280 *l*. 14*s*. 2*d*. in arrears: his six ' beagles ' joined him in petitioning Parliament for this sum.[1] A Government that did not pay its executive officers regularly had no right to expect its laws to be regularly executed.

Parliament Dispenses its own News

Experience had shown that whenever the news-books were laxly controlled false news spread rapidly as a result. The experience was repeated in 1654, and an old remedy applied. Parliament ordered (October) from an old prescription : ' some mistakes having been committed in ' reference to Parliamentary Proceedings, a Committee ' hath been appointed to consider of the manifold errors of ' the press, and it was ordered, that no man should print ' any passages of the House but by direction from the ' Clerk of the Parliament '.[2] Thus Parliament carried the Act of 1653 to a logical conclusion and proclaimed itself the sole dispenser of its own news. *Mercurius Politicus* became the official news-book.

It was the surest way to make the country suspicious. Anything might be happening behind the closed doors of the House. It was a breach of privilege for any member to reveal the transactions of the House. The Journals of the House had long been shut to the public, and when it came to supplying the Nedhams and the Henry Walkers

[1] *C.S.P.D.*, Vol. 1654, p. 170.

[2] *Weekly Intelligencer*, 26 Sept.-2 Oct.

with material for their news-books, the Clerk of the Parliament might not be 'in a vein'. There was an immediate proof of the country's suspicion. Single sheet versions of *The Speech of Colonel Shapcott in the Parliament House in behalf of K. Charls the second*[1] were multiplied and widely distributed. The speech, which was purely fictitious, was an attack on the Protector rather than an appeal for the return of Charles. Colonel Shapcott was aggrieved and acquainted the House with the matter, and the pamphlet was voted treasonable, false, scandalous and seditious, and the serjeant-at-arms was sent to seize copies. Troubles of this sort were naturally provoked by the decision of Parliament to be its own dispenser of news.

The Failure of Mercurius Politicus

English ambassadors abroad wrote to secretary Thurloe about the importance of having a thoroughly reliable news-book to circulate in foreign countries, a great number of the inhabitants of which were then 'infected with the 'scurvy disease of hearkening gladly to ill-contrived and 'improbable tales of false news'.[2] Pell, the ambassador, was plainly not impressed with *Mercurius Politicus*, whose version of foreign affairs was, although authorised, often inaccurate. The Government would, he thought, be well advised to have it 'thoroughly sifted and well circum-'stantiated before allowing it to be printed by public 'authority'.[3] The Government continued to pay Nedham

[1] 6 November, 1654 (*Thomason Tracts*, 669 f.19.34).

[2] Pell to Thurloe, March, 1655 (*Thurloe's State Papers*, Vol. 1, p. 159).

[3] *Ibid.*, Vol. 2, p. 47.

a hundred pounds a year for his journalistic services, and had a right to expect accuracy in return : there should have been at least one news-book of unimpeachable veracity every week. It seems that Nedham also gave advice to the Council of State how to make their control of the press effective[1]. In August, 1655, a stricter censorship of news was promised.[2]

Prosecutions of News-Writers

Democritus, 1-8 February, 1654, hopefully foretold that ' there would be a calm when the storm was over '. Evidently he was once more in prison. It was the end of *Mercurius Democritus*, but the beginning of the yet more indecent *Mercurius Fumigosus*. John Crouch was responsible for both of them—in the first issue of *Mercurius Fumigosus* he spoke of Democritus's ' resurrection from the dark and dolefull Grave of Porta Nova ', that is, Newgate. After his release he walked more warily and did not venture to sign the new pamphlet with his name. But he was not the only printer or stationer in trouble. R. Wood and G. Horton were both in like state. Horton and Huby petitioned the Protector on 31 March ' to save them from ' ruin : they had been three months in custody of Mr. Hol- ' den, messenger, for printing and publishing scandalous ' and unlicensed pamphlets : they were heartily sorry, had ' confessed all they knew, and promised never to do the

[1] See, e.g., *C.S.P.D.*, Vol. 1655, p. 139, April.

[2] *Severall Proceedings*, No. 261.

' like again but to make discovery to their utmost power '.[1] Through their information, others were discovered and proceeded against. In March, also, a woman was arrested for vending two unlicensed news-books, *A Perfect Account* and *The Moderate Intelligencer* ; she disclosed the name of the printer and he was examined.[2]

Thus there was an occasional prosecution to remind the writers, printers and vendors of news-books that the Government intended the Act of 1653 to be obeyed.

Religious Disputes in News-Books

By June, 1654, there were already several unlicensed news-books in circulation, despite the new laws, when the *Weekly Abstract* was added to their number. It appeared without printer's or licenser's name and was, of course, not registered at Stationers' Hall—but then neither were its licensed contemporaries (apart from the four mentioned above). The writers of news, also, assumed a larger measure of freedom than they were entitled to by law, and interpreted Cromwell's avowed doctrine of the liberty of conscience more generously than Cromwell intended or deemed expedient. The Quakers were attacked in nearly every news-book, most frequently and virulently in R. Wood's *Weekly Post*, and by Henry Walker : to which charges the Quakers replied in numerous pamphlets. Liberty of conscience was interpreted as meaning freedom for all the

[1] *C.S.P.D.*, Vol. 1654, p. 62. They were released on 6 April. Yet on 23 May Horton printed *A Declaration to the Freeborn People of England*, Lilburne's plea for *Habeas Corpus*. Horton escaped prosecution. (E.735.18.)

[2] *Ibid.*, p. 59.

numerous sects into which puritanism had sub-divided to engage immediately in a complicated and unlimited religious controversy. The children of light grappled with the children of darkness ; Anabaptist closed with Quaker, and the noises of battle reverberated in the news-books.

A Lost Petition from the Stationers' Company to Parliament

A draft ordinance for regulating the abuses of the press was drawn up by Parliament in June, 1654. After so many failures Parliament could have had but little heart for the melancholy task of preparing yet another ordinance, when so many perfectly good ones had been disregarded as soon as they were made. The Stationers' Company, however, had not lost interest : they produced a petition the text of which is lost, so that it is impossible to say what it was about. Most likely it was a piece of advice. *Severall Proceedings*, 3-10 August, related : ' A Committee of the ' Councell sate early this morning about Printing, and the ' Proposals presented by the Stationers were considered '. The stationers made no attempt to resist control by the Government. The prosperity of their business would be helped forward by the belief that the powers that be are ordained of God ; and when those powers were strong and assertive, authors of unlicensed books had difficulty in finding a printer. Hence *Mercurius Fumigosus*[1] in a rhymed litany besought the Lord to deliver him from printers as well as from the usual ' devils, serjeants, jailors, Ranters and preaching weavers'.

[1] 22-30 Nov., 1654.

Cromwell's Solution of the News-Book Problem

Cromwell turned Parliament out of doors in January, 1655, and became thereafter solely responsible for the government of the country. In August he had his plans laid and carried for regulating the press. His Order[1] contained nothing new, it was simply an order for putting in speedy and due execution the old laws. He had no fault to find with the former Acts which provided for an adequate control. The trouble was that, except during 1649, they had never been applied ; the control which had been provided for had never been exercised. John Barkstead, lieutenant of the Tower, John Dethick, alderman, and George Foxcroft were commanded to put the law into practice, and were given military command.

At once, so far as news-books were concerned, the law was obeyed. Only two news-books were to be authorised, *Mercurius Politicus* and the *Publick Intelligencer*—and only these two appeared. The others disappeared. The two privileged news-books were to be entered in the Stationers' Register—and they were duly entered every week. And that was the end of the matter.

CROMWELL AND THE SUPPRESSION OF SCANDALOUS PAMPHLETS

' Liberty of Conscience ' and the Press

The problem of reconciling liberty of conscience with a closed press had for many years pressed upon Parliament.

[1] See Appendix, E.

251

It became acute just before Cromwell ousted Parliament in January, 1655.

The publication of *A Twofold Catechism* by one, John Biddle, brought matters to a head. Biddle was made the object of a heresy hunt that was fast and furious and prolonged for over a year before the unfortunate theologian was landed in gaol. When his first book came out the Council of State commanded Dr. Owen of Oxford to see that Biddle was fully answered, lest the babes of grace be carried away by the wind of his blasphemous doctrines. John Biddle, however, persisted in teaching heresy. In December Parliament voted his books about the Trinity blasphemous, ordered them to be burned and the author to be arrested. At his examination he refused to betray the name of his printers, and was returned to the Gate-house where he was deprived of the comfort of pen, ink or paper. The printers were, nevertheless, discovered : they were Richard Moon and John Cottrell, men of a not unblemished reputation. Together with Biddle they were brought before the Committee, to whom they gave offence by refusing to tell their names or to give any answers. The Commons' Journals mention but withhold details of their ' rude and obstinate behaviours and misdemeanors '.[1] But none of them seems to have followed the strange precedent of Coppe who, being examined by a similar committee about his authorship of a blasphemous book in 1650, replied with a volley of fruit to their heads.[2] A special Bill for the punishment

[1] *H.C.J.*, 19 Dec., 1654.
[2] *Supra*, p. 206.

252

of Biddle was brought in, and the three men were sent to prison (February, 1655).

The trial and conviction of Biddle aroused great interest. Cromwell was now at the head of the Government. Biddle had been so vigorously assailed by Parliament that he gained a lot of sympathy even from men who were shocked by his blasphemous writings. Not that his writings were really blasphemous. They were heterodox in 1654, but would possibly have been welcomed to-day as a thoughtful contribution to Higher Biblical Criticism, though perhaps a little old-fashioned and conservative in places. The main charge against him was that he taught men that Christ was not God, to which he answered ' that he did heartily ' acknowledge Jesus Christ to be his Lord and God, and ' hoped in Him, and honoured Him, believing whatsoever ' he[1] or any other could bring him out of the Holy Scripture ' concerning Christ '. Bail was not allowed.

Men of all parties, from Anabaptists to Fifth-Monarchy men, suspecting a return of the spirit of persecution, joined in protesting. A pamphlet was published in July for (it is interesting to notice) Richard Moon at the Seven Stars in Paul's Churchyard and entitled *The Spirit of Persecution Again broken loose, By An Attempt to put in Execution against Mr. John Biddle Master of Arts, an abrogated Ordinance of the Lords and Commons for punishing Blasphemies and Heresies. Together with, A full Narrative of The whole Proceedings upon that Ordinance against the said Mr. John Biddle and Mr. William Kiffen Pastor of a*

[1] i.e., his accuser.

253

baptised Congregation in the City of London.[1] The author accused the Beacon-Firers of being solely responsible for the persecution of John Biddle. Friends of Biddle, he said, went to the Court of Aldermen :

> ' Whereupon being come thither, they there found certain Booksellers of *Paul's* Church-yard, *viz. Tho. Underhill, Luke Fawn*, and *Nathaniel Web*, notoriously known for their preposterous zeal, and former opposition unto Christian liberty, under the Name of Beacon-Firers. These men being called into the Husting-Court, and having there stayed for some time, came afterwards out again from thence, and went away ; but soon returned back to their attendance at the Door of the Court ; and upon notice given, were soon called into the Court again.'

Biddle, however, refused to discuss the matter with them, ' they three being his mortal Enemies ', and (added the author) ' men that would set this poor Nation in the ' burning Fire of persecution. Oh ! what miserable desola- ' tions would be made in this Land, were not Liberty of ' Conscience allowed ! It had been better for us, never to ' have seen a day of Liberty, than now again to return to ' Bondage '.

Cromwell had promised liberty of conscience, and when he dissolved Parliament did he not intimate this as one reason, namely, ' That nothing would satisfie them, unless ' they could put their finger upon their brothers conscience ' to pinch them there ' ! Surely he would not allow himself to be ridden by persecuting Presbyterians :

> ' Sure will his Highness and the Council now take these Men into favor, credit, and be their stalking Horses to carry on the old Presbyterian designe of persecution. . . .'

Cromwell's government was founded on a promise to give to all men liberty of conscience :

> ' and what is the Protestant Cause the Presbyterian Dominion and Lordship ? to force all People to be of your Opinion and Judgement. What

[1] Brit. Mus. E.848.27, July, 1655.

hath my Lord Protector gone thorough, Fire and Water ? the greatest difficulties that can be imagined for the sake of liberty of Religion, which he calls a natural Light, hath he not made this superceed all Laws, and Constitutions whatsoever in this Land, in opposition to such Men as these, and will he now give all away into their hands. . . .'

The author of the pamphlet concluded by reminding the Council of the clause in the *Instrument of Government*, ' That whosoever professeth Faith in God, by Jesus Christ, ' though differing in judgement from the Doctrine, Worship, ' and Discipline, publickly held forth, shall not be res- ' trained from, but protected in the profession of the Faith ' and exercise of the Religion, &c. And all Acts and Ordi- ' nances to the contrary are to be esteemed Null and Void '. *A Short Discovery of His Highness the Lord Protector's Intentions Touching The Anabaptists in the Army*, a libel which, according to Thomason, was ' scattered about the ' streets in the night about the middle of August ', declared that the *Instrument of Government* was not worth the paper it was written on if it could not save Biddle from prison ; and the Fifth-Monarchy man who produced the equally libellous *The Protector Unvailed*[1] (October) agreed, though he added that Parliament in this were not acting with Cromwell's consent, yet Cromwell was to blame for not interfering sonner than he did :

' *Mr. Biddle* was sent to Prison, and his Book burn'd ; and it was press'd strongly he should be put to death ; and none were suffered to come to him.

' Things being so, it was look'd upon by many who fear the Lord, to be very unsuitable to the dayes we live in, which should be dayes of Liberty. Whereupon, some Pastors, and several Members of Churches, being very much affected with it, after their meeting together, did agree to come to the Protector to complain of it, and to get a Redress. In the mean time the Parliament bore the brunt of all the hard Censures of the godly People for

[1] Brit. Mus., E.857.1.

these things ; whereas they did no other, than what their Principles and Judgements led them to ; and nothing less could be expected from them.

' Now if any were to be blamed for this, it was the Protector, because the fault clearly was in him : first, in giving way that such a Parliament should be chosen. And secondly, that he suffered them so long to go on in the doing of such things. . . .'

The ' Beacon-Firing ' Controversy Revived

The famous Beacon, first fired by Webb, Fawne, Underhill and their fellow stationers, quenched by Independents and Quakers and then relit, had been smouldering silently since December, 1652. The prosecution of Biddle was a reminder that the beacon-firers had not changed their creed. They still believed in rigid licensing laws. *A Second Beacon Fired* (October, 1654)[1] exhorted the Protector to suppress popish, socinian and quaker books, and to extend and enforce the licensing system. There is no proof that this appeal for licensing was itself licensed. But neither is there any proof that any book or pamphlet, apart from news-books and some few others, was licensed, since the licenser's *imprimatur* was not printed at the beginning or end of book or pamphlet. If the printer's name was published and the publication also entered in the Stationers' Register, the licenser's consent may be assumed to have been granted. The appearance of licensers' names, however, becomes rare in the Register after July, 1653 ; and a succession of dots is added to indicate the omission, the name of the master or warden of the Company alone appearing. A likely explanation is that the master or warden had become the licenser of pamphlets, having

[1] *Brit. Mus.*, E.813.1.

already become by the Act of 1653 a state official : and if
a book was not entered in the Register it must be regarded
as unlicensed. If that be so, then none of the pamphlets
contributing to this ' jangling controversy ' was licensed.
Yet each contained the name of the printer, which should
have made it easy for the Government had it wished to
prosecute. No one, however, was prosecuted ; which
proves how little the law was regarded. At the universities there was a strict censorship of the press, and in
London the licensing system was applied with varying
degrees of carefulness to news-books and to books of law,
medicine and astrology ; but the multitude of miscellaneous
books and pamphlets on other subjects were in practice
unhampered by licensing restrictions.   Printers were
obliged to put their name to their publications and expected
also to submit them to the master or one of the wardens of
the Stationers' Company, who, if he approved of them, would
enter them in the Register at the trifling cost of sixpence
per pamphlet. And if later such a book or pamphlet was
found to contain matter offensive to the Government, there
was no difficulty in discovering who was to blame : the
printer could say for whom he had printed it.

It was not a satisfactory state of affairs : hence the interest
of the Beacon-firing controversy. The Beacon, relit by the
Presbyterian stationers in October, 1654, was not allowed
to burn itself out. Beacon-quenchers set to work at once.
One, ' called after the flesh Francis Howgil ' and ' a witness
for the truth against Gog and Magog ', replied with a

quenching stream of denials mingled with abuse,[1] but he had singularly little to say about the licensing dispute. A month later John Goodwin almost extinguished the beacon with his *Fresh Discovery of the High Presbyterian Spirit*[2] which demonstrated to the saints that licensing was unscriptural. The pamphlet was not written with the same literary skill as the *Areopagitica* nor decked with the same finery of classical illustration, but it was no less powerful and enlightened a plea for unlicensed printing. The arguments of Goodwin and Milton were similar, their methods different. Goodwin was writing to convince the saints, therefore he kept to the Word ; whereas Milton examined the question in a secular spirit and in the light of political expediency. They came to the same conclusions. Goodwin found no warrant in the Bible for appointing anyone with a power of life and death over the press. A licenser he defined as one who had parliamentary authority for saying to the Holy Ghost, ' nothing which Thou ' revealest unto other men, be it never so much for the ' glorifying of the name of God, of never such worthy and ' sacred concernment unto the world, shall publickly go ' forth into the world, unless Thou wilt reveal the same ' unto me also, and make me a partaker of the Vision as ' well as others '. Then, further, who was to determine what should be regarded as orthodox, and what qualifications were meet for licensers ? Surely the Government was

---

[1] *The Fiery darts of the Divel quenched*, by Francis Howgil. Nov., 1654. (*Brit. Mus.* E.817.16.)

[2] See Appendix, F.

not so foolish as to expect to suppress heresies and blasphemies by such means ?   As well set a company of armed men about a house to keep darkness out of it at night, as set watchmen with authority at the door of the press to keep errors and heresies out of the world. Better to give errors and heresies freedom and fresh air—they would die sooner in the sunlight : permit them, they perish—forbid them, they flourish, *quod licet ingratum est, quod non licet, acrius urit.* Let them die of exposure. The surest and swiftest method of nullifying the evil effects of Biddle's doctrines would have been to allow him to state them freely, for then he could have been fully answered in every particular by men of greater knowledge and piety : the best way of dispelling darkness is to bring it into contact with light. Biddle would not then have been a martyr, with the public sympathy which martyrdom *per se* always commands, but would have cut a poor figure and his fallacious doctrines would have been unfashionable.

' Nullius Nominis ', as the author of *An Apologie For The Six Book-Sellers,*[1] signed himself, considered that Mr. Goodwin's tract cast foul and unjust aspersions upon six worthy Presbyterians, and he protested against the worship by Goodwin and too many like him of the accursed Idol of Toleration—the new Diana whose devotees were as disinclined to listen to reason as the Ephesians whose dialectical method had been to continue shouting ' Great is Diana of the Ephesians ! ' till they had drowned the arguments they could not refute. This was unjust of Nullius

[1] 28 Jan., 1655 (*Brit. Mus.*, E.826.8).

Nominis—it was Goodwin who argued and Nullius Nominis whose dialectics were lamentably Ephesian.

The controversy closed in July, 1655, with R. Moon's *The Spirit of Persecution Again Broken Loose,* which held the six booksellers responsible for the prosecution of Biddle—' a demonstrable evidence that the Presbyterian ' had as much rankour and bitterness in his spirit as ' Papist or Prelate '.

Cromwell's Intervention

On the twentieth day of August Cromwell gave ' orders ' for putting in speedy and due execution the laws, statutes ' and ordinances made and provided against unlicensed and ' scandalous books and pamphlets and for further regulat- ' ing of printing '. Pamphlets were to be licensed by such as should be appointed thereunto by Cromwell or his Council. Licensers for news-books were appointed, but no one except the master and wardens of the Stationers' Company seems to have licensed pamphlets in London—the universities, of course, had their own licensers.[1] Stationers

[1] Leonard Lichfield, Oxford's printer, acknowledged his indebtedness to Cromwell in some verses affixed to his edition of *Musarum Oxoniensium,* June, 1654 (E.740.1) :—

> ' . . . I want the Riming trade,
> My Art speakes through those Poets which I made ;
> I owne their Verse, only your Name can give
> My printing life, by whom all others live.
> Oh that I had the Pen of Fate to write,
> Or the same Ardour which you use in Fight !
> Then I might tell the World how great you are,
> And whil'st I tell them, in those glories share :
> But since my Fortunes made and form'd by You,
> Aske more than I can say though less than's due,
> Doe You, Great Sir, accept of what I showe
> As part o th' Tribute I to Caesar owe.
>   LEONARD LICHFIELD.

took responsibility for what they published. Every printer was registered and the law demanded that the printer's name should be printed on every publication. Presumably the master or wardens of the Stationers' Company could object to the publishing of any book or pamphlet they considered undesirable, but it is not recorded that they ever did. If the Government found fault with a pamphlet, the printer whose name was published on the title-sheet would be examined, and the names of the stationer and author soon discovered. Then the authorities would know whom to prosecute. The beacon-firers could not have been wholly satisfied, for though news-books were strictly censured, pamphlets of general interest were not : no one was specially appointed for the sole purpose of supervising them. It was left to the master and wardens of the Stationers' Company to do so, and presumably they had other duties as well to perform. Licensers as a class were unpopular. They were, said Milton in his *Second Defence of the People of England*, ' generally men of little learning or judgement '. The country would be well rid of them : they served a useful purpose in censoring the news-books, but they should not be allowed to interfere with the free discussion of other matters in print.

Cromwell's Tolerance

From the beginning of his rule as Protector Cromwell sought to introduce a spirit of tolerance in his attitude to the press. He treated Arise Evans, a fanatic preacher and author of pamphlets abusing him, with a kindness he did not deserve.

261

' The *Bloody Vision* interpreted by Arise Evans, was presented to his Highness the Lord Protector by the said Author, who notwithstanding the high invectives therein contained, proving that the late Parliament was the mark of the Beast, mentioned in the Revelations, and that the fift Monarchy should suddenly be established under the power of *Charles Stuart &c.* yet did the favourable clemency of his Highness extend so far, that he graciously remitted this imperious Representation, and permitted him his liberty. Nevertheless, when he departed, he went to White-hall, and there made Proclamation of what was published by him.'[1]

Walter Gostelo, like Arise Evans, presented a book to Cromwell in favour of a restoration of monarchy and the house of Stuart in particular, and in an accompanying petition added :

' Worthy *Protector* and Council, read, know, and see clearly ; the *Honourablest, wisest, best,* and *most considerablest people* of this *Kingdom* desire *Kingly Government,* the *Person,* none but him, whose unquestionable *Right the Crown is,* CHARLS STUART.'[2]

No harm came to Gostelo, although he assured the Protector that he would proceed with his utmost endeavour to possess all Christian kings, the Jewish Rabbies, the Universities, and the See of Rome with the book, and expose copies for sale in the cities of the three kingdoms.

Less fortunate was Philip Dancy who delivered copies of *Dissertatione Pace* at the door of the House. He was detained and the serjeant-at-arms visited the printers, R. Moon and J. Cottrell, in search of copies.[3] The book was regarded as likely to cause dissension among the churches. Major-General Overton, however, said that Cromwell laughed at abuse of himself by poets and pamphleteers and did not take them seriously :

' Objection III. But, say some, you made a company of scandalous verses upon the lord protector, whereby his highness and divers others were offended and displeased for your so doing.

[1] *The Grand Politique Post,* 10-17 Jan., 1654.
[2] *Brit. Mus.,* 669.f.19.66. Jan., 1654.
[3] *H.C.J.,* Dec., 1654.

Reply III. I must acknowledge I copied a paper of verses, called the Character of a Protector ; but I did neither compose, nor (to the best of my remembrance) shew them to any, after I had writ them forth. They were taken out of my letter case at Leith, where they had lain a long time by me neglected and forgotten. I had them from a friend, who wished my lord well, and who told me, that his lordship had seen them, and I believed laughed at them, as (to my knowledge) heretofore he hath done at papers and pamphlets of more personal and particular import or abuse.'[1]

George Wither the poet was treated with indulgence by Cromwell, who suffered his boring attentions with remarkable patience when most men would have repulsed him from their doors. Wither was not satisfied with the protectorate as a form of government, and in *A Declaration to these Nations* he signified unto Cromwell how a more righteous Government might be established. Wither's account of how he was received by Cromwell is remarkable, as it was published at a time when he was desperately anxious to be off with the old love, Cromwell, in time to be on speaking terms with the new, Charles, whose restoration was imminent. He says in *A Cordial Confection*[2]:

' Though that *Discourse* [i.e. *A Declaration to these Nations*] was very large, he with much seeming Contentment, heard me read it over to the last word ; and then protested, according to his usual manner, that it answered to his very heart, as the *shadow of his face* in the Glass (then hanging before him in the room) answered to his *face* ; and pretended he would publish that *Declaration*, and act accordingly, as soon as he with one in whose discretion he much confided, had considered what alteration it might need, (or words to that effect) and then received it of me, promising to return it with his final resolution within a week.'

Wither complained of Cromwell's temporising with the affair as though it were not urgent. Wither was not the man to admit on the eve of the Restoration that he had been well treated by Cromwell. He was kept, he said, in

---

[1] *Thurloe's State Papers*, Vol. 3, p. 111, Major-General Overton's letter from the Tower to a friend of his.

[2] 23 Dec., 1659. This tract has, so far as I know, been entirely overlooked. See Appendix, G.

constant attendance at Whitehall waiting to hear whether
Cromwell approved of the Declaration :

' [Cromwell] pretended many moneths together, a firm adherence to what
he had seemingly resolved on, keeping me all that time in attendance :
gave me the Key of his Closet at the end of the *Shield Gallery* in *White-hall*,
(wherein his Books and his Papers lay) to retire unto when I came thither ;
carried me often to his own Table ; frequently discoursed with me concerning my *Proposal* ; and appointed many set days wherein to review the
said *Papers*, but failed always in performance ; wherewith I being a little
discontented, told him, I thought his mind was changed ; and giving him
back the Key of his *Closet*, purposed never to wait again upon him in relation
to that business.'

The business was never attended to. Wither, however, was
otherwise well treated. He was given the Statute Office,
though he complained (in 1659) that it was little worth to
him because he expressed his thankfulness for it by declaring unto Cromwell ' those truths which he was not willing
' to hear of '. Altogether, a fractious, unquiet poet, defici-
ent in the power of self-criticism, better treated than he
deserved !

It was only consistent with his speech in Parliament
in defence of Prynne's servant long since that Cromwell
should now favour the giving of as much freedom to the
press as possible. On that occasion he had declared for the
liberty of the subject. Sir Philip Warwick described him
as he appeared then :

' his countenance swoln and reddish, his voice sharp and untunable, and
his eloquence full of fervour ; for the subject matter would not bear much
of reason ; it being in behalfe of a servant of Mr. Prynn's, who had disperst
libells against the Queen for her dancing and such like innocent and courtly
sports ; and he aggravated the imprisonment of this man by Council-
Table unto that height, that one would have believed, the very Government
it selfe had been in great danger by it. I sincerely professe it lessened much
my reverence unto that great councill ; for he was very much hearkened
unto.'[1]

[1] Sir Philip Warwick's *Memoirs*, 1701 edition, p. 247.

The Presbyterians were less tolerant than Cromwell. They were not satisfied that he was keeping the door of the press well enough guarded against the approach of errors and heresies ; and by errors and heresies they meant the notions and beliefs of most, if not all, other sects. There were petitions that the Government should suppress certain specified books. For example, Richard Baxter asked for the suppression of Hobbes' *Leviathan* :

> ' Lay a penalty on him that Prints or sels any Books against the Fundamentals or Essentials of Christianity ; and that slander or reproach Magistracy, Ministry, or Ordinances of Christ. And burn some more of this nature, that you may manifest a disowning them. Specially *Hobbs* his *Leviathan*.'[1]

That was in January, 1655, and in October, after Cromwell's Orders for the regulating of printing had been passed, the old beacon-firers, Underhill and Webb, were still found protesting. They agreed that the Council of State should protect men of all religions, but surely not blasphemers ! Therefore they asked for the suppression of a book, *Praeadamitae*, then printing by F. Leach.[2]

There was a successful raid on a printer's shop in January, 1655, which *Mercurius Fumigosus* reported :—
' Some of their Quaking Tenents were last Saturday night
' seized on at the Press, and with the Printer and Publisher,
' carried before Authority to answer for venting such errors
' to deceive the simple '. But prosecutions were remarkably few. Abuse of Cromwell by pamphleteers continued both at home and abroad, but he took no serious action against

[1] *Humble Advice, Or The Heads of Those Things which were offered to many Honourable Members of Parliament By Mr. Richard Baxter*, Jan., 1655 (Brit. Mus., E.821.14.16.).

[2] *C.S.P.D.*, Vol. 1655, p. 393, 24 Oct.

them. Abroad, the States General forbade the sale of a scandalous pamphlet deriding the Protector and his Government, and offered 500 *l.* reward for the discovery of the author.[1] At home, Cromwell was frequently abused by pamphleteers who preferred to remain anonymous.[2] There were occasional arrests—some printers were taken into custody in April[3]—yet too few probably, and those not prosecuted with enough vigour, to please the presbyterians.

The only really serious disturbances were caused by Anabaptists and Fifth-Monarchy men. At the end of August, 1655, a ' well-wisher to the Anabaptists' prosperity ' anonymously published *A short Discovery Of His Highness the Lord Protector's Intentions Touching the Anabaptists in the Army. . . . Upon which there is propounded 35 Queries for his Highness to answer to his own Conscience.* His highness was accused of scorning the base degrees (i.e. the Anabaptists) by which he had ascended. They had ' made a leg ' for Cromwell, and were themselves now likely to be kicked. Immediate action was taken against the contrivers of this pamphlet. On 4 September *The Weekly Intelligencer* announced that the two printers were found,[4] and added : ' it is likely they will ' suffer as they justly do deserve, and so will those Men who ' were neither ashamed nor afraid to disperse them up and

[1] *Mercurius Politicus*, 2-9 March, 1654.

[2] *Severall Proceedings*, 25 Jan.-1 Feb., 1655.

[3] *Ibid.*, 5-12 April, 1655.

[4] See, also, information of John Harris (*Thurloe's State Papers*, Vol. 3, p. 149). Larner the printer was involved in the charge (*Ibid.*).

' down the *City*, and in *White-Hall* itself, where two of them
' were taken, and committed to *Lambeth-House* '. The
Anabaptists were for the moment exceedingly bitter
against Cromwell and would certainly have done him a
mischief if they could, but their chiefs were in prison and
the rest ' could not do him much hurt by theire brawl-
' ings and splenatique pamphlets—and therein they did
' not spare him '.[1]

Equally abusive of Cromwell was another pamphlet,
The Protector Unvailed, by ' a late member of the Army ',
of strong fifth-monarchical convictions. It was published
at the end of October, 1655. Cromwell was accused of
tyranny, for ' by his orders Major-General Harrison,
' Mr. Carew, Col. Rich, Quartermaster-General Courtney,
' Mr. Feake, Mr. Rogers and others were in prison only for
' their witness to the kingdom and coming of Christ '.
Once again Major John Harris, the former play-actor and
printer, proved his worth to Cromwell by discovering who
were the printers of the pamphlet. Jones, who had helped
to print both these pamphlets (*Queries*, and *The Protector
Unvailed*), was called to account and punished.[2] John
Harris offered his services to Cromwell :

' . . . if your honour be pleased to certify by some private intimation
your pleasure herein, he doubteth not but to be instrumental in the prevention or discovery of many scandalous papers, he having been bred a printer,
and knowing the methods that are and must be observed in the discovery
thereof.'

And once more John Harris changed his profession.

[1] *The Correspondence of Sir Edward Nicholas* (letter from Col. R. Whitley
3/13 Oct., 1655).

[2] *Thurloes' State Papers*, Vol. 3, p. 149.

CHAPTER X

THE PROTECTORATE, 1656-1658

The Licensing System

JOHN Barkstead and George Foxcroft were diligent executors of the laws regulating the press and visited the printing houses frequently : which must have been very disturbing to the disorderly, who found the risks attached to unlicensed printing alarmingly increase. A man with a family might be pardoned for not taking the risks. The correct and orderly method of procedure was for the printer to submit his manuscript to the licensers before setting up his type. Presumably he applied to Stationers' Hall, and if neither Barkstead nor Foxcroft nor the Council had appointed men especially to licence books, then the printer would have to rely on the Warden's decision. Peter Cole the printer's petition to the Council in January, 1656, shows that the licenser, though his identity cannot now be discovered for certain, made his presence felt at the time. Having many sermons of Mr. Burroughs, Mr. Hooker, and others to print, Peter Cole told the Council :—' the writing ' is too bad to be read by a licenser, yet no book can be ' printed without license. Petitioner begs to be a licenser ' of his own copies, on security not to pass anything that ' is seditious '.[1]

[1] *C.S.P.D.*, Vol. 1655-6, p. 149, January.

The number of books entered in the Stationers' Register rapidly increased, but rarely was an *imprimatur* printed on the copies exposed for sale. Here are two of the exceptions to the rule :—*An Elegy on the Archbishop of Armagh*,[1] printed by Francis Leach, claimed to have been ' licensed and entred according to order ' ; and ' that so much expected book, *The Life and Death of Nathaniel Butler* ' who was executed for murder, was advertised in *Mercurius Politicus* to come forth ' by special Order of the Lord Mayor, ' attested under the Hands of severall eminent ministers, ' and will be duly Licensed and Entred '.[2]

When a book was licensed the author did not cease to be responsible for the matter it contained. He could not shelter behind an *imprimatur* : as Sir Harry Vane, junior, discovered when his *Healing Question* was the subject of debate. He had published it in the hope that it might help the Government to solve its difficulties. The governors had called the nation to a day of public humiliation, of fasting and prayer, ' to invite to the giving in of Light and convic-' tion, with a free and open profession of a ready subjection ' of mind thereunto '; and as a result of that day's meditation Sir Harry Vane proffered his *Healing Question*. The manner of its publication he explained in *The Proceeds of the Protector (so called) and his Councill against Sir Henry Vane, Knight* :

'. . . being asked for from me by one of the *Councill*, I delivered in writing and it continued in their hands about a Months space, without any prohibition to Print, & then was put to the Presse in the ordinary way of

[1] 21 March, 1656 (E.875.2).

[2] *Mercurius Politicus*, 3-10 Sept., 1657.

all other bookes, and had the usuall warrant for the comming forth, and nothing laid to its Charge ever since, till (for what reason of State I know not) it is now thought meet to be called *seditious*, and occasion is taken thereby to threaten me with *Bonds*. . . .'[1]

Refusing to give in security not to disturb the peace of the Commonwealth, he was sent prisoner to the Isle of Wight.

Vane had delivered his unfortunate *Healing Question* to a member of the Council before printing it. Members of Cromwell's Council also received other men's manuscripts, upon which they gave their opinion on whether or not they contained anything seditious. In March, 1657, Hodgkinson, a printer, asked one, Mr. Whiting, for the Copy of *King James his time* which he was ready to begin printing. Mr. Whiting ' told him it was in Just. *Hales* hand for ' perusall, but promised faithfully to bring it to him in a ' fortnight '.[2] Members of the Council, if not official licensers, were at times ready to give expert advice to authors and stationers who were in doubt.

Of unregistered, and presumably unlicensed, books and pamphlets there were plenty on sale, but nearly all of them carried the printer's name and colophon. There was no prosecution of the printer or author unless his book was found to be either blasphemous or seditious. At a meeting of the Council in June, 1658, a draft warrant for executing the Acts against unlicensed books was read and approved and sent up to his Highness ; Fleetwood, Wolsley, the Lord Chamberlain, Jones, Desborough, Lisle and Strick-land were appointed ' to consider fit persons to be added

[1] B.M., E.937.2., 1656.

[2] B.M., 669.f.20.74.

for licensing books and to report their names '. Cromwell signed the warrant committing to the Master and Wardens of the Stationers' Company, and to Henry Hills and John Field, printers to his Highness, the execution of the said Acts (14 June, 1643, 28 September, 1647, 20 September, 1649 and 7 January, 1653); but nothing more was heard of the fit persons which were to have been added for licensing books. The committee's report, if it was ever made, has now vanished.

CROMWELL'S INTERPRETATION OF THE FREEDOM OF THE PRESS

There were still several private printing-presses at work in London : Livewell Chapman, the printer, was found by Barkstead to be using one[1]—and his press was broken. However, there were other presses with nut and spindle still intact that continued to evade Barkstead and Foxcroft. In October, 1656, a Committee was called ' to consider of a way to suppress private presses '.[2]

Cromwell had no desire to restrain the discussion of religious questions in print. His Council was less tolerant. It is by no means certain that he agreed with the Council's prosecution of offenders under the press-acts. Once or twice he interfered, but as a rule the Council was free to exercise its own discretion and to enforce its own judgments. Both the protector and his Council, however, agreed in

[1] *Thurloe's State Papers*, Vol. 4, p. 379, Jan., 1656. Chapman was in trouble again in Oct., 1657—for printing ' an erroneous book denying the moral law and covenant of grace '. (*C.S.P.D.*, Vol. 1657-8, p. 134.)

[2] *H.C.J.*, 20 Oct., 1656.

January, 1656, that the newly printed popish books seized by Barkstead and Foxcroft were justly and rightly condemned to be burned by the common hangman.[1]

No sanction whatever was given to popish books, or to what were technically known as malignant books. Neither Cromwell nor his Council would suffer the royalists to print attacks on the Commonwealth. These, however, were printed in spite of the vigilance of the commissioners for printing, and were the chief cause of the Order of August, 1656, banishing to a distance of twenty miles from London all who had been in arms against the state :—' We ' foreseeing the dangerous consequences to the public of ' the freedom of access to London of malignants (who sow ' sedition) as appears by the books they boldly publish ' from time to time. . . .'[2] Royalist propaganda had been going on for some time. Libels ' abusive and derisive of the present government ' were printed and sent by post to seamen stationed at Dover. Some of these pamphlets came to the notice of the authorities, who regarded them as ' liable to corrupt the minds of the seamen and others ', and letters addressed to the Dover seamen were intercepted and opened ' so that the authors and dispensers of ' such villainous pamphlets might be discovered, insurrec- ' tions prevented and the honour of his Highness vin- ' dicated '. The Council had ten such printed libels passed on to them and noted their ' malignant tendency '.[3]

[1] *C.S.P.D.* Vol. 1655-6, p. 119.
[2] *Ibid.*, Vol. 1656-7, p. 91.
[3] *Ibid.*, p. 56.

' Merry ' books were also banned, and that, it should be observed, at a time when ballads were permitted to reappear and to enjoy their own again. The Stationers' Register shows that the Cromwellian Government gave official warrant to ballad-makers to sell their songs. But merry books were deemed offensive. Some of the ballads were coarse enough, but the coarseness of the merry books must have surprised even readers of *Mercurius Fumigosus* and *Democritus* who, whatever they were, cannot be accused of prudery or squeamishness. Saints of the seventeenth century, not delicate nor over-nice, had—at least the best of them had—' that good digestion which turneth all to health ', and could ' pick out of mirth, like stones out of the ground, profaneness, filthiness and abusiveness '.[1] They were of their age no less than the unregenerate, and shared in the general appreciation of a certain type of broad humour which the average reader of the twentieth century would find merely disgusting. *Sportive Wit*, first of these merry books, although it passed the licenser and was duly entered at Stationers' Hall, was, however, too coarse to be palatable even to a Government which permitted ballads: parts of it were frankly obscene. A committee of the Council reported that it contained ' much Scandalous, Lascivious, Scurrilous, and Profane matter ', and copies of the book were ordered to be seized and to be ' forthwith publickly burnt '.[2] The same fate was reserved for *Choice*

[1] George Herbert's *The Church-Porch.*
[2] *Publick Intelligencer*, 21-28 April, 1656.

273

Drollery, Songs and Sonnets,[1] entered in the Stationers' Register on 9 February. It was suppressed for being ' stuffed with profane and obscene matter tending to the corruption of manners ' : and R. Fletcher's *Ex Otio Negotium, or Martial's Epigrams Translated*, although it had the usual warrant for coming forth, was seized at the press, ' being stuff tending to the corruption of manners '.[2] The objection was not to Martial's epigrams but to Fletcher's sundry poems which supplemented the translation. The sundry poems included some clearly ' malignant ' satire against Cromwell's Government : which goes to prove that even licensers nod.

Religious tracts gave more trouble to the authorities than did the secular merry books. The Quakers, most persistent of controversialists, replied to every charge made against them, carrying the war into the enemy's camp and aggressively agitating against spiritual wickedness in high places. Few of their books were entered in the Stationers' Register, and nearly all of them were presumably unlicensed. But printers put their names to them, and, if the Council had been vindictive, could easily have been prosecuted ; yet Giles Calvert, who printed most of their tracts, seems to have been the only sufferer. In April he was prosecuted for printing an indecent merry-book, in May he was summoned to answer for uttering ' books reflexive on the present government '.[3] These had

[1] *C.S.P.D.*, Vol. 1655-6, p. 314.
[2] *Ibid.*, p. 325.
[3] *Ibid.*, p. 308.

been written by Quakers who sought to apply quaking principles to political and secular affairs, being convinced that Cromwell and his Council were men who walked in darkness. The vitality of Quaker pamphleteers was admirable. Reports reached the Council that Quaker pamphlets were circulating in all parts of the country.[1] Barkstead and Foxcroft did what they could to suppress them in London, but the Quakers were not easily subdued—as the following extract from the *Publick Intelligencer* shows :—

'. . . It seems now, that subtle and dangerous Heads began to creep in among them [i.e. the Quakers], to drive on designes of disturbance, as appeared this day by a Book that was brought by an Officer to Major General Sir *John Barkstead*, which is notably Penned, and entituled, *A trumpet of the Lord sounded out of Zion, being an Alarm and preparation for Warr, &c.* The *Author* pretends to have had a Message come to him from God (as hee lay upon his Bed in *Kilkenny*-City in *Ireland*) to bee declared against all sorts of People. First, he fals upon his Highnesse and the Councill ; then hee hath a Controversie against the Judges, Lawyers, and all that handle the Law ; Astrologers, Magicians, Soothsayers, and Wisemen ; against Generals, Colonels, Commanders, Officers and Souldiers in *England, Scotland,* and *Ireland* ; Priests, Prophets, and Teachers of the people ; all Papists, and their whole Body and head at *Rome* ; all that are called Old Protestants ; all that are called *Presbyterians* and *Independents* ; all that are called *Anabaptists* ; all that are called *Frewillers,* all that waite for Christ's personall Reign upon Earth ; all that are called *Ranters* ; all that are called *Seekers* and *Waiters* ; all these he hath a Controversie against ; yea and against the *Cavalier-party,* to whom hee thus addresseth himself (*To all you who are and have bin alwayes Enemies to the very appearance of Righteousness, who are called Delinquents and Cavaliers* ;) . . . Thus saith the Lord. . . .'

The Quakers alone are excluded from this list of those whom the author had a controversy against. It is not surprising that the Government found in his book a cause of controversy against *him.*

[1] e.g., Desborough seized Quaker pamphlets in the West of England (Feb., *Thurloe's State Papers,* Vol. 4, p. 531) ; and Monk wrote to Cromwell asking him to use his influence to stop the printing of Quaker pamphlets, witness those found in the possession of George Fox when arrested at Edinburgh. Monk had to pay 14s. for the transport of those books and papers to Newcastle. (*Ibid.,* Vol. 6, p. 811.)

There were other Quakers who found fault with the rest of mankind as obstreperously as did this ecstasied author of the *Trumpet of the Lord* ; the Government cannot be blamed for attempting to silence them.[1] Samuel Chidley's minatory *Thunders from the Throne of God against the Temples of Idols*, with an epistle directed to the Protector, was suppressed[2]: it deserved, no less than the *Trumpet of the Lord*, to be silenced. There were questions in Parliament in October (1656) about the blasphemies of the Quaker, James Naylor, whose doctrines were being circulated in pamphlets in London and the West country. His blasphemous books received further advertisement from his triumphal entry into Bristol. He rode into the city seated on an ass and preceded by women crying ' Holy, Holy, Holy ! ' Parliament found him guilty of blasphemy, his books were burned and a cruel sentence was executed on his person. Cromwell interfered after part of the punishment had been inflicted, and abated the edge of his sufferings.[3]

Seven Quakers appealed from Horsham gaol to the Protector in January, 1657. Three of them had been committed by justices for owning some books set out by Quakers and publicly sold, containing an account of the

[1] See *The Libertine School'd. . . . In Answer to some Fallacious Queeries Scattered about Limerick by a Nameless Author*, etc. (Aug., 1657 : B.M., E.923.4), by Claudius Gilbert, printed at London :—' They [i.e. Quakers] had spread multitudes of Pamphlets, Libels and Papers, full of their sad stuffe, and by all possible ways labored to gather a strong party ' . . . (p. 56).

[2] *H.C.J.*, 20 Oct., 1656.

[3] For full details of the affair see M. Brailsford's *James Naylor* (1927).

state of regeneration, which seemed to the justices to be highly seditious. The others were committed for ' endeavouring to publish scandalous books '. Their gaoler proved to be a man of a very free and easy spirit, or else he was a Quaker, for he allowed great assemblies of people to have access to the prisoners and to disperse seditious books among them : wherefore the gaoler was locked up in his own gaol. Cromwell ordered the release of the prisoners ' because of the insufficiency of their crimes, and because ' they had not been brought to trial the next session '.[1]

' *Killing No Murder* '

The last years of the Protectorate produced three noteworthy seditious pamphlets. The first, *Killing No Murder*, written by Colonels Sexby and Titus[2], printed in Holland and brought over to this country by Sexby and widely circulated, appeared immediately after the failure of the Syndercombe plot to murder Cromwell. The escaped plotters hoped that where the plot had failed the pamphlet might succeed. A day of national thanksgiving was proclaimed for Cromwell's miraculous deliverance from death. Syndercombe was committed to the Tower, where he perished before the date legally fixed for his execution. Sexby renewed his efforts to despatch Cromwell ; and *Mercurius Politicus* gave notice on 18 May of the dispersing up and down of

[1] *C.S.P.D.*, Vol. 1656-7, p. 229.

[2] See Prof. C. H. Firth's article in *The English Historical Review*, Vol. 17, 1902, p. 308-9.

' divers abominable desperate Pamphlets, many of them being sealed up in brown paper covers, laid in the streets, and scattered in the Mews by Charing-Cross, and other places in and about the City, striking at the honor and safety of His Highness and the Commonwealth ; it seems to have been written by some Jesuited Villain, both in regard of the stile, and the subject matter.'

Further revelations were made in the next issue of *Politicus*:

' Some discovery was made about the dispersing of the Treasonous Pamphlets formerly mentioned, written to infect mens minds with that inhumane and damnable Doctrine of Privy Murther and Assassination.

' Beyond the Tower, six or seven parcels of the said Books, made up like Bales of Silk, and which seem to have been brought from beyond Sea, were seised by some Officers, who attending there to observe such as might convey away customable Commodities, and perceiving such a man slily to convey the said parcels a shore, questioned him, and he betaking himself to his heels, ran away, leaving the parcels behinde him.

' There was also one *John Sturges* apprehended, with a bundle of the same Books under his arm. This man was formerly one of his Highnesses Life-guards, but being found to have a hand in that seditious Pamphlet, published two years ago, entituled *Quaeres*, written on purpose to pervert those who are called Anabaptists, and disaffect them against the Government ; he was for this cause a while imprisoned, and cashired : But being afterwards set at liberty, he of late hath betaken himself to more desperate courses, being more than suspected to be privy to *Sindercome's* business, since which time he hath been beyond Sea, and now being returned, was found going to scatter these devilish Books, which seem written on purpose to promote the same design. The said *Sturges* being this day brought hither hath been under examination before his Highness, and stands committed to the Tower of *London*.'

Six months later he died in the Tower and was reported to have confessed himself guilty of the Syndercombe plot and responsible also for the publication of *Killing No Murder*.[1]

The Fifth-Monarchy Men and the Press

The second seditious pamphlet of remarkable interest, though it created less stir than *Killing No Murder*, was the work of Fifth-Monarchy men at the time when Cromwell was considering an offer of the Crown (February-May, 1657). The Fifth-Monarchy men feared he would accept it. To

[1] *A Narrative Touching Col. Edward Sexby Who Lately Dyed A Prisoner In The Tower*, Jan., 1658 (B.M., *Burney Collection*).

the number of about eighty, they rose in arms against him. First, a pamphlet, *The Standard Set Up*, was prepared by William Medley. *Mercurius Politicus*, 16-23 April, 1657, reported :

' . . . That Printed Book lately taken with them, entituled *The Standard*, with their Declaration annexed to it, was subscribed by the said *William Medley*. . . . the Book contains *The Principles and Declaration of the Remnant, who have waited for the blessed Appearance and Hope*. . . . they intended with Sword in hand to give their judgment of Things (as they declare in Print) in respect of Power, Laws, Government, Exercise of Magistracie, Administration of Justice, Rights and Priviledges.'

The Insurrection failed, the leaders found themselves in the Tower. And Cromwell refused ' the bauble '.

The Excluded Members and the Press

In September, 1657, after the passing of the military despotism under which the country had been divided into districts controlled by major-generals, there was a return to parliamentary government. The result of the elections displeased Cromwell : so a purge was administered to Parliament, and about a hundred members were excluded. Denied the freedom of the press, they published a declaration[1] in print nevertheless, appealing to the country's sense of justice. In defying the Government the excluded members were only doing what many pamphleteers and petitioners had been doing in a milder way for some time. It had been a common practice for men with a grievance against the Government to air it in single broadsheets that were printed and circulated in the same manner

[1] The pamphlets (about 1000 in number) were sent in great white boxes to be left at several houses in London to be delivered out when called for. The government got wind of it and sent men to collect the boxes, which were unsuspectingly handed over to them (*Thurloe's State Papers*, Vol. 5, p. 456).

as pamphlets. Quite evidently such petitioners were more anxious for the general public, than for Parliament, to read what they had printed. There had been trouble with the petitioners before. In December, 1656, an order against them was renewed :

' that the order against printing private Petitions, before they are presented to this House, be duly observed ; and that the Serjeant attending this House shall seize upon such printed Petitions, in the Hands of any Person that shall deliver or disperse the same.'[1]

Trivial Offences Ignored

In March, 1658, the incorrigible Livewell Chapman was again in trouble, this time for printing ' a book reflexive on the Government '.[2] He could not have been very seriously dealt with for his former irregularities, or else he would have taken greater care to avoid discovery. Dr. Peter Heylin was prosecuted for his *Respondet Petrus*.[3] The Council ordered a search to be made for the author of a book defending the ' natural polygamy of man ' ; and the latest books of William Saunderson and Mr. Harrington were narrowly eyed.[4]

Yet many unlicensed and mildly libellous books and pamphlets were ignored by the Government. One of Thurloe's agents could write to him from Edmondsbury, ' I send you one of the libels dispersed in the country, which do no great good, nor much harm : '[5] and Thurloe would agree with him.

[1] *H.C.J.*, Dec., 1656.
[2] *C.S.P.D.*, Vol. 1657-8, p. 339.
[3] *Ibid.*, Vol. 1658-9, p. 71.
[4] *Ibid.*
[5] *Ibid.*, Vol. 1656-7, p. 56.

The Dispute about the Printing of the Bible

The rights of the Stationers' Company were well safeguarded by the Government, his Highness's printers, Hills and Field, coming in for specially favourable treatment. Hills and Field, by special command of Cromwell, prepared a new edition of the Bible. Their right to the copy was vigorously contested. They proceeded to advertise the new edition in *Mercurius Politicus* on 6 November, 1656 :

' Whereas for the space of about Twelve years past, the Printing of the Bible lay in common ; so that every man presumed to Print it at pleasure (which was never permitted before in any Country, the Magistrate in all States and Kingdoms, ever committing it to the care of persons of his own appointment) it so fell out through the Arbitrary and Licensious custom of Printing, that many Hundreds of very gross Errors are escaped in the Common Impressions now abroad, to the great scandal of *Religion* and *Government* and abuse of the people.

' For remedy whereof, due care hath been had to settle the Printing of *the Holy Scriptures*, in an orderly way for time to come ; and ther is now a Bible finished, *By His Highnesses special Command*, corrected and amended, according to the Original Manuscript Copy of the *Translators*.

' And to the end, that a Book of so sacred concernment, may be exactly and truly Printed for the future, there are two Correctors kept to correct all Bibles that shall be Printed hereafter ; and over and above, there is a very learned person appointed by his Highness, carefully to revise every sheet before it be wrought off at the Press.

' Such regard hath been had likewise to the Publick, and ease of the people, in the price of Bibles, that his Highness Printers (notwithstanding they have purchased the translated Copy in the Manuscript, which cost them Twelve hundred pounds ; and by entring it in the *Stationers* Register Book, have a Legal Title to the sole Printing of it, and are at the great Charge aforesaid of Correcting it) are obliged to sell Bibles in the Common Volumes, without Notes (called *Twelves*) at no more but Two shillings a Book in quires. At which price, the Corrected Impression aforesaid, is now to be sold at the House of *Henry Hills* in *Aldersgate street*, next door to the sign of the *Peacock*.'

William Bentley, printer at Finsbury, declared this to be an infringement of his copyright.[1] Since 1644 he had, he said, printed Bibles ' by the favour of the parliament ',

[1] B.M., 669.f.20.34., Nov., 1656.

and his press at Finsbury had supplied the army which had been sent to Ireland in 1649, with Bibles at 2s 4d each, and the army that invaded Scotland in 1650, with a cheaper edition costing 20 d. *per* book. He reminded the Government of how Robert Barker's claim to the sole printing of ' the translated copy of the Bible called the New Translation ', had been decisively rejected in 1652 by a Parliament which ' in no ways intended to monopolise the printing of the Bible '. On 6 March, 1656, ' by some irregular ' dealings, and upon misinformation, the Company of ' Stationers were enforced to make an undue Entry in ' their Registry, contrary to their custome, to Henry ' Hills and John Field (his Highnesse Printers) of that ' Individual Copy of Barker '. Bentley protested to the Stationers' Court, but he was denied a hearing. Meanwhile Hills and Field ' obtained deputations to themselves ' from Sir John Barkstead, and Mr. Foxcroft (his Highnesse ' Commissioners for regulating of printing) to search for ' and seize all scandalous and unlicensed books and Pamph- ' lets ' : which power Bentley accused them of prostituting to their own private ends by suppressing all printing of Bibles and Testaments which interfered with their own trade. They had also raided Bentley's house, assisted by red-coats, and carried away the form and materials used for printing part of the New Testament, together with those sheets that were already printed. Bentley appealed to Cromwell.

Hills and Field replied[1] with a vigorous *argumentum ad*

[1] B.M., 669.f.20.35., Nov., 1656.

hominem—Bentley was a man of no standing in the book trade, a ' forreiner as to the art and mystery of printing, a mere paper-seller ' : for if he had been a lawful master-printer he would have been long since disabled for ever from the exercise of printing. That would have been his punishment for having employed his printing-house in printing popish books, some of which had been discovered, condemned and publicly burned by the hangman, and for having continued to print popish books afterwards. A shabby fellow, hardly worth replying to ! It was only necessary to point out that the sole printing of Bibles was by purchase of the original manuscript of the Translation, and this purchase Hills and Field had made. His highness, by special warrant to the Company of Stationers, had given direction for the entry of the said copy for his printers, as the lawful proprietors thereof ; which had been done accordingly. Bentley's charges were dismissed as both frivolous and false, and he was not able to carry them any further.

Cromwell's Use of Writers

Cromwell did not underestimate the power of the press. He had been often reminded that the influence of a book cannot be destroyed by ordering a hangman to burn copies in Cheapside or Palace Yard. Weapons of the flesh do not avail against spiritual foes. And a book can outlive its covers and its material form. From the beginning of their rule the saints had realised that it was not enough to burn their enemies' books and pamphlets : they must reply to them, refute their specious arguments, present the case in their own defence. Cromwell understood this, and had his ' writers'—men who held themselves ready to reply to scandalous books, and to present the case for the Government. Michael Hawke regarded himself as one of these. Having rendered service to Cromwell, he petitioned for some reward to be given him :—' Petitioner has always ' acted in the interests of the Commonwealth, has written ' a book on public law defending the present Government ' from attacks of the envious : Has thereby induced several ' Royalists and other seditious persons to change their ' opinions, but has brought on himself the hatred and ven- ' geance of many, by reason of whose threats he has not a ' farthing. Is ready to meet death on behalf of the chief ' of the State '.[1] Hawke was not discouraged from render- ing further service, for in August, 1656, he published a reply to Vane's *A Healing Question*. The reply was entitled *A Letter from a person in the Countrey to his friend in the City giving his judgment upon a Book commonly supposed to be Sir Henry Vanes, entituled A Healing Question*, and in October, 1657, he was still friendly enough with Cromwell and his Govern- ment to issue *Killing Is Murder*, in reply to *Killing No Murder*. His services had received some sort of recognition, else they would not have been continued. Cromwell him- self may have privately encouraged him.[2] Anthony à Wood relates that in 1649 Cromwell tried to engage

[1] *C.S.P.D.*, Vol. 1655-6, p. 338.

[2] One, Richardson, seems to have been another of these ' writers ' : Major General Goffe in a letter to Thurloe expressed the hope that some reward would be given to one, Mr. Richardson, who had written a book exonerating Cromwell from the charges brought against him by Vavasor Powell (*Thurloe's State Papers*, Vol. 4, p. 445).

Casaubon to write a history of the war for him, offering him 300 *l.* if he would do so. The offer was refused.

Harrington's Oceana *and Cromwell's* Imprimatur

Cromwell took a personal interest in the affairs of the press, and his personal instructions were frequently invited by his subordinates when their own efforts to stop seditious pamphleteering had failed. He kept in touch with his agents at Edinburgh who were trying to suppress hostile pamphlets. And it was to Cromwell himself that John Harrington applied when the licensers had refused to pass his *Oceana* for the press. In his preface to the 1737 edition of *Oceana* John Toland gave the following account of this incident :—[1]

'. . . In the mean time it was known to som of the Courtiers, that the Book was a printing ; whereupon, after hunting it from one Press to another, they seiz'd their Prey at last, and convey'd it to *Whitehall.* All the solicitations he could make were not able to relieve his Papers, till he remember'd that OLIVER'S favorit Daughter, the Lady CLAYPOLE, acted the part of a Princess very naturally, obliging all persons with her civility, and frequently interceding for the unhappy. To this Lady, tho an absolute stranger to him, he thought fit to make his application ; and being led into her Antichamber, he sent in his Name, with his humble request that she would admit him to her presence. While he attended, some of her Women coming into the room were followed by her little Daughter about three years old, who staid behind them. He entertain'd the Child so divertingly, that she suffer'd him to take her up in his arms till her Mother came ; whereupon he stepping towards her, and setting the Child down at her feet, said, Madam, 'tis well you are com at this nick of time, or I had certainly stolen this pretty little Lady. Stolen her, reply'd the Mother ! pray, what to do with her ? for she is yet too young to becom your Mistress. Madam, said he, tho her Charms assure her of a more considerable Conquest, yet I must confess it is not love but revenge that promted to commit this theft. Lord, answer'd the Lady again, what injury have I don you that you should steal my Child ? None at all, reply'd he, but that you might be induc'd to prevail with your Father to do me justice, by restoring my Child that he has stolen. But she urging it was impossible, because her Father had Children enough of his own ; he

[1] p. xix.

told her at last it was the issue of his brain which was misrepresented to the Protector, and taken out of the Press by his order. She immediately promis'd to procure it for him, if it contain'd nothing prejudicial to her Father's Government ; and he assur'd her it was only a kind of a Political Romance, so far from any Treason against her Father, that he hop'd she would acquaint him that he design'd to dedicat it to him, and promis'd that she her self should be presented with one of the first Copys. The Lady was so well pleas'd with his manner of Address, that he had his Book speedily restor'd to him ; and he did accordingly inscribe it to OLIVER CROMWELL, who, after the perusal of it, said, the Gentleman had like to trapan him out of his Power, but that what he got by the Sword he would not quit for a little paper Shot : adding in his usual cant, that he approv'd the Government of a single Person as little as any of 'em, but that he was forc'd to take upon him the Office of a High Constable, to preserve the Peace among the several Partys in the Nation, since he saw that being left to themselves, they would never agree to any certain form of Government, and would only spend their whole Power in defeating the Designs, or destroying the Persons of one another.'[1]

The *Oceana* was not popular with many of the more ardent Cromwellists. *Mercurius Politicus*[2] published discreetest animadversions on it—' the jolly crew of *Oceana* and the learned author ' were careful terms which he used to disguise his disapprobation. It was evident that only Cromwell's *imprimatur* kept Harrington out of the Gatehouse.

Cromwell and Cleaveland

Cleaveland, the poet and diurnalist, was generously treated by Cromwell, whom he had persistently libelled for many years. The most damaging attacks on Cromwell had come from him. He had had one narrow escape long since, when, having fallen into the hands of the enemy, he had been brought before Leslie, the soldier. His accusers

[1] Stat. Reg., 19 Sept., 1656, ' Entered under hand of Master Thrale, a book entitled, *The Commonwealth of Oceana*, dedicated to his highness the Lord Protector of the Commonwealth of England, Scotland and Ireland, by James Harrington '.

[2] *Mercurius Politicus*, 12 March-9 April (*Burney Collection*).

produced a bundle of his verses which they considered to
be sufficient evidence against him. ' Is that all ', said the
general, ' ye have to charge him with ? For shame ;
' for shame ! Let the poor fellow go about his business and
' sell his ballads '. Granger, who reports the affair in his
Biographical History, adds : ' This contemptuous slight
' affected Cleaveland so much, that he is said to have
' drowned the remembrance of it in strong liquors, which
' hastened his death '. The comment is not justified—or
else the remembrance took an unconscionably long time
a-drowning—for he was vigorous enough in October, 1657,
to petition Cromwell for release from his enemies into whose
hands he had again fallen. Cromwell, the libelled, it is
refreshing to note, evidently bore no grudge against one
of his most malignant libellers. The petition was dignified,
and Cromwell honoured himself in granting his request.
' My crime ' (argued Cleaveland) ' is my fidelity to my
' sovereign, my late lord and king, and that is my defence ' :

'. . . My *Lord* you see my crimes ! As to my defence you bear it about
you ! I shall plead nothing in my justification but your *Highnesses* clemency, (which as it is the constant inmate of a valiant breast, if you
graciously please to extend it to your Suppliant in taking me out of this
withering durance,) your *Highness* will find that mercy will establish you
more than power ; though all the days of your life were as pregnant with
victories, as your twice auspicious third of *September*.'[1]

Cromwell and the Intolerants

Cromwell, it was generally believed, was more tolerant
than his advisers but for whom there would have been a
freer press. J. Croope, one of the Liberty-of-Conscience
party, wrote in the preface to his *Conscience-Oppression ;*

[1] B.M., 669 f.20.69., and E.746.4., October, 1657.

Or, A Complaint of Wrong done to the Peoples Rights, etc.[1] in February, 1657 :

‘ Reader, whilest I put my self in thy stead, and consider my self, looking upon the Title of this little Book, I find these thoughts arising, *viz.* This is some new *Faetus* of some hot brain, and adds to the infinite number of those Libels, which the abuse of Liberty of the Press hath brought forth ; and it shall content me to read the Title, I know better how to spend my time than to hazard it in looking through these sheets. . . .’

The reader who ignores this warning not to waste his time in looking through the ensuing sheets will find that the author blames men like Goffe and Peters for introducing ‘ the old Popish and prelatical spirit of persecution ’ into Cromwell’s council of advisers :

‘ . . . Col. *Goffe*, a man famed enough for Religion, and interest in religious men (which is none of the weakest bonds that ties him to the Protector) to discover his judgment about liberty, at a private Fast kept by the General and his Officers at Whitehall, blames the civil Magistrate (grounding his Speech upon the 34 of *Ezek.*) because he did not intermeddle in matters of religion, and judg between the fat cattle and the lean ; also he applies that which is spoken to the Church of *Thyatyra* about their toleration of the woman *Jezebel* in Rev. 2.20. to the Magistrate. How easie this goes down with the present Power, see by a late Expostulation made with some Teachers of Churches, concerning Dissenters in doctrine, &c. “ Will not you excommunicate such ? Some said, they would. *Then if you take care for your Bodies and Societies to keep them clear, shall not I accordingly take care of the Commonwealth ?* ” ’

And Peters counselled short shrift for heretics, rather than freedom to promulgate their heresies :

‘ . . . he [i.e. Peters] saith, he found, *That so long as Calvin and the Presbyters in Geneva dealt courteously with Servetus by perswasion, and argument, his Heresies spread and prevailed ; but the cutting off of Servetus was the overthrow of the Heresie* : Whence he observes, *That as the blood of the Martyrs is the seed of the Church, so the blood of Hereticks is the destruction of Heresie.* . . .

‘ . . . He [i.e. Peters] is brought in not to be disputed with. But to shew that the Protector is not free from temptations ; no not from these of his own house ; and when they are persecuted by men of such intimacy, and appear so fitly accommodated to a desire of Ruledom, let the wise fear, they may sometimes be admitted.’

Croope would have had ‘ a free way open for the Dissenters

[1] B.M., E.903.8.

' from the approved religion to profess and publish their
' opinions, which being published, should contract no other
' evil to the publishers than an advantage thereby to be
' taken for their better instruction, not for their destruction,
' imprisonment or banishment '.

Marchamont Nedham was one of those same intolerant
men, a Boanerges to call down fire from Heaven upon
people with whom he disagreed. His profession as journalist
brought him into close touch with Cromwell, and with
Goodwin against whom he launched a violent but carefully
prepared attack in July, 1657. In March of the same year
he met Cromwell in Goodwin's house—' Nedum, our news
' writer, being last night in Dr. Goodwin's chamber at
' Whitehall, the Protector asked him the news. . . .'[1] Four
months later he published *The Great Accuser cast down ; Or,
A Publick Trial Of Mr. John Goodwin Of Coleman-street,
London, At the Bar of Religion & Right Reason.   It Being
A full Answer to a certain Scandalous Book of his lately
published, Entituled. The Triers Tried and Cast, &c. Whereupon being found Guilty of High Scandal and Malediction both
against the present Authority, and the Commissioners for
Approbation and Ejection, He is here sentenced and brought
forth to the deserved Execution of the Press.*[2]   In a fulsome,
vaunting, dedicatory address to Cromwell, Nedham observed
that there was no need now to send Goodwin to the Tower
for his scandalous pamphleteering, there was no danger in
him now, he (Nedham) had handled him—pestilent fellow
that he was, paper-worm, with a windmill in his brain that

[1] *C.S.P.D.*, Vol. 1656-7, p. 57, 19 March.
[2] B.M., E.920.1.

kept the press always going as if it were his handmill ! He would be quiet now.

It is gratifying to know that Nedham received a hearty drubbing in return. Goodwin's *Triers Tried* had been the protest of an old and willing servant in the cause of freedom, and had not deserved Nedham's violent censures. A friend replied for him with *A Letter of Addresse To The Protector*,[1] which was unlicensed. The author confessed himself but an ' idle spectator upon the deck of State ', but he could see clearly enough that Nedham was ' a State Porter, a *venalis* ' *anima*, a mercenary soul that for a handful of earth ' could be hired to assassinate the greatest fame and reputa- ' tion ' : all the influence of the Protector with the best advice of the Council was required to keep him in his wits. Goodwin's friend besought Cromwell to shake himself free from a man like Nedham, and to deny that he had set him on to write *The Great Accuser cast down* :

. . . . ' Had *Needham* been in pay to *Aristides, Scipio*, or some of those great-minded Heroes, and should have been sent abroad into the world with the prefix of their honourable names, such a trivial and scurrilous Pamphlet, in return to a sober and weighty discourse, they would certainly have cashiered him their service, and condemned him to the mines, though it had never so much concerned them.'

But he need have had no fear. Cromwell could shake himself free of the influence of intolerant men, though he could also use them for his own purposes.

Cromwell's Services to Literature

Cromwell was well disposed towards men of letters, too, though he ' placed piety above learning ';[2] and respected the

[1] B.M., E.923.7., August, 1657.
[2] C. H. Firth's *Cromwell*.

piety and learning of men whatever their religious creed or political party. For example, he paid the funeral expenses of Archbishop Usher as a mark of respect although he had disagreed with him in his lifetime on nearly every possible topic. He encouraged study and University education by considerable grants of money to Glasgow, Edinburgh and Durham. He numbered poets among his friends and servants—Milton, Marvell, Waller, Davenant. He permitted opera to be revived, and presented at the Cockpit so discreetly that the more rigid of his puritan subjects might not suspect that the theatres were re-opening or dream that *Hypocrites* had come to town. To the press he had granted as much freedom as the times would permit, with the one reservation that there be no news published which the Government had not first examined and declared authentic.

In the general excitement at the Restoration, all this was forgotten. Cromwell's services to literature were emphatically denied : for instance, the following passage from *The English Devil* (i.e. Cromwell) is typical of Restoration abuse:

. . . 'We hold it as a great disparagement to our Quill to bestow a Copy of Verses on him, as he was a grief and trouble to the Loyal party of the Nation. And indeed, how can any Son of Phoebus imploy his time so ill, as to salute his dead Corps with an Epitaph, that was so great an enemy to them whilest living ; Who had a real design to extirpate all literature, and implunge us into as deep a Gulph of ignorance and prophaneness as the Turk is cast into ? He hated all Learning, and the Learned, because his Crimes were so black and horrid, that they went far beyond the mercy of the Book. He granted a tolleration for all Religions, because his own was to choose. . . .'

Against which must be placed eulogistic estimates, equally extravagant as the above, such as the following which appeared in 1659 :

' . . . Was there ever a more bountiful Benefactor, than he has been to all the virtuous persons of it ? To instance in one for all ; What obliging favours has he cast upon our *English Virgil* here (I mean Mr. Edm. Waller) and merely for that, and his other virtues, having in some other relations, little capacity enough to deserve them. My Lord has sufficiently shewed his most excellent judgment in Poetry, by his approbation and election of him, to be the object of his great goodness, who is clearly one of the ablest, and most flourishing wits, that ever handled a pen, and he does it with that natural dexterity and promptness, as if he had begun to write, so soon as to live. . . . his [i.e. Cromwell's] favours likewise were extended most liberally, to all those that did deserve them, either here, or in either of his Universities : He was a perfect *Philomusus*, and why not by that, qualified for a Poetical Prophet ? . . .'[1]

Nearer the truth is George Wither's estimate of Cromwell's attitude to the press, which appeared in *A Suddain Flash*, 1657 :

' These wayes, thou wert Victorious heretofore ;
And, I will mention one great Conquest more,
By few observed : Thou hast stood the Shock
Of malice and detraction, like a Rock,
On which the waves and billows of the Main,
Have spent their strength, and foam'd out rage in vain.
I, very often, have observ'd the fell,
Fierce, raging, and three headed dog of Hell,
With his three double rows of teeth, assay
To tear thine honour, and thy pow'r, away ;
With his foule tongues, bespattering thy fame,
To turn thy blooming honour into shame ;
I've seen this Cur oft, dog thee in the dark,
In hope to bite thee, when he durst not bark ;
And, I have heeded, by what sacred Charms,
Thou hast been hitherto, preserv'd from harms.

    This Helhound, thou hast tam'd without so much
As giving him a crust, a spurn, or touch ;
Meerly by meekness, and, as passing by
With disregard of causelesse injury ;
And now he sometimes fawns on thee and those,
Who are thy friends : and, snarleth at thy foes,
As if he were appeas'd : which, I believe
Is but a cunning dog trick, to deceive.'

The Restoration proved that in this, at least, Wither was right.

[1] *History of the Life and Death of the Lord Protector* by S. Carrington, 1659.

APPENDIX

APPENDIX

A

Star Chamber Decree for the Regulating of Printing, 1637

SUMMARY

1. Seditious, schismatical or offensive books or pamphlets to the scandal of Religion, or the Church or the Government or Governors of the Church or State, or Commonwealth or of any Corporation, or particular person or persons whatsoever not allowed to be printed or circulated in this realm or in any of his majesty's dominions.

2. All books and pamphlets and every title, epistle, preface, proem, preamble, introduction, table and dedication thereunto annexed to be licensed and entered on the Stationers' Register before being printed.

3. Books of Law to be licensed by the Lords Chief Justices : Books of History or of State affairs by the principal Secretaries of State : Books of Heraldry by the Earl Marshall : and all other books by the Archbishop of Canterbury or the Bishop of London, or by the Chancellors of the Universities. The Chancellors to license books printed within the limits of the Universities.

4. The licensers to have two several written copies of every book in its approved form : license to be allowed only to books containing nothing contrary to the Christian Faith and the doctrine of the Church of England, or against the State or Government, or contrary to good life or good manners : licensers' name and *imprimatur* to be imprinted on every copy.

5. The Archbishop to be furnished with a catalogue of imported books before they are offered for sale.

6. No such packs or fardels of books to be opened except in the presence of one of the Chaplains of the Archbishop or of the Bishop of London.

7. Books which the Stationers' Company or any person by the Letters Patent have the privilege to print not to be printed either at home or abroad by the unprivileged.

8. Names of printers and authors to be printed on all books, ballads, etc.

9. The name, title, mark or vinnet of the Stationers' Company not to be printed on any book without the consent of the Company.

10. No buying, bartering or selling of books to be carried on by haberdashers, ironmongers, chandlers or other persons not having been seven years apprentice to the trade of Book-seller, Printer or Book-binder.

11. English books not to be printed abroad.

12. No foreigner unless a freeman of the Stationers' Company to bring in books to vent in England.

13. No press or printing-house to be erected nor any printing to be done in any house, vault or cellar without the Wardens of the Company being notified thereof.

14. No press to be made or letters cast without the Wardens of the Company being notified thereof.

15. Twenty Master Printers appointed for London, each to have the use of one press only. In addition are the King's printers and University printers.

16. Every owner of a press to give 300 *l.* surety not to print anything not licensed.

17. No printer to keep more than two presses unless the Wardens of the Company who may keep three : all supernumerary presses to be suppressed.

18. No book to be reprinted unless re-licensed.

19. No printer to engage more than the specified number of apprentices.

20. ' The Court doth likewise declare, that because a great part of the secret printing in corners hath been caused for want

of orderly imployment for journeymen printers. . . . Master
Printers be compelled to take on one each of such unemployed
journeymen seeking work.'

21. Master Printers who refuse this obligation and reluctant
journeymen to suffer imprisonment.

22. The Universities not to be restrained from taking any
number of journeymen they think fit.

23. None but freemen and apprentices to the trade to be
employed in printing.

24. Unallowed printers to be set in the pillory and whipt
through the City.

25. Master and Wardens of the Company to have power and
authority to search for and seize unlawful presses, and to view
what is printed in the Printing houses and to call for the license
to see whether it is licensed or no.

26. Books suspected by the searchers to contain matter contrary to State and Government, or contrary to the doctrine and
discipline of the Church of England, to be brought before the
Archbishop of Canterbury or the Bishop of London.

27. Four founders of letters for printing allowed and nominated.

28. No Master founder to keep above two apprentices.

29. The same regulations affecting journeymen printers to
30. apply to journeymen founders.

31. Transgressors, over and above their fine and punishment,
to give good security never after to transgress.

32. Books to be imported into London only.

33. A copy of every published book to be sent to the Bodleian
library.

B

A Briefe | Treatise | Concerning | The Regulating | Of | Printing. | Humbly presented to the | Parliament of | England. | By William Ball, Esq. | Lond, | Printed in the year 1651.[1]

Amongst many temporall Benefits which Divine Bounty hath in severall ages manifested to mankinde, the invention of *the Mystery, or Art of Printing* may rightly be acknowledged one of the greatest, as an exact and exquisite Instrument, opening to the understanding, not onely all naturall Sciences, but even super-naturall Mysteries ; by the means whereof the mindes of men have been endowed with many excellent gifts. Yet even as the best things have been abused, so hath this beneficiall Art been notoriously depraved by vaine, contentious, and seditious Persons ; to the great confusion of Doctrinall Tenets, and Disturbance of State-Affairs : For prevention (as much as may be) of so dangerous extravagancies, the most regular Christian *Potencies* (or Republicks) and Illustrious *Potentates* have thought fit *to comprehend the liberty of Printing, (even as of Coyning) within the sphere of their severall Powers* : Wherein (amongst others) the late Q. *Elizabeth*, and her successors have (not without mature deliberation, and sage presidents in this point) been most vigilant, well perceiving *that the Eye of understanding might be subject to be deceived by erroneous principles in Print, as may the bodily Eye by counterfeit Coyne* ; In Regard whereof they propagated wholsome Orders, and Decrees for the Regulating of Printing, and Printers ; which rightly considered, cannot be defaced, no not blemished by the notion of *Tyranny*. Moreover it is an *Axiom* of State, that, *Acta legitima Tyrannorum et Hostium Reipublicae rata esse oportere.* (Bodin. de Republica, L.I.C.5.) The lawfull Acts of Tyrants, even of (over-Lording) enemies ought to be observed in a Commonwealth : so that admitting Oppression, or Tyranny in some Trans-actions of these Later

[1] B.M.E. 1295.3., 24 November.

Princes, yet their prudent, and just Ordinances are not to be Rejected, but rather (*mutatis mutandis*) to be carefully conserved.

Wherefore with all humble submission to the High Representative of this Nation, I have tendred these subsequent Proposalls and clauses concerning the Regulating of Printing, and Printers, unto their grave Considerations, and censures ; part whereof I have collected out of former Ordinances, and have partly proposed somewhat of mine owne ; as hereafter ensueth.

I.

That no person or persons whatsoever Print, or cause to be Printed any offensive Bookes, Pamphlets, Papers, or Ballads to the Derogation of this present Government, or seditious disturbance of this Common-wealth, or of any Dominion, Member, or Corporation thereof, nor shall sell, or dispose of any such Bookes, Pamphlets, Papers, or Ballads, upon Paine that he, or they so offending shall forfeit for every such Booke, &c. the summe of 10 *l.* The one halfe to the use of the Common-wealth, the other to the party discovering the same, and suffer such farther punishment as the Demerit of the Offence, or Offences shall deserve.

II.

That no person or persons whatsoever shall Print, or cause to be Printed any Booke or Pamphlet whatsoever, unlesse such Booke or Pamphlet, and all, and every the Titles, Epistles, Prefaces, Proems, Preambles, Introductions, Dedications, Tables, and all other matters, and things thereunto annexed, or therewith imprinted shall be first lawfully Licensed, and Authorised by such Person, or Persons as the Parliament of *England* shall in their wisdomes constitute, and appoint ; and that all, and every such Book, or Pamphlet be also first entred into the Register Book of the Company of Stationers ; upon Paine that every Printer offending therein shall be hereafter for ever disenabled

to exercise the Art, and Mystery of Printing, and suffer imprisonment by the space of one whole yeare : provided that this extend
not to the Printers of the Parliament of *England*, and Councell of
State, for or touching any Booke which they shall command, or
allow of.

III.

That all the Books concerning Divinity, Phylosophy, and Poetry
shall be Printed by speciall Allowance of the Chaplaines in
ordinary to the Councell of State, or by one of them ; And in
case of no such Chaplaines in being, then by three Divines for
that purpose appoynted, or by one of them ; All Books of State
Affaires and History (except Diurnalls) to be licenced by the
Secretary of State, with two more of the Councell of State joyned
unto him, or by one of them : All Books concerning Law to be
Licenced by the Lords Commissioners of the greate Seale, Lord
Chief Justices, Master of the Rolls, or by one of them ; All Books
touching Phisicke to be Licenced by three of the Colledge of
Phisitians appointed for that purpose, or by one of them ; All
Books of Mathematicks to be Licenced by three professed Mathe-
maticians, being appoynted thereunto, or by one of them ; All
Books of Military Discipline to be Licenced by three of the
Councell of War, or otherwise of the Grand Committee for the
Militia, or by one of them ; All Books of Heraldry to be Licenced
by the Principall Herald at Armes with two other Authorized
Heralds joyned unto him, or by one of them ; All Books con-
cerning forraigne Languages to be allowed by three Linguists
for that purpose appoynted or by one of them.

Provided that the Chancellors or Vice-Chancellors of the
Universities shall Licence onely such Booke, or Books that are
to be Printed within the Limitts of the Universities Respectively,
but not in LONDON or else-where, not medling with Books of
Common Law, matters of State, Military Discipline and Heraldry.

IV.

That every Person, or Persons which are, or shall be appoynted, or Authorized to Licence Books, shall have two severall Copies *entirely* written ; one of which Copies shall be kept in a *Publicke Office, or Registrie* for that purpose to be appoynted, the which Copy every such Person, or Persons who shall Respectively allow of, or licence for Printing shall send into the said *Office, or Registry* testified under his or their hands, to the end that he or they may be secured, that the Copy so licensed by him, or them, is not altered without his or their privity ; the other Copy Licensed shall remaine in his hands whose Copy it is ; and all Stationers, and Printers that shall Print, or cause to be imprinted any Copy, or Copies whatsoever differently from this Rule, to incurre the penalties contained in the second clause.

V.

That every Merchant of Books, or Person, or Persons whatsoever who shall Import any Book, or Books from beyond the seas into this Common-wealth of England, shall before he, or they deliver, or cause to be delivered forth any such Book, or Books out of his, or their hands, or expose them to sale, deliver in a true Catalogue in writing of all and every such Book, and Books unto the Master of the *Office*, or *Registrie* for Copies aforesaid ; upon paine of forfeiture, and Confiscation of all, and every such Book and Books, and twenty shillings fine for every such Book delivered forth, or exposed to sale ; the one half to the use of Common-wealth, the other to the Party discovering the same.

VI.

That no Merchant of Books, or Person, or Persons whatsoever shall import, or cause to be imported from beyond the Seas any offensive or scandalous Books, Pamphlets, Papers, Portraitures, or Ballads into any part of this Common-wealth of England, upon incurring the penalties contained in the first clause.

VII.

That no Person, or Persons whatsoever shall within the Precincts, and Dominions of this Common-wealth, or elsewhere Imprint, or cause to be imprinted, or shall Import or cause to be imported into this Common-wealth of England, or any part thereof, any Copy, Book, or Books, or part of any Copy, Book or Books Printed beyond the Seas, or elsewhere, which the Company of Stationers, or any other Person, or Persons have, or shall have Rights unto by Order or entrance in their Register-Book ; or otherwise by speciall Order of Parliament, or by Letters-Patent, being *unnulled* by this present Parliament ; nor shall binde, stitch, or expose to sale any such Book, or Books, upon paine of forfeiture all the said Books, and twenty shillings fine for every such Book, to be issued by Writ, or Action, Bill, &c., by the Person, or Persons aggrieved.

VIII.

That every Person who shall hereafter Print, or cause to be printed any Books, Ballads, Charts, Portraictures, or other thing, or things whatsoever, shall thereunto, or thereon set his, and their owne name, or names ; as also the Name, or names of the Author, or Authors, Maker, or Makers of the same ; and by, or for whom any such Book, or other thing is, or shall be printed, upon payne of forfeiture of all such Book, &c. And having his, or their Presses, Letters, and other Instruments for Printing to be utterly defaced, and made unserviceable, and twenty shillings fine for every such Books, &c. The one half to the use of the Common-wealth, the other to the Party discovering the same.

IX.

That no person, or persons whatsoever shall Print or cause to be Printed, forge, put, or counterfeit, in or upon any Book, or Bookes, &c. the name, title, marke, or vinnet of the Company of Stationers, or of any particular person, or persons which hath, or shall have lawfull Priviledge, Authority, or Allowance to Print the same, without consent of the said Company, or of the Party, or Parties which shall be so priviledged, and Authorized, first had, and obtained, upon paine of incurring the Penalty in the seventh clause.

X.

That no Tradesmen, Shop-keepers, or any other person or persons whatsoever, not being a free Stationer of the City of *London*, or not having served 7 years apprentice to the trade of Book-seller, Printer, or Book-binder, shall within the City, or Suburbs of *London*, receive, take, or buy, to barter, sell againe, exchange, or doe away any Bibles, Testaments, Primers, Psalm-books, Almanacks, or other Book, or Books whatsoever, upon paine of forfeiture of all such Books, and twenty shillings fine for every such book, to be sued by Writ, or Action, Bill, &c. by the person, or persons aggrieved.

XI.

That no Stranger, or Foreigner whatsoever, be suffered to bring in for sale, barter, or rent, here, any book or books printed beyond the Seas, in any Language whatsoever, either by them-selves, or their secret Factors ; except such onely as be free Sta-tioners of *London*, and such as have been brought up in that profession, upon paine of confiscation of all such Books so im-ported, and twenty shillings fine for every such Booke to be sued by writ, or Action, &c. by the Master and Wardens of the Com-pany of the Stationers.

XII.

And for as much as there may be great abuse committed by Searchers, and other Officers of the Customes by seizures of Books, who (as I have heard credibly reported) seize *English* Bibles, Testaments, & other Books, Printed in *Holland*, and in other

parts beyond the Seas very erroniously, to the dangerous introduction of severall Heresies within this Common-wealth, and
great Injury to such, to whom of right the Copies or Originalls of
such Bookes belong ; and after such seizure (having as it is said
first exacted custome in Grosse) vent, and disperse the said
Bibles, Testaments, and Books in *England, Ireland,* and other
Dominions of this Common-wealth : for prevention whereof, no
Searcher, nor other Officer of the Customes or excise whatsoever
shall hereafter seize on any Books (if discovered) before he first
acquaint the Master of the *Office, or Registrie for Copies* aforesaid,
together with the Master, and Wardens of the Company of
Stationers, (upon pain of forfeiture of his, or their Places, and
Imprisonment) who shall have Power to accompany such Searchers, and Officers of the Customes : and shall forthwith upon
discovery, take a true Catalogue of such Bookes, and present it to
the Honourable Councell of State : And to prevent the farther
venting, and dispersing of such erronious Bibles, Testaments,
and other Bookes as aforesaid, after notice given unto the Honourable Counsell of State, the said Master of the *Office,* or *Registrie
for Copies,* together with the Master, and Wardens, of the Company of the Stationers, or some of them, shall cut, or cause to be
cut into waste paper, or otherwise utterly deface the said *English*
Bibles, Testaments, and other Bookes printed in *Holland,* and
in other parts beyond the Seas, and deliver the said waste paper,
or defaced Bookes, to such to whom of right the Copies, or
Originalls doe belong.

XIII.

Moreover for farther prevention of Importation, venting, and
dispersing of Seditious, Schismaticall, and Offensive Bookes, as
well as of the Bookes aforesaid ; That no Driefats, Sacks, Maunds,
Chests, or Fardells of Bookes whatsoever Imported into this
Common-wealth be permitted by any Officers of the Custome or
Excize, to be opened or conveyed away before notice given unto

the *Master of the Office, or Registry for Copies*, and also to the Master, and Wardens of the Company of Stationers (upon paine of such Officer, or Officers forfeiture of his, or their Places, and Imprisonment ; And the said *Master of the Office, or Registrie for Copies*, as also the Master and Wardens of the Company of the Stationers shall have Power to accompany the Searchers and other Officers of the Customs, and excise within 48 houres after such notice given (Sabbath-Dayes, and dayes of publick Thanksgiving, and of Humiliation being excepted out of the sayd 48 houres) and shall also have Power to seize on all Seditious, Schismaticall and offensive Books, and forthwith take a true Catalogue of such Books ; and present it to the Councell of State ; and after that carry the said bookes into the Stationers' Hall, there to remaine in safe custody, untill farther order taken by the Councell of State ; And the said Master, and Wardens of the Company of the Stationers, if they cannot performe the same by themselves, shall have Power to depute and nominate from time to time, sufficient persons in his, or their stead provided that at all times one of the said Masters or Wardens be present at every search : And the said Master of the *Office or Registrie for Copies*, and the Master, and Wardens of the Company of the Stationers, shall have power to appoint some convenient place where searches shall be made ; and if the said Master *of the Office, or Registrie for Copies*, Master, and Wardens of the Company of the Stationers shall neglect, or omit on their parts any thing or Duty which they ought to performe herein, they shall incurre such penalty as the Councell of State (upon Information of such their neglect, or offence, shall in their wisdomes thinke fit, be it by fine, or Imprisonment.

XIV.

That no person, or persons within the City of *London*, liberties thereof, or elsewhere, shall erect, or cause to be erected any Presse, or Printing house, or shall demise, let, or suffer to be held, or used any House, Vault, Seller, or other roome whatsoever to, or by any persons for a Printing house, or place to print in, unlesse he, or they who shall demise, let, or suffer the same to be used, shall first give notice to the Master, and Wardens of the Company of the Stationers of such Demise, or suffering to work, or print, upon paine of forfeiture of 20 *l.* for every such offence, the other halfe to the use of the Common-wealth, the other to the party discovering the same.

XV.

And for the better discovering of printing in corners without Licence, the Master, and Wardens of the Company of Stationers, or such whom they shall depute and trust, shall have Power, and Authority to search what houses, shops, vaults and rooms (and at what time they shall thinke fit) especially Printing houses, and to view what is in Printing, and to call for the Licence to see whether it be Licenced or no, and if not, to seize upon so much as is printed, together with the Presses, and all Instruments for printing, and to carry the offenders before the Councell of State, or the L. *President* thereof for the time being, to take such farther order therein as they shall in their wisdomes see cause.

XVI.

That no Joyner, Carpenter, or other person shall make any printing presse, nor Smith shall forge any Iron-worke for a printing presse, nor Founder cast any letters for any person or persons whatsoever, nor shall any person or persons bring in from any parts beyond the Seas any letters founded, or cast nor buy any such letters for printing, unlesse he, or they respectively shall first acquaint the said Master, and Wardens or some of them for whom the said Presse, Iron-works, or Letters are to be made, forged, or cast ; upon paine of Imprisonment, and such farther penalty as the Councell of State shall think fit.

XVII.

Whereas the multitude of printers is greatly increased by the late licencious and by-printing of unlicenced pamphlets, and other seditious and impertinent books, and papers, to the great scandall of this Common-wealth, and their owne disgrace, ignominy, and want of good, and sufficient employment, and maintenance ; for present remedy whereof, the Printers attempt a cure as bad, or worse than the disease, by petitioning the Honourable Committee for regulating of Printing, that they would be pleased to report to the High Representative of this Nation, that the said Printers might be made a Fraternity, or Company distinct from the Stationers ; against, and in opposition of such their not only unsound, but even dangerous Petition, and desires, I have thought fit to insert these ensuing Reasons, *viz.*

That Printing being of great concernment, and of important consequence, by meanes whereof this Common-wealth may either enjoy benefit, or receive notorious detriment ; Printers therefore ought to have some carefull, and exact supervisors over them, even as Apothecaries (who have the Colledge of Physitians, and Doctors of Physique over them, not only to prescribe, but also to peruse their Medicines) lest the first poyson the mindes of the People by erronious principles in print ; as may the last their bodies, by evil Medicines, and also by self-compliance (in case they should be a Fraternity, or Company distinct from the Stationers) Print undecently, how, and as they please according to Letter, and Paper (as do some Printers in Amsterdam and Geneva) to the dishonour of this Common-wealth, discontent to the people, and pre-purposed detriment of the Stationers whom they maligne, and inveigh against, and would (in regard of their present pressures occasioned by themselves) undermine by specious pretences : who notwithstanding are chiefly the men which this Common-wealth can subordinately intrust (in respect of their skill, abilities and long continued industry that waies) to supervise the Art and

Mistery of Printing, and Printers. And if they should say that the Apothecaries seperated themselves from the Grocers, and became a Company distinct, and why may not the Printers doe the like ? I answere, that the case is not alike, for the Apothecaries sell for the major part compounds for Medicaments, and the Grocers simples for Nutriment, being things of a distinct nature, and quality ; but the Printers, Book-binders, and Stationers make, and sell nothing but a booke, &c. However the Apothecaries are subject to the Doctors of Physique as aforesaid, and if the printers should exempt themselves from the Stationers, there would be none found, who might subordinately Regulate, and reforme such abuses, and disorders which those Innovating, and meane undertakers may in all probability from time to time commit.

XVIII.

Moreover, it is a *Maxime* of Policy, as well as of Philosophy, that *Frustra fit per plura, quod potest fieri per pauciora* ; *modo ita bene fiat* : That thing is in vaine done by more, which may be done by lesse, in case it may be as well accomplished : The Regulating of Printing, and Printers, may, not onely for the welfare of the Publique, but even for the good of themselves (if not exorbitant in their desires) be subbordinately performed by the Stationers, without any creating, or making the Printers a distinct Company. If the number of the Printing-houses in *London* were stinted, and none of them suffered to be without the liberties of the Citty of *London*.

If the number of Printing-presses were limitted.

If the number of Apprentices were also limited.

If the Master and Wardens of the Company of the Stationers take good care, that Journeymen-Printers (who are free of the Company of Stationers) of honest behaviour, and able in the Art or Mysterie of Printing, be employed and set on worke ; and in case such Journeymen Printers are in want of worke, Apprentices to be removed from such employments as any Journeymen-Printers of good behaviour shall offer themselves unto.

Lastly, if the Printers themselves will be subject to the good Orders and Constitutions of the Company of Stationers concerning all which (as also the price of useful Books) I conceive the Master, Wardens, and others able and experienced Stationers, are the fittest men to be consulted with.

XIX.

But it may be greatly suspected, that the Bible, Testament and some of the Stationers Copies and Originalls, are the Baits which the Printers would catch, or compasse : As touching the Bible, I take it to be a book of so high consequence, *wherein the Mysteries of Salvation are contained, that it ought to be regularly, and exactly, and not communicatively printed, lest in a Book of so high importance not onely dangerous Errors, but even pernicious Heresies be imprinted, and propagated, and the Book itself be also undecently Printed in Letter, and Paper* ; And for as much as *Propriety* (rightly considered is) *Relatio Legalis cujuslibet in Bonum Temporale*, A legall Relation of any one to a Temporall good ; I conceive *the sole Printing of the Bible, and Testament, with Power of Restraint in others*, to be of Right the *Propriety* of one MATHEW BARKER, Cittizen and Stationer of LONDON, in regard that his Father paid for the *Amended* or *Corrected* Translation of the *Bible* 3500 *l.* by reason whereof the *Translated Copy* did of right belong to him, and his Assignes ; yet for the better carrying on of so Important a Work, and the Regulating of an Impression of so great concernment, in the fourteenth yeare of *King James* his Reigne, he continued Letters Patents granted to *Robert* his Sonne ; since when in the yeare of our Lord 1635, for the farther carrying on, & Regulating of the said Important Impression, there hath beene payed by *Mathew Barker* aforesaid 600 *l.* for a Reversionary Patent.

If it be said, that *Mathew Barker* his Father made, or might have made benefit enough by his sole Impression of the *Bible*, &c. For the costs, and charges which he was at for the *amended*, or *corrected Translation* thereof, so that *Mathew Barker* himself neede not have a farther benefit thereby : I answere, so doth every one of the Stationers who purchaseth a Copy, or Copies make benefit enough thereby, and yet he enjoyeth such Copy, or Copies for himself, and his Assignes, and so ought to do, or else any other might invade his Right : so also every one who purchaseth Land at the valuation of 18. or 20. yeares Revenew, be it more, or lesse ; make at or about the determination of such time sufficient benefit for his purchase, yet there is no Law, nor any reason that himself, his Heires, or Assignes should be excluded, or debarred of the Remainder, &c. That were to *Null* all *Law, violate all Right.* And certainely according to equity (if not Law) *Mathew Barker* ought to succeede his Father in the sole printing of the *Bible*, &c. both in regard of his Fathers costs & charges ; as also in respect of his owne Patent Purchased dearely enough, in regard it was for Reversion.

But it may be some will say, that divers may make benefit by *Printing of the Bible, and Testament*, whereas if *Mathew Barker* enjoy the sole Printing thereof, himself will also enjoy the sole benefit thereby for him, or his Assignes ; to the which I answere, the same may be objected against *Miles Flesher*, and his Partners, sole Printers of all Law-Books ; against *John Feild* sole Printer of all Acts of this present Parliament ; against *William Dugard* Sole Printer for the Councell of State ; against *Richard Cotes*, sole Printer of all Acts, Proclamations, and other matters for the City of *London* ; against the University-Printers of *Oxford*, and *Cambridge*, who enjoy also the printing of the Bible by Patent ; against the Company of the Stationers themselves who enjoy by Patent four severall Books, *viz.* The Psalter, Psalmes, Primmer, and Almanack ; yea this may be objected against very many Stationers, and some Printers, who notwithstanding ought not

310

thereupon to be deprived, or debarred of their rights ; for it is, and ought to be held a *Maxime* in Law, and Equity, as in Divinity, *that not any shall doe bad, that good may come thereof* ; and consequently not to violate any one of his Propriety, or right, that thereby some or any benefit may accrew to others : moreover all well Regulated Polities (especially Republiques) *doe conserve the particular Right of every Person Individually, so farre as such Right opposeth not the Generall Good* ; *and thereby preserve the Generall Good, without violating any ones particular Right unjustly or indirectly*, according to which Rule, neither *Mathew Barker*, nor other the Stationers, or Printers nominated ought to be debarred, or deprived any their Originalls, or Copies.

If any one should object (as lately a Stationer did unto my selfe) that the Bible cannot properly be called a *Copy*, because it is the written Word of God : although such objection be frivolous, yet to such I answere, that the severall Translations thereof are properly copies, as are the singing, or Meetred Psalmes also belonging to the Stationers aforesaid, *Erasmus* his Latine Translation of the Testament, and many others of the like nature.

XX.

Peradventure some greedy, and it may be needy Printers, and Stationers, will not be satisfied with Reason, unlesse they may against reasonable equity, invade other mens Proprieties, and Rights. But I hope the High Representative of this Nation, at what time they shall in their wisdomes thinke fit to passe an Act, or Acts for the *Regulating of Printing*, will therein by expresse *Provisoes* confirm, and ratifie not onely the propriety of *Mathew Barker* aforesaid, for him, and his Assignes, but all such other Propriety and Proprieties which belong to the Company of the Stationers, to every free Stationer respectively ; whereby the Prudent care of the *Parliament* will suppresse Licencious Incroachments upon many considerable Copies, and avoyd therein future debate and controversy.

WILLIAM BALL.

Certaine Additional Answers | to such
Objections, as may perad/venture be made.

I.

If it should be said that the Penalties which I have proposed are too great, and also that Penalty left to discretion, in some cases may seeme Rigor.

I answer, that Abuses are seldome reformed without great Penalties ; and in Regard as great Detriment may ensue to a Common-wealth by scandalous, and erroneous Printing, as may by counterfeit and debased Coyning ; The Penalty for the one, ought in some measure to æqualize the Penalty of the other : And Penalty in some cases left to the Discretion of grave Personages is not Rigor, but *Prudent Terror*, which may be regulated by *Neutrall Equity.*

II.

If it should be said, that the Commissioners of the Great Seale, Judges of the Law, Secretary of State, and some others whom I have nominated for Licencing of Bookes, may in Regard of their great and weighty Affaires want leisure to peruse, and Licence Books, &c.

I answer, that every one of the said Persons and others who shall have power to licence, may have power to entrust, and depute one for them, provided themselves will be responsible for the errors which such Deputies shall Commit ; and that such Deputies set their owne names, and the names for whom they are deputed unto such Bookes, &c. which they shall Licence.

III.

If it should be said, That requiring double Copies, and an Office for Registry thereof would be vexatious, &c. I answer, that the abuses to Licensers, as also to Authors have been so great, (as my selfe amongst others can testifie in a late Booke of mine owne) that no safer way can be found ; moreover why should not those things which appertaine to the minde be kept upon *Record*, as are many things that appertaine meerely to Livelyhood ; and whether men write for the Glory of Almighty God, and good of others (which ought to be the chiefe ends) or the profit of themselves, let them take so much paines as to write the subject twice, or otherwise spare their paines for once. And if it should be said, that by that meanes fewer bookes will come into the Presse, I answer, not the numerous multitude of Bookes, but the solid validity of them will benefit a Common-wealth.

WILLIAM BALL.

C

Printing Act of 7 January, 1653

The following amendments to the Bill were rejected by Parliament :—

1. ' That the Act be not interpreted to the Impeachment, Annulling, Diminution, or Prejudice, of the Title or Interest of Robert Barker the younger, and all claiming under him, to the sole Printing of the translated Copy of the Bible, commonly called the New Translation.'

2. ' That the Council of State fix a reasonable price for unbound Bibles.'

3. That hawkers be severely punished.

4. ' That no Books, after the same are searched, should be seized, or taken out of the Possession of such Persons as are employed in the Printing or Keeping thereof, by the Master and Wardens of the Company of Stationers alone, unless the Book be scandalous.'

An Act for reviving of a former Act, Entituled, An Act against Unlicensed and Scandalous Books and Pamphlets, and for Regulating of Printing, *with some Additions and explanations.* [7 *January*, 1653.]

Whereas a late Act, Entituled, *An Act against Unlicensed and Scandalous Books and Pamphlets*, and for better *Regulating of Printing*, hath appeared by experience to be a good and profitable Law for the ends therein expressed ; and that the discontinuance thereof hath occasioned some lewd Pens and Presses to reassume their former boldness, in Writing, Printing and Dispersing Unwarrantable, Seditious and Scandalous Papers, Books and Pamphlets, to the great dishonour of God and offence of the Parliament, and insufferable contempt of all good Order and Government ; And whereas many of the Evils and Exorbitances complained of in that Act, appear to have been occasioned through the multiplying of Printing-houses, without any Warrant or Authority, and by reason of the Artifice and Subtilty of restless Spirits, unwilling to be confined within the limits of orderly Government ; The Parliament of England taking the premises into their serious consideration, finde it requisite to revive and explain the said Law, and to supply the further Remedies following ; Be it therefore by the Authority of this present Parliament Enacted, Ordained and Declared, That the said Act, Entituled as aforesaid, and all the Clauses therein contained, Saving for so much thereof wherein alteration shall be made by this present Act, be from henceforth revived, and remain in full force and vertue.

And be it by the Authority aforesaid Enacted and Ordained, That the Council of State for the time being, be Impowered to inquire how many, and which of the said Printing-houses now in being shall be continued ; and how such others of them, as shall be by the said Council judged meet to be suppressed, shall be disposed of ; and what number of Apprentices and Presses every Master-printer (to be allowed by the said Council of State) shall have at one time ; and to have full Power to take such Order therein, as to them shall appear just and convenient.

And forasmuch as the Life and Growth of all Arts and Mysteries consisteth in a due Regulation thereof, Be it therefore Enacted and Ordained by the Authority aforesaid, That the Government and Regulation of the said Mystery of Printing and Printers, shall from henceforth be and remain in the Council of State for the time being ; and that the Master, Wardens and Assistants of the Company of Stationers London shall follow and observe such Rules, orders and Directions concerning the Regulation of Printing, as they shall from time to time have and receive from the said Council successively : And the said Council of State for the time being, and Master, Wardens and Assistants of the said Company, according to such Rules and Directions as they shall receive

315

from the said Council, are hereby Authorized and Required to use all good means with care and diligence, for the preventing and punishing of Offences and Misdemeanors against this Act, and the Laws, Statutes and Ordinances heretofore made and now in force, against Unlicensed and Scandalous Books and Pamphlets, and for the better Regulating of Printing.

And be it further Enacted and Ordained by the Authority aforesaid, .That no person or persons shall or may at any time or times hereafter, Excepting such as shall be Licensed and Authorized by the Parliament or Council of State, or may claim a Priviledge thereunto by Patrimonial Right, Use or Exercise the Art, Trade or Mystery of a Printer of Books, unless he or they heretofore have, or hereafter shall have served as an Apprentice by the space of Seven Years in the said Art, Mystery and Science of Printing, with some Lawful Master-Printer of this Commonwealth of England ; and that every such person and persons who shall be so qualified and enabled to be a Printer, and shall take upon him the Trade or Mystery of Printing as a Master-Printer, shall Use and Exercise the same in his and their respective Dwelling Houses, and not elsewhere, Any Law, Statute, Priviledge, Usage or Custom to the contrary thereof in any wise notwithstanding, under the Penalty of Forty Pounds for every Moneth, and so proportionably for any shorter or longer time, to be forfeited by every person offending against the Provision aforesaid.

And whereas by the said recited Act, it is provided amongst other things, that no Dry-fats, Packs, Maunds, Chests, Fardels of Books imported into this Commonwealth, be permitted by any Officers of the Customs or Excise to be Opened or Conveyed away before Notice given ; and that the same be Searched and Viewed (within Forty eight Hours after such notice) by the said Master and Wardens of the said Company of Stationers, or such as they shall appoint ; It is hereby now Enacted and Declared, That the Lords-Days, and Days of Publique Thanksgiving and

Humiliation (if any such shall happen within the said Forty eight Hours next after such Notice as aforesaid) be not accompted nor reckoned as part of the said Forty eight Hours.

And be it further Enacted by the authority aforesaid, That what Books or other things prohibited by this or the said recited Act, the said Master and Wardens, or such as they shall appoint, shall finde and seize upon their search and view as aforesaid, they are hereby authorized and required to bring them, or cause them to be brought to Stationers-Hall London, there to remain and to be disposed of as by the said Act is directed : And to the end that the said searches and views may be made without Spoil or Damage to the Owners of the Goods so Imported, Be it further Enacted by the Authority aforesaid, That the said Master and Wardens, or any of them, shall have Power to appoint some convenient place where the said Search shall be made ; and that no Merchant or Owner of any such Books Imported, shall open their said Goods, or permit them to be opened, but in the presence of the said Master and Wardens, or such as they shall appoint, upon the Penalty of Forfeiture of Five pounds for every such Offence ; Provided that such Search and View be made within the time above limited after such Notice as aforesaid.

And be it further Enacted by the Authority aforesaid, That all and every the pecuniary Forfeitures and Penalties mentioned, as well in this Act as in the said other recited Act, which shall be incurred by any Offender or Offenders against either of the said Acts, shall and may be Sued for in any Court of Record whatsoever, within the Jurisdiction whereof such Offence shall be committed, by Action of Debt, Bill, Plaint or Information, wherein no Essoyn, Wager of Law, or Protection shall be admitted or allowed to the Defendant or Defendants : The one Moyety of all which Forfeitures, if recovered by the Prosecution or Appointment of the said Company of Stationers, after Deduction and Satisfaction of the Charges of Recovery, shall be by them received and reserved, shall be for the Use of the Poor of their Company ;

and if by the Prosecution of any other person, then to the Use of the Prosecutor ; and the other Moyety or one Half shall be to and for the Use of the Commonwealth, and be accompted for accordingly.

And it is further Enacted and Ordained by the Authority aforesaid, That the Council of State for the time being, shall hereby have like Power as in the said former Act is contained, to all Intents and Purposes, for the more full and effectual Execution of the same.

And be it further Enacted and Declared, that the Agent for the Army for the time being, in stead of the Secretary of the Army formerly appointed, shall have Power to License such Intelligence as may concern the Affairs of the Army onely, under the like Rules and Directions as are contained in the said Act of September, One thousand six hundred forty and nine.

Provided always, and be it further Enacted by the Authority aforesaid, That no Clause or Clauses, either in this or the said recited Act of September, One thousand six hundred forty and nine, shall be construed to extend to the Prejudice or Infringing of any of the just Rights and Priviledges of any of the Printers of either of the two Universities in this Commonwealth ; But that the same shall be full as large and effectual to all Intents and Purposes, as if this and the said recited Act of September, One thousand six hundred forty and nine, had not been had or made.

D

The Humble Remonstrance of the Stationers' Company to Parliament[1]

As the mistery and Art of printing hath proved of great concernment to the advancement of Religion & learning of all sorts, for the better enabling of the students thereof, for the well and peaceable governing of the Commonwealth and the instruction of men in good manners, the same being well ordered and Regulated. Soe the disorderly & unlimitted tolleration & licence given to all persons to Imprint what they please, hath proved not only to be a meanes for the Corruption of Religion & good manners, but of scandall Ignominy and reproach of the present Government, it being most true that in things most precious & excellent the abuse if not prevented is commonly more dangerous than the use is advantageous. And therefore in all ages since the invention thereof in this nation it hath been thought very expedient as a flower of the present supreame power, that not only the Regulation thereof but the sole power for the graunting of the Impression of all Bookes especially those of most common & publique use, and the restriction of all others than such to whom the supreame power should vouchsafe to grant the same, should remayne in the sole dispose of the present supreame power, And such grauntes in all successive ages amongst us were ever held to have a full & absolute interest in such impressions so graunted unto them and no others to pretend interest in the same. And to the end this may appeare not to be a bare suggestion but the reall truth, the sd Company are ready to make it appeare by many instances & examples of graunts of that nature, for above this Hundred yeares successively, and the enjoyment of the fruit of those graunts without the least interruption, untill by some irregular persons since the tymes of the late publique destractions, and more especially by Robert White a printer of the Citie of London, who

[1] Transcribed from the original document in the Public Record Office.

hath petitioned you the Right hono^ble the Councell of State against divers of the same Company, having done nothing at all against him but what is warrantable by Law, as they hope it will appeare to you hono^r by their Case which is as it followeth.

Queene Elizabeth late Queen of England (taking into her Consideration that divers great abuses and many fantasticall and fond prophesyings had crept in by the great Libertie which was takeing in the Printing of Almanacks and pamphlets of that nature) by her Letters Patents bearing the date the third day of Decemb in the One and seventieth yeare of her Raigne did graunt unto Richard Watkins and James Roberts for the tearme of One and seventieth yeares the sole Impression of all Almanacks, and prognostications whatsoever, & of all manner of Bookes and pamphlets tending to the same purpose thereby restrayning all others for the printing of the same which tearme being expired King James by his Lettrs Patents dated the Eighth day of March in the thirteenth yeare of his Raigne for the releife of the sd Company of Stationers (amongst other things) did graunt unto the Mr Wardens & Coyalty of the same Company & their successors full power priviledge and authority from tyme to tyme forever to print or cause to bee printed All manner of Almanacks and prognostications whatsoever in the English tongue, and all manner of Bookes, & pamphlets tending to the same purpose, with straight comandment & prohibition to all other printers and others to print the same ; under the which two before mentioned graunts the said graunts respectively have ever since quietly & peaceably enjoyed the sole Impression of all Almanacks being above sixty yeares whereby the poore of the sd Company have received great releife and succour, and the which if it shalbe interupted they must of necessity perish.

Afterward the late parliament taking into consideration the great care of the said Company in the discovery of the Authors & Printers of unlicensed & scandalous Bookes & Pamphlets, for the better releife of the poore of the sd Company they did ordaine &

appoint that no person or persons whatsoever should from the fourteenth day of June 1643 print or cause to bee printed any Booke or Bookes, or part of any Booke or Bookes before that tyme allowed of, & graunted to the sd Company of Stationers for their releife and maintenance, without the Licence and consent of the Mr Wardens and Assistants of the same Company upon paine of forfeiture of the same and with power to seize the same.

Afterwards by an Act made the same Parliament the 20th of 7ber 1649 (amongst other things) it was Enacted, that no person or persons whatsoever within this Common-wealth should from thenceforth Print or reprint any Booke or Bookes or part of any Booke or Bookes legally graunted to the sd Company for their releife or maintenance of their poore without the Lycence & consent of the Mr Wardens & Assistants of the same Company, upon paine of forfeiture of the same and six shillings & eight pence for every Booke printed or stitched bound or put to sale.

And by another Act made the 7th of January 1652[1] the said last mentioned Act is made perpetuall & enlarged & power given to the sd Mr and Wardens and such as they shall appoint to seize such Bookes as are prohibited by the sd first Act and to bring them to the Stationers hall London there to remaine to bee disposed of according to the sd Act first mentioned.

The Mr Wardens & Coyalty of the same Company being Interested in the printing of Almanacks as is aforesaid, and the sd Mr & Wardens being impowered to seize as aforesaid, and being commanded by the present Councell of State to seize all unlicensed & prohibited Bookes, In pursuance thereof the One & Seventieth day of September last past haveing certaine knowledge that the sd petitioner Robert White had formerly printed or caused to be printed A scandalous Almanack called Whartons Almanack : they did repaire to the house of the sd Robert White to search for aswell scandalous as prohibited Bookes by the sd severall Acts & to seize the same where after a faire demand made

[1] i.e. 1653, according to the modern reckoning.

to the sd White to come into his house for to search according to their power & a refusall they did according to the power given by the sd first mentioned Act brake open the Doores & upon search did find divers Almanacks which the said White had printed contrary to the aforesd graunt made unto the said Company, and without any Licence or Entry made with them at their hall according to the Custome, which Almanacks according to Law (as they humbly conceive) they did seize & carry away to their Common Hall where they all remaine in specie undefaced to bee disposed of according to law ;

All which premises considered the said Mr and Wardens & the rest doe humbly conceive that they have done no Injury to the said petitioner but that what they have done is warrantable & agreeable to Law & Justice.

*Orders of His Highness the Lord Protector, made and
published by and with the Advice and Consent of
His Council, for putting in speedy and due Execution
the Laws, Statutes and Ordinances, made and provided
against Printing Unlicensed and Scandalous Books and
Pamphlets, and for further Regulating of Printing.*

Whereas in default of the speedy, due, and effectual execution of
the many good Laws, Statutes, and Ordinances heretofore made
and published, against Unlicensed, Seditious, and Scandalous
Books and Pamphlets ; divers evil-minded persons, and of
malicious, insolent and restless Spirits, have assumed to themselves, and do continually take upon them a licencious boldness,
to Write, Print, Publish, and Disperse several Dangerous, Unwarrantable, Seditious, Blasphemous, and Scandalous Pamphlets,
Books and Papers, to the high Dishonor of Almighty God, the
endangering of the peace of this Commonwealth, the violation of
all good Order and Government, and in manifest Contempt and
Scorn of the Government and Laws of the Land ; which we
having into Our Consideration, do hold Our selves obliged to
provide Remedy to the aforesaid Evils : And therefore (having
Confidence of the Care, Diligence, Discretion, and good Affection
of you, *John Barkstead*, Esq ; Lieutenant of Our Tower of
London, *John Dethick* Alderman of Our City of *London*, and
George Foxcroft, to Us, the present Government, and Peace and
Welfare of this Commonwealth) We have thought fit, (as we
hereby do) to intrust, and commit unto you, jointly and severally
the Execution of these Orders and Directions, touching the Premises, with the several Powers and Authorities hereafter mentioned, as well for the punishment of such Offenders, as the
timely preventing and suppressing of all Seditious, Blasphemous,
and other Libellous pamphlets, Books and Papers whatsoever.
And for your better and more effectual proceeding therein, Our

Will and Pleasure is, And We do hereby Authorise, and straitly Charge and Command you carefully to observe these Orders, Rules, and Directions following :

I.

That without delay you diligently search and inquire concerning the Printing-houses, Presses, and Master-Printers, as well for the certain number of them, as also for the names of the Master-Printers, and of the names and number of Servants, Workmen, and Apprentices, each Master Printer hath or shall hereafter retain, and how many Presses each Master-Printer hath, within Our Cities of *London*, and *Westminster*, and Borrough of *Southwark*, or the Liberties, Suburbs, or the Precincts thereof, and of what fame, quality, conversation, or condition every such Master-Printer is, and how he, and his Servants, and Work-men stand affected to the present Government ; And that you make Certificate of all the premises unto Us, or Our Council within eight and twenty daies after your Receipt hereof.

II.

That you carefully inform your selves what person or persons (not having a lawful license in that bealf) do take upon them to print, or use, or put in practice, or cause to be used or put in practise the Art or Mystery of Printing, or do use or employ, by themselves or others, any Printing-Press, Rolling-Press, or other Instrument for Printing, in any, and what place or part of this Common-wealth. And where any such shall be found, That you cause all their Printing-Letters and Materials for Printing to be immediately defaced, and the Offendors prosecuted, for recovery of the forfeitures, summes of money, and penalties by them incurred in this behalf, and cause them to be otherwise punished according to the Laws and Statutes of the Land in such cases made and provided.

III.

That you also inform your selves whether the Printers and other Persons in Our City of *London*, and Liberties thereof or elsewhere, who keep Printing-Houses, or are owners of Printing-Presses, Rolling-Presses, or other Instruments for Printing, have entred into Bonds respectively with two sufficient sureties, according to the purport and direction of the Act of Parliament, Intituled, *An Act against unlicensed and scandalous Books and Pamphlets, and for better regulating of Printing* ; And in case they have entred into such Bonds accordingly : Then whether they have, since that time offended ; or shall hereafter offend in any of the premises or particulars mentioned in the said Act of Parliament : or broken the conditions of those respective Bonds, to the end, you may in like manner prosecute them, and their sureties in Our name for recovery of the penalties in the several obligations mentioned, and by them forfeited by the said conditions broken, and otherwise according to Law and their respective demerits.

IV.

That you take especial Care and see, That no person or persons presume to Print, Reprint, or Publish, or cause to be Printed, Reprinted, or Published, any Pamphlets, Books of News, Occurrences, or other such like Papers whatsoever, unless he, or they shall be hereafter thereunto lawfully Authorized by Command from Us, or Our Council, or unless such Newes, Occurrences or such like Papers be Licensed by such as shall be appointed thereunto by Us or Our Council. And whosoever shall offend in the premises, shall be proceeded against by you, according to the Laws established against unlicensed and scandalous Pamphlets for such their contempt and disobedience in the premises.

V.

And further, Our Will and pleasure is, And more particularly We do hereby require, Authorise, and Command you, for the better execution of the premises, That you put in speedy and effectual execution in all things not hereby altered or otherwise directed, the Ordinance of the Lords and Commons Assembled

325

in Parliament, of *Septem*. 1647. Intituled, *An Ordinance against unlicensed or scandalous Pamphlets, and for the better Regulating of Printing*, As also one other Ordinance of the Lords and Commons in Parliament, of the 14. of June 1643. for Regulating of Printing, and suppressing the great abuses and frequent disorders therein, and the Act of the Common-Council of Our City of *London*, bearing the date the ninth of October, 1643. prohibiting all persons whatsoever from crying or putting to sale about the streets within the said City of *London*, and Liberties thereof, any Pamphlets, Books, or Papers whatsoever, by way of hawking, and for punishment of the Offendours therein ; And if any person or persons hath or have heretofore offended, or hereafter shall offend in the premises, or shall abet and countenance the same, contrary to the said Acts or Ordinances, or any other Act or Ordinance now in force, We do hereby Will, Authorise, and Command you, that immediately you repair to the place or places where they are or shall be abiding, aswel within Liberties as Without, and to apprehend, and arrest, or cause to be arrested the bodies of them, and every of them so offending, and their Complices and Abettors, and to cause them to be sent in safe and secure Custody unto Bride-well, And to cause all such corporal and pecuniary punishments to be speedily and impartially inflicted on such of the Offenders in the premises, and the penalties duly levied for their several offences, as therein and thereby are mentioned and provided ; And we will they shall not be thence discharged until they shall have made full payment and satisfaction, and received the said punishment accordingly. And the Governors of Bride-well, are hereby required to see such Offendors as shall be sent to them punished according to the Law. And you are hereby also Authorised and required from time to time to make diligent search in all places where you shall think meet for all Printing Presses, any way employed in Printing such scandalous, seditious, and unlicensed Papers, Pamphlets, Books, or Ballads whatsoever, and to seise, and carry away such Printing-Presses

326

and Letters, with the Nut, Spindle, and other Materials of every such irregular Printer, which you shall finde so mis-employed, unto the Stationers Hall in our said City of *London*, there to be defaced, and made unserviceable, according to the said Acts and Ordinances of Parliament in that behalf : As also to make diligent search and inquiry in all suspected Printing-Houses, Warehouses, Shops, and other places whatsoever, for such unlicensed Books, Papers, Sheet or Sheets of News whatsoever, as is herein before directed ; And the same to detain and keep, to be disposed of as We or Our Council shall think fit ; And in case of any opposition or resistance in the premises ; We hereby Authorise and require you, to break open all or any locks or doors, and to apprehend all and every person and persons whom you shall finde so opposing or resisting, to convent or cause to be brought before the Lord Mayor of Our City of *London*, or any other of Our Justices of Peace to be examined and proceeded against according to the Law. And all Our Justices of Peace, Mayors, Sheriffs, Bailiffs, Constables, Head-Boroughs, and all and every other Our Officers, and Ministers of Justice both Civil and Military, and other persons whatsoever, are hereby required and commanded to be aiding, and assisting unto you, or your Deputies, in the execution of the premisses, as they and every of them will answer the contrary at their utmost perils. And We do hereby give you full power and authority to assign, depute, and employ any fit and discreet persons under you by writing under your hands and seals, for the better execution of these Orders and Directions, and to reward prosecutors (allowance whereof shall be made unto you by the Council) and do all and every such other thing and things as are meet and requisite to the effectual performance of this Our service, so much conducing to the preservation of the publique peace : For all which, these presents shall be a sufficient Warrant and discharge in this behalf.

Given at *White-Hall* the eight and twentieth day of August, 1655.[1]

[1] B.M., E.1064.58.

F

[1]*A Fresh Discovery/Of The/High-Presbyterian Spirit./ Or The/*Quenching *of the* second Beacon fired./*Declaring/*

1. *The Un-Christian Dealings of the Authors of a Pam/phlet, Entituled,* A Second Beacon Fired, &c. *In present/ing unto the Lord Protector and Parliament, a falsified/passage out of one of Mr* John Goodwins *Books, as con/taining, either Blasphemie, or Error, or both./*

11. *The Evil of their Petition for subjecting the Libertie/of the* Press *to the Arbitrariness and will of a few men.*

111. *The Christian Equity, that satisfaction be given to/the Person so notoriously and publickly wronged./ Together with the Responsatory Epistle of the said Beacon Firers,/to the said Mr* Goodwin, *fraught with further revilings, falsifications, scurrilous language ; &c. instead of a Christian ac-/knowledgment of their errour.*

Upon which Epistle some Animadversions are made, | By John Goodwin, *A Servant of God in the | Gospel of his Dear Son./ . . . London, Printed for the Author, and are to be sold by H. Cripps,/ and L.Ll. in Popes head Alley.* 1654.

[p. 4.] 2. That pernicious Counsel against the liberty of Printing and for the subjecting of all the learning, gifts, parts and abilities of all the worthy men in the Nation, unto the humor and conceit of a few men, who for their comporting with the Religion of the times, shall be sirnamed, Orthodox, which the said Beacon-firers do (in effect) very passionately suggest and commend unto the Parliament, (p. 11.) and which, were it put in execution according to the terms of the suggestion, would certainly fire both Citie, and Countrie, as well as *Beacons,* should (me think) argue the *second Beacon* not to be of your *firing.* For you are reputed friends

[1] (*B.M.,* E.821., 18 January, 1655.)

unto *Jesus Christ*, and to the truth : and consequently who can imagine that you should give any such advice, especially unto a Parliament, which is of an obstructive, at least of a threatening import, to the advancement, and further discovery of *Jesus Christ* unto the world, yea and which, were it pursued by those, to whom it is given, cannot (in greatest likelyhood) but sort to an issue or consequence, quite contrary to that, whereunto it pretends ; I mean, to a further propagating and spreading of errors and unsound Doctrines and Opinions in the Land ; and for the justification whereof, there is neither footing nor foundation in the Scriptures. For,

1. Where doth the Lord Christ, authorize any person, or persons, of what capacity soever, to authorize or appoint any number of men, whom they shall please to call Orthodox (whether they be such or no) yea or those, which are such indeed, to say unto the Holy Ghost ; nothing which thou revealest unto other men, be it never so much for the glorifying of the name of God, of never such worthy and sacred concernment unto the world, shall publickly go forth into the world, unlesse thou wilt reveal the same unto us also, and make us partakers of the Vision, as well as others ? Or doth not the *Beacon-firers*, very passionately and importunely tempt men in authority to assume unto themselves such an exorbitant and prodigious power, as this ; I mean, to authorize a certain number of men, who shall, in their sence, be Orthodox ; though according to the sence of as understanding men, and (probably according) to the truth it self, be as erroneous in their judgement as other men, to word it is (in effect) at such a rate with the Holy Ghost ?

2. What ground is there in the Word of God for the investing of *Edmund* (for example) *Arthur*, and *William*, with a *Nebuchadnezzarean* power over the Press, to stifle or slay what books they please, and what they please, to keep alive, more than there is for the investing of *Joshuah*, *Peter*, and *Tobiah*, with the same ? Or if the three latter be altogether as religious, as judicious, as

329

learned, as the three former, by what rule of equity, reason, or conscience, should they be more obnoxious in their writings, and publication of them, to the censure and disapprobation of these, than these in their writings unto them ? Or by what rule delivered in the Word of God shall any man judge the three former, either more religious, learned, or judicious, and so more meet for the intrustment under consideration, than the latter ?

3. Whether hath the Holy Ghost any where characterized, or declared what qualifications are requisite and meet, to be found in such persons, who shall bee set over the Press and be intrusted with such a soveraignty of power, as by which they shall be inabled to fill the world with books and writings, for the advancement of their own faction, or for the propagation of their own erroneous, (and perhaps dangerous) conceits, and on the other hand, to suppresse whatsoever shall bee prepared by men of solid and sound judgements for the detection, and eviction of their folly in such cases ?

4. Is not the granting of such a power over the presse, as the Beacon firers in the great heat of their devotion and zeal, sollicite the Parliament to vest in a certain number of men, ill consistent with the interest and benefit of a free Commonwealth, and of like nature and consideration with the granting of Monopolies ? Or may not the Commonwealth deeply suffer by the exercise of such a power, in being thereby deprived of the use and benefit of the gifts, parts, experiments, diligence and labours of many her worthy members ?

5. Who are in a regular capacity of power, to nominate and appoint such persons, to whom the said power over the Press ought to be committed ? If it be said, the Civil Magistrate.

1. I would gladly know of the *Beacon-firers*, who hath delegated such a power or authority unto him, or in what part of the Word of God, any such power is asserted unto him.

2. Whether the said power over the Press bee an Ecclesiastick or civil power ? If it be the latter, how are men set apart for the

ministery of the Word of God, and prayer, capable of the investiture ? If it be the former, how is the civil Magistrate in a capacity of conferring it, or investing any man with it ?

6. If the Supream Magistrate in a State or Commonwealth, be allowed a power to invest what persons he pleaseth with such a power over the Press, as the *Beacon-firers* demand, is it not to be expected that onely such persons shall be deputed to this trust by him, which are of his own sence and judgement in matters of Religion, and consequently who shall comply with a State Religion ? And are men of this character competent Arbitrators, between persons of their own party and perswasion, and those who are contrary minded to them, in their contests about truth and errour ? And in case the Magistrate himself shall be unsound in the faith (as men of this Order have no priviledge of exemption from errour, more than other men ; nay, they are under more and greater temptations, than other men, to be carried aside in their judgements from the truth) if then (I say) the Magistrate be of an unsound judgement in things appertaining unto God, shall not our Press-Masters be unsound also ; and consequently, shall we not have errour countenanced and set at liberty, and truth imprisoned, and condemned to silence and obscurity ?

7. Shall not such men who shall undertake the administration of such a power, by which the Press shall be suffered to speak when they please, and be compelled to keep silence when they please likewise, run an extream hazard of fighting against God ? Or to reject and repel the Holy Ghost, when he shall at any time be desirous to come forth by the way of the Press, into the world with any new Discovery of Truth, is this anything lesse (being interpreted) than a fighting against God ? Or do they, who know but in part, universally or infallibly know, when the spirit of truth, and when the spirit of errour is desirous to come abroad into the world ?

8. Doth not a power of gagging the Press, when men please, carry a dangerous Antipathy in it to that Evangelical charge, or

331

APPENDIX

precept, imposed upon all men, whereby they are commanded by God to try all things, and particularly to try the spirits, whether they be of God or no ? For if many things, or many spirits of Doctrines be not suffered to come to the knowledge of men, how shall they be able to try them ? Do not then the Beacon-firers, by their counsel given to the Lord Protector and Parliament, for the restraining of the Presse, render that great commandement of God for the trial of all things, of none effect ?

9. And lastly, That great evill of the infectious spreading of errours and heresies in the Nation, the prevention whereof the said advice given touching the Press, pretendeth unto, is not likely to be at all prevented, but promoted rather, by it, should it be followed and put in execution. For,

1. (As the saying is) *Quod licet ingratum est, quod non licet, acrius urit.*

> *What Laws permit to do, to do*
> *Men do not much desire :*
> *But what restrained is, to do*
> *They burn as hot as Fire.*

And the Apostle *Paul* himself saith : That *Sin taking occasion by the commandement, wrought in him all manner of concupiscence. For without the Law, Sin is dead.* Rom. 7. 8. And little question there is, but that in case the liberty of the Press shall bee by any law restreined, they who otherwise would be but indifferent whether they published in Print their weak, it may be their erroneous and wicked conceptions, or no, will be hereby admonished and provoked to do it, though more secretly. Stollen Waters are sweet.

2. In case they shall by any such law of restraint, be kept from venting their fond and uncouth notions by the Press, or shall by the Masters of the Press bee prohibited the Printing of them, they will by way of indignation and revenge be so much the more zealously diligent and intent to propagate them underhand, and

332

privately ; and probably gain many more disciples this way, than by the other. *The prophane and vain babling* of Hymeneus *and* Philetus *fretted like a Canker*, although they wanted the opportunity of a Press for their propagation.

3. When the generality of people shal understand that the publishing of such or such notions, or Tenents, hath been restrained and obstructed by those, who shall exercise an arbitrary dominion over the Presse, it will (in reason) both occasion them to think the better of them, or at least to think that there is somewhat more than ordinary in them, in one kind, or other ; and consequently, they will be awakened and stirred in their spirits to inquire more narrowly after them, and to acquaint themselves with them. So that in this respect also there is little like to be gained towards the suppression of errors and heresies, by subjecting the Presse unto a Test.

4. The setting of Watchmen with authority at the door of the Presse to keep errors and heresies out of the world, is as weak a project and design, as it would be to set a company of armed men about an house to keep darknesse out of it in the night season. For as the natural darknesse cannot be prevented, or dispelled, but by the presence of light, nor needeth there to be any thing, either for the preventing or dispelling it, but light onely : So neither is it possible either to prevent, or to remove, errors and heresies, which are spiritual darknesse, but onely by shining spiritual light in the hearts and understandings of men ; neither needeth there any thing but this to effect either.

5. Errors and Heresies, the lesse they play in sight, are like to defend themselves upon terms of more advantage, and to lengthen out the daies of their continuance amongst men for the longer time. For by this means they are kept from the clear and distinct knowledge of judicious and learned men, who otherwise, being both able and willing to perform so worthy a service both unto God and men, would publickly detect and confute them. And I verily beleeve that the printing of *J. Biddles* most enormous

333

and hideous notions, and conceits about the nature of God, and some other very weighty points in religion, will bring the judgement of *bloody and deceitful men upon them*, which (according to *Davids* Award) is, *not to live out half their daies*. *Psal*, 55. 23, For as the great Apostles reasoneth concerning such Teachers, whom he calleth men of corrupt minds ἀδόχιμοι ωἐὶ τιὼ πιϛιν *injudicious*, or without judgement, *about matters of Faith, But* (saith he) *they shal proceed no further for their madnesse shall be manifest unto all men, as theirs also was* ; so is it very reasonable to conceive and judge, that the more generally and publickly any vile, wicked, or blasphemous conceit shall discover and manifest it self unto men, it is so much the nearer to become the loathing and abhorring of all men. Nor do the *Beacon-firers* argue like worthy men, when from the number of buyers, and from hence conclude the number of persons, either infected with, or inclined to, the errors contained and pleaded for, in those books. For who knoweth not that many men, especially Ministers, Schollars, and learned men, buy many books, not with any intent to say as they say, or to side in opinion with their Authors, but partly to inform themselves concerning the spirits that come abroad into the world, partly to rebuke and confute them upon occasion, in case they see cause for it ?

6. (And lastly for this) The Gospel, and the truth never flourished, prospered, & triumphed at a higher rate in the world, than when errors and heresies were no otherwise restreined, punished, or opposed, than by those spiritual means, which God himself hath sanctified and prescribed in this behalf, as *viz.* by the effectual preaching of the Gospel, the stopping of the mouths of the gain-sayers of truth by arguments of conviction, and solid demonstration ; by casting out of their respective Churches, and delivering up unto Sathan, all such, who after admonition and conviction, shall persist in their errors, and in the teaching and spreading of them. But certainly amongst all the means, Offices, and Officers, which the Lord Christ hath directed or established,

for the perfecting of the Saints, for the work of the Ministry, for the edifying of the body of Christ, till we all come in the unity of the faith, and acknowledgement of the Son of God, unto a perfect man, &c. neither restraint of printing, nor Licensers of the Presse, are to be found ; these are Apocryphal, both Names and Things. This for the second particular.

For the third and last, He, or they (whether it be some other, others, or your selves) who have represented you as the firers of the second Beacon, and consequently, the Authors of the advice given (in the Pamphlet mentioned) touching the monopolizing of the Presse, do insinuate you as men, who can be too well content that others of the same craft with you, should suffer in their trade, so you may advance in yours. For it is not much to be doubted, but that your desire is, that such men as you count Orthodox, should be recommended by you, or by your motion & interest, to the high preferment over the Presse, who by the opportunity of their standing on this ground, shall be in a good capacity to gratifie their friends and benefactors in their way. But in this I shall spare you.

For a cloze, I shall make this reasonable and Christian request unto you, that in case you be fellow-sufferers with me, and have not been privy or consenting to the framing or publishing of that unworthy Pamphlet, intituled, *A Second Beacon fired, &c.* you will publickly, and in print, wash your hands from the guilt hereof, and declare unto the world, that you had neither right hand nor left, either in the inditing, or venting, of that Pamphlet. Or if your consciences be not at liberty to accommodate you in this (for by somewhat I have heard since I began this Epistle to you, I am little lesse than all thoughts made that you are the true, and not the personated, *Beacon-firers* your selves) that then you will with your own hands, quench your Beacon on fire. . . .

335

APPENDIX

Mr. John Goodwins Notes on the Six Book-sellers Letter (in reply
to the above)

[p. 48.] Your Cavil at my *investing Doctor Whichcote, Doctor
Cudworth* &c. with a *Nebuchadnezzarean Power over books and
opinions*, is extreamly childish and futile. . . . I do not any
where use the expression of a *Nebuchadnezzarean Power*, in all my
Epistle to them. Nor secondly, do I *invest* them with any power,
priviledge, prerogative, or the like ; but only declare, or affirm,
them to be *invested* already. . . .

. . . Nor is it any better than a putid or silly cavil, not worthy
the *Genius* of a School-Boy of ten or twelve years old, to charge
me with *the grossest Blasphemy*, because I ascribe unto the
University an *Autocratorical majesty over Books and opinions*, in
such a sence, as I declare and explain in the period immediately
following, at large. Nor would your Committee of Licensers,
should the Parliament indulge you in your Anti-*Christian*[1]
request about them, (which I trust is found among the *Absits*
of all considering men) be able to accommodate you in your expec-
tations, or desires, if they should not invest them with such an
Autocratorical Majesty over Books and Opinions, as I ascribe to
the Doctors of *Cambridge* : Should then the Parliament be guilty,
either of *base flattery*, or of the *grossest Blasphemy*, in case they
should invest them with such a power *over Books and Opinions*,
as that which I Rhetorically term, an *Autocratorical Majesty* ?
Or have I not every whit as much ground of *hope*, that there will
be found none (at least no wise men) who will take that power and
glory, to themselves, without which Licensers of the Presse
cannot be established to do their work effectually, and with

[1] *I call your request,* Anti-Christian, *because a restraint of the Press is generally
practised, where* Anti-Christ *hath his Throne. The same Engine was made
use of by the late Prelacy, to support their Kingdom of unrighteousness. Is
it meet to bring in the methods and artifices, invented and practised by Satan
for the support of his tottering State and Kingdom in the world, into the Kingdom of* Jesus Christ, *for the establishment of this, as if it were not able to stand
but upon* Satans *legs* ?

authority, as you have to hope that the *Cambridge Doctors will not take that glory to themselves, which I ascribe to them* ?

[To the following clause in the Book-sellers' letter—' We might gain by selling Biddles Books, but we had rather see them burnt by the hand of the Hangman '—Goodwin replied :—]

If you saw the Books that you speak of *burnt by the hand of the hangman,* do you think that the *Errors, Heresies* and *Blasphemies,* contained in them, would *burn* with them ? If you do, I confess I am of a far differing mind from you. I verily beleeve that the ashes of these Books would be much more propagative of the said Errors and Heresies, than the Books themselves.

G.

*A Cordial Confection./ To strengthen their Hearts whose Courage
begins /to fail, by the Armies late dissol/ving the Parliament./
It is wrapt up in/An Epistolary Discourse,/Occasionally written
to Mr. Ro. Hamon, Mer/chant, by Geo. Wither, Esq.; about a
week after the/said Parliament was dissolv'd ; and is thus com/
municated by a Copy thereof, as very pertinent/ to these distracted
times, and tending to pre/servation of the Common-Peace./ . . .
Printed at London, by James Cottrel, 1659.*[1]

. . . p. 6. [G. W. has given his view of reasons why Common-
wealth failed—non-attendance to the needs of *individuals*—too
much for ' public '—O.C's failure to do God's Will etc.]

Somewhat of this Nature, and to the like purpose, I offered to
their consideration, whom it concerned to take notice thereof,
but with little or no regard ; for, not remembring that but a
while since, some of themselves, then in power, were as inconsiderable persons as I am, they were so elevated, that they thought
it a disparagement to take advice in such matters, from so obscure
a person : yet, knowing my self concerned in the *Publick Welfare*,
I persisted in endeavouring what I thought pertinent thereto :
And when *Oliver Cromwel* late Lord Protector had taken upon
himself the *Supreme Authority*, (thereto providentially admitted
both for his own Probation and our) I submitted (according to
my *Principle* grounded upon Divine Precepts) to that Power
which was in *being*, and complyed with him in things tending to
preservation of the *Commonwealth*, in hope to insinuate thereby,
somewhat into his Consideration, for Publick Advantage : And,
because, I had not such a measure of the *Spirit* which rested upon
Elias, as might warrant me to say unto my *Soveraign Prince*,
in plain terms, *Thou art wicked*, (when I saw him prevaricate from
what he had professed) yet I endeavoured, as *Paul* did to work

[1] 23 December.

338

upon King *Agrippa*, first, by publishing somewhat whereby I might preserve and encrease a good opinion, without any sordid flattery, (though some who misunderstood my Poems, have conceived otherwise) and then I sought by private Addresses, to screw into him a serious Consideration of his Duty, in many particulars relating to GOD, to the *People*, and to *Himself* ; declaring boldly and plainly (not a little to my personal disadvantage) that the power conferred upon him was not vouchsafed for his own sake ; but, that he might thereby glorifie GOD, and settle upon his People those Rights, which were so anciently and naturally their due, that no Prescription could be a just bar to their Claim. And though perhaps he surreptitiously and unjustly hastned to get possession of that power which GOD had designed him, (as *Hazael* did, after the Prophet of GOD had foretold him he should be King) yet I perceiving, by his honourable new *Title*, and by other Circumstances, that GOD had permitted a more absolute Arbitrary Power to be devolved upon him, than any of our Kings ever had, because without such a *Power*, it was impossible for him to bring as to a perfect *Settlement*, (being so unsettled and divided as we then were, and yet are) I presumed both to declare unto him, to what intent that *exorbitant Power* was permitted ; how long he was to enjoy it ; in what manner he should thereby proceed ; and what would follow if he employed it to any other end.

But, (before I had presumed so far, or declared any thing, to the making ineffectual my good *Intents*, by ought which might be distasteful) I then perceiving he took as little notice as the *Parliament* had done before their first *Interruption*, of that course which I thought pertinent to the introducing of a *Righteous Government* ; and that he probably intended rather to establish it for his own and his Posterities advantage, than for the Peoples Accommodation, (or else, that he might trifle away the Opportunities then given, by prosecuting his own *Designes* until they were lost.) I signified unto him in a *Discourse* prepared in form of a *Declaration* to these *Nations*, how he might settle a *Righteous Government* (as I believed) with safety and honour, if he would engage himself to the *People*, by publishing a *Remonstrance* to that effect for their satisfaction. This Overture being made at a time wherein his fears and hazards were very great : Though that *Discourse* was very large, he with much seeming Contentment, heard me read it over to the last word ; and then protested, according to his usual manner, that it answered to his heart, as the *shadow of his face* in the Glass (then hanging before him in the room) answered to his *face* ; and pretended he would publish that *Declaration*, and act accordingly, as soon as he with one in whose discretion he much confided, had considered what alteration it might need, (or words to that effect) and then received it of me, promising to return it with his final resolution within a week.

At the weeks end, or thereabout, he, or Mr. *Thurloe* then Secretary, (who seemd also to approve thereof) delivered back unto me my *Papers* ; and the *Protectors* Answer, which then was, That he himself, together with the said *Secretary* and *my Self*, would within a few days, examine it over, to see what *verbally*, might require alteration, or what addition would be necessary ; and that being done, he would then without fail, take order for Publication thereof. But, afterward he apostatiz'd from that *Resolution*, to his own dis-advantage, and to the occasion of what hath since befallen to the *Publick Detriment* ; yet, pretended many moneths together, a firm adherence to what he had seemingly resolved on, keeping me all that time in attendance ; gave me the Key of his Closet at the end of the *Shield Gallery* in *Whitehall*, (wherein his Books and his Papers lay) to retire unto when I came thither ; carried me often to his own Table ; frequently discoursed with me concerning my *Proposal* ; and appointed many set days wherein to review the said *Papers*, but failed always in performance ; wherewith I being a little discontented, told him, I thought his mind was changed ; and giving him back the key of his *Closet*, purposed never to wait again upon him in relation to that business. He then, with very respective words to me excusing his delays, assured me that at six of the Clock next morning, he would send for his *Secretary*, and dispatch that which he intended, before he would admit any other person into his presence. I came before the appointed hour, but was then also put off, until a little past three in the afternoon, at which time I attended till past four ; and then, hearing that *He*, and his *Secretary*, were gone forth in a Coach to take the Air, I purposed to depart, and loose no more time on that occasion : and as I was leaving the room, one informed me, that about the same hour, in which I was appointed to attend *Him* and his *Secretary*, their necks were both in hazard to be broken, by the *Protectors* usurping the Office of his *Coach-man* ; and that they were both brought in so hurt, that their lives were in danger. Of that imprudent, if not disgraceful attempt mis-beseeming his person, I endeavoured to prevent as much of the dishonor, as I might, by a little *Poem*,[1] as I thought it my duty, in regard he executed the *Supreme Office* at that time. After this, he called on me again, as if his mind had not been wholly changed, and referred the said Papers to his *Privy-Council*, who referred them to a *Sub-Committee*, of which Sir *Gilbert* Pickering being one, gave it a high approbation, and was pleased to say he did not flatter me ; but from that time forward, I heard no more of it. Another service I did, which much tended to *His* and the *Publick Safety*, whereto Sir *Gilbert Pickering* is privy likewise ; and in consideration of the fore-mentioned

---

[1] *Vaticinium Causale, A Rapture Occasioned by the late miraculous Deliverance of His Highness The Lord Protector from a desperate danger.* Oct., 1654, Printed for T. Ratcliffe and E. Mottershed :

' His *Acte*, was not *unseemely*, nor a *Crime*,
As they suppose, whose Memorie forgets,
What, others or what best themselves befits
For, 'twas not judged an *Unprincely Game*
To drive a *Chariot*, when th' *Olimpian Fame*
Was thirsted after ' ;

N.B.—G. W. was still obtaining *access* to O.C. and presenting advice as late as 1657 (authority—*The Prisoner's Plea* by G. W., 1661).

services, the said *Protector* having, without my asking that, or any thing else, (but to be relieved according to Justice from my oppressions, which I could not obtain) gave me the *Statute-Office*, and afterward made it little worth unto me, because (as I conceive) I exprest my thankfulness for it, in declaring unto him those *Truths*, which he was not willing to hear of. Pardon this digression, for it is somewhat pertinent.

INDEX

INDEX

Abuses Discovered, 187
Accuser Shamed, 207, 209
Act for Establishment of Governors of the English Print, 17
Actors, Peter, 1
Acts and Ordinances of the Interregnum, 188
Adjutators, 118
Adlinghill, 238
Agreement of the People, 151, 172
Allnutt, W. H., 68
Almanacks, writers of, prosecuted, 233-5 ; copyright of, 320-2
Alsop, B., 199
Amsterdam, 22, 23, 307 ; suppression of libellous books at, 43 ; Bibles printed at, 52, 53 ; Lilburne buys printing press at, 239
Anabaptists, 114, 250, 253, 255, 266-7, 275
Answer, by W. Prynne, 39
Apologie For The Six Book-Sellers, An, 259
Arber, E, 5, 12, 13, 14, 15, 16, 18, 20, 30, 35, 65
Archbishop of Canterbury, 7 ; and Censorship, 295-7
Archbishops, as licensers, 13 ; as supervisors of Customs' searchers, 30
Areopagitica, 77 etc., 165, 173, 185, 211, 258
Aristides, 290
Aristophanes, 137
Armagh, Archbishop, of 56 ; *Elegy on Archbishop of*, 269
Army, and control of press, 117-119, 130, 163-4 ; and publication of news, 119-120, 124 ; Agent of, licenses news, 241 ; supplied with copies of Bible, 282
Army's Grievances, 118
Ash, Francis, 176, 194
Ash, Ned, 158-9
Ashton, William, 67
Assembly, of Divines, 101

Aston, John, 57
Athenae Britannicae, by Myles Davies, 58
Athenae Oxonienses, 167
Audley, T., 45, 88-94
Aulicus His Hue and Cry, 89
Austin, Robert, 238

Bachiler, Mr., 161
Ball, William, 1, 203, 298 etc.
Ballads, Cromwell permits, 273, 299; W. Ball's proposals concerning, 301 etc.
Ballad-singers, and hawkers, prohibited, 188, 191
Ballad stanzas in royalist newsbooks, 140
Barker, Christopher, queen's printer, 2
Barker, Christopher (' the Third '), 282
Barker, Matthew, 309-311
Barker, Robert, 6, 7, 8, 309
Barkley, Mr., 97
Barkstead, John, 251, 268, 271, 272, 275, 282, 323
Barnes, Henry, 238
Bartlet, John, 239
Bastwick, Dr., 39, 47, 49, 103
Baxter, Richard, 265
' Beacon Firing ' Controversy, 225-233, 265, 328-337 ; and Biddle, 254 ; revived, 256-260 ; and licensing, 256-7, 261
Beacon Flameing, The, 232
' Beacon Quenchers ', The, 229-233
Beacon Set on Fire, A, 221, 225-6
Beacons Quenched, The, 229-233
Beaumont and Fletcher, 137
Bedfordberry, 238
Bellamy, John, 162
Bellum Hibernicale, 125
Bentley, William, 281-3
Berkenhead, Isaac, 239
Berkenhead, John, 70, 89, 121, 122
Bethan, Francis, 158, 159, 164

Bible, printing of, 7, 10, 24, 107 ;
foreign editions of, 23, 73, 188,
224, 303 etc. ; disputes about
printing of, 281-3, 309-311 ; army
supplied with copies of, 282
Bibliographica, 68
Biddle, John, 252-6, 259-60, 333,
337
Bishop of London, 2, 7, 15 ; and the
press, 295
Bishop of Winchester, 5
Blackfriars, King's printing house
at, 27
Blaiklock, 97, 98
Blasphemous books, and press,
206-8, 221, 276 ; laxity of govern-
ment in dealing with, 228 ;
Biddle's, and the press, 252-6 ;
Goodwin's proposal for dealing
with, 258-60, 328-337
Blayden, William, given monopoly
of printing Irish news, 62
Bloody Vision, The, 262
Bloomsbury, 45
Bodleian Library, 297
Bond, John, 63
Border, Daniel, 197
Bostock, R., 95, 96, 97, 130, 170
Bourne, Nicholas, 8
Bradshaw, John, 176 ; and the
press, 167, 185-6
Bray, Dr., 53
Brayne, Mr., 194
Brent, Sir Nathaniel, 123, 160-1, 208
Brewster, T., 239
Bridge, Major, 229
Briefe Relation, 189, 196, 198, 201,
202, 211
Briefe Treatise concerning Printing,
1, 203, 298-311
Brightman, Dr., 83
Bristol, printer at, 73 ; popish
books at, 227 ; Naylor at, 276
British Lightning, by G. L. V., 54
Brittanicus, his welcome in Hell, 122
Brown, a vendor, 112-113
Brown, David, a bookseller, 218
Browne, John, 120
Brudenell, Thomas, 186
Buchanan, Mr., 96, 97, 135

Buckingham, Duke of, 239
Bucknell, Thomas, 215
Buckner, Mr., 37
Bulkley, Stephen, 68
Burghley, Lord, 29
Burgoyne, Sir R., 88
Burney Collection, 93, 174, 198, 208,
244, 245, 286
Burton, Henry, 39, 47, 49
Bustian, 46
Butler, Nathaniel, 269
Butler, Samuel, 71, 93, 141, 143

Caesar, Julius, 136
Calamy, Edward, 232
Caley, Robert, 14
Calvert, Giles, 230, 239, 274
Cambridge, printing at, 3, 74, 310
Cann, ' the sectary ', 240
Carew, Mr., 267
Carisbrooke Castle, 118
Carrington, S., 292
Carter, W., 15, 16, 18
Caryes Book, Dr., 176, 194
Caryll, Joseph, licenser, revolts,
167-9 ; why not dismissed by
Parliament, 168
*Case of the Commonwealth of England
stated*, 211
*Cases in Star Chamber and High
Commission Courts*, 7, 26, 36
Catechisis Ecclesiarum Poloniae,
221 ; reprinted after being
banned, 221
Caxton, 1
Censorship (*See* Licensers, Sta-
tioners' Company and Stationers'
Register), papistical books and,
12, 15, 221, 224-233 ; first puritan
protest against, 16 ; a woman's
protest against, 149-150 ; Parliament's inadequate, 150-2, 157
etc., 236 ; religious disputes in
news-books and, 249-250 ; at
Universities, 257 ; Cromwell and,
260-1 ; religious disputes and,
271 etc. ; malignant books and,
272 ; ' merry books ' and, 273-4 ;
' excluded members ' and, 279-
280 ; bishops' methods of, 295-7 ;

INDEX

Mercurius Pragmaticus, 121, 134, 140, 158, 166-8, 174, 185, 222; counter mercury to, 126; committee appointed to suppress *Melancholicus* and, 127; popularity of, 129; reward offered for discovery of, 131; and other royalist news-books, 133; on ballad stanzas in news-books, 140; attacked in *Anti-Mercurius*, 142; author examined by Milton, 172-3; author discovered, 180-1; counterfeited, 182; written by Cleaveland, 184; blames Bradshaw for press restrictions, 186; warrant for arrest of author, etc., 191; suppressed 197; counterfeited, 217

Mercurius Pragmaticus for King Charles II., 182, 186

Mercurius Rusticus, 71, 93

Mercurius Urbanus, 129

Meredith, Christopher, 162

Merest, Adjutant-Gen., 229

'Merry' books, banned, 273-4

Mesole, a printer, 113

Metropolitan Nuncio, 141

Militia, called in to control press, 157-161

Miller, George, 109, 162

Milton, John, and Stationers' Company, 77 etc.; his Divorce Tracts, 78, 185; and censorship of news, 79, 172-3, 261; and copyrights, 80; and licensers, 81-2, 261; and Mabbott, 172-3; influence of, 185; his *Eikonoklastes*, 196; and Dugard, 202-3; and Salmasius, 211; and Goodwin, 258; and Cromwell, 291

Moderate, The, 169, 190; started by R. White, 146; and execution of Charles, 166; suppressed, 173

Moderate Intelligencer, attacked in pamphlets, 138, 142-3; and Stationers' Register, 144, 180; Dillingham's quarrel about, 145-149; and execution of Charles, 166; revived, 217; vendor of, arrested, 249

Modest Narrative of Intelligence, 195

Monk, George, 275

Moon, Richard, 236, 244, 252-3, 260, 262

Moore (John ?), 164

Moore, Richard, 236

Mottershed, E., 341

Mumford, a bookbinder, 168

Musarum Oxoniensium, 260

Muzzle for Cerberus, 127

McDowell, ambassador, 200

M'Kerrow, R. B., 22

Nalson, J., 50

Narrative Touching Col. Edward Sexby, A., 278

Naylor, James, M. Brailsford's biography of, 276

Nedham, Marchamont, 70, 92, 246; libels the king, 89; author of *Pragmaticus*, 181; author of *Politicus*, 198; attacked in pamphlet, 199; official news-writers, 247-8; his intolerance, 289-290

Netherlands, ambassadors from, and the press, 86

New Marriage between Mr. King and Mrs. Parliament, 159

New News from the Old Exchange, 205

New Testament of Lords and Saviours at Westminster, 151

Newcastle, 275; seditious books at, 44; Marprelate press at, 69

Newcombe, Thomas, 209

Newhouse, William, licenser, 123, 146

News, not common property, 58-9; inexpedient publishing of, 74, 241; effects of uncensored publication of, 85, 200, 246; publication of false, 120; Fairfax asks Parliament to publish its own, 124; parliament accused of counterfeiting, 152; public thirst for, 181; false reports in royalist news-books, 182

News from Ipswich, by W. Prynne, 39, 42

INDEX

Perfect Diurnal, 66, 98, 128, 150, 153, 173-4, 178, 179 ; attacked in *Anti-Mercurius,* 142
Perfect Diurnall of some Passages, 189, 190, 197, 198, 224 ; and Stationers' Register, 212-4, 241, 243 ; attacked by Sheppard, 214
Perfect Occurrences, 119, 131, 147, 186 ; quarrel about, 178-180 ; not perused by licenser, 180 ; counterfeited, 182-3 ; suppression of, 197 ; and Stat. Reg., 241, 243
Perfect Passages, 138, 214
Perfect Weekly Account, 197
Peter, Mr. Secretary, 12
Peters, Hugh, 194 ; anonymous libels on, 223-4 ; stationer's apology to, 223-4 ; presbyterians accused of libelling, 230 ; blamed for restraining freedom of press, 288
Peters Keys, 224
Petition, in favour of puritan books, 34 ; attacking the bishops, 35 ; of puritans to Parliament, 53 ; of ministers to Parliament, 54 ; of Mary Blaithwaite to Protector, 73 ; of Stationers' Company, 73 ; of Mary Overton, 114 ; of Mabbott to Parliament, 145 ; of R. White to Parliament, 145 ; of H. Walker against Mabbott, 147-8 ; of Gentlemen of Bucks to Parliament, 150-1 ; of Stationers' Company to Parliament, 160-1, 236 ; of freemen of Stat. Coy. to Parliament, 162-3 ; of Levellers to Parliament, 164-5, 171 etc., 211, 220 ; of John Hall to Protector, 177 ; of Hackluyt, 184 ; of Wardens of Stationers' Company to Council of State, 203 ; of Josiah Prymatt, 208-9 ; of Horton and Huby to Protector, 248-9 ; a lost, of Stationers' Company, 250 ; of Cole to Council, 268 ; of M. Hawke to Cromwell, 284
Petitions, for privilege to print, 5, 8; printing of, a way of evading press restrictions, 171, 208-9, 279-280
Philanglus, by James Howell, 83
Pickering, Sir Gilbert, 341
Plautus, 137
Playford, J., 170, 194
Plays, licensers and publication of, 209-210
Plomer, H. R., 23, 25, 68, 95, 103, 202
Poets' Knavery Discovered, 61
Poet's Recantation, The, 63
Pocklington, Dr., 53
Political events, and publication of news, 118
Pollard, A. W., 73
Pope, Mistress, 150
Pope, The, 176
Powell, Vavasor, 284
Practice of Piety, 43
Praeadamite, 265
Prelatical tyranny over press, 33
Presbyterian tyranny over the press, 100 ; shown by ' Beacon Quenchers ', 229-233, 257-260 ; compared with Cromwell's toleration, 265
Presse Full of Pamphlets, A., 60
Price, Thomas, 172
Pride, Col., 229
Printer, ' wicked enticements ' of a, 184
Printer, the Parliamentary, 75
Printers, foreign, 11 ; arrogance of, 133 ; news-writers complain of tyranny of, 183, 250 ; a meeting of, 186 ; power and self-importance of, 201-3 ; proposal for separate Company of, 203, 307 etc. ; and the Government (1652), 220-1
Printing, royal prerogative of, 2, 4, 298 etc. ; proposal for regulating, 27 ; Government's prerogative of, 238 ; Bishops and, 295-7
Printing-press, costs 30 *l.,* 239
Printing trade, 1637 Decree and, 295-7 ; W. Ball's proposals concerning, 298-313 ; 1653 Act and, 314-8 ; Cromwell and, 323-7

356